Communal Riots in India

Communal Riots in India

Editor

N. L. Gupta

Gyan Publishing House

Delhi-110002

Communal Riots in India
(Political Science, History)

ISBN : 81-212-06448

Published in 2000 in India by
Gyan Publishing House
5, Ansari Road
New Delhi

Laser Typeset at Manas Typesetter, New Delhi
Printed at Cahwla Offset Press, New Delhi

For my wife

Sharda

Contributors List

1. N.L. Gupta (Rtd), Department of Political Science, Kirori Mal College, University of Delhi, Delhi.
2. K.B. Garg, Professor, Department of Physics, University of Rajasthan, Jaipur.
3. H.C. Bhartiya, Associate Professor, (Rtd) Department of Zoology, University of Rajasthan, Jaipur.
4. Late S.S. Oberoi, Deputy Chief Mechanical Engineer, Indian Railways; Secretary General, Hindustani Manch, Jaipur.
5. K.C. Pandey, Social Scientist (Rtd), University of Rajasthan, Jaipur.
6. Dalip S. Swaney, Professor, South Campus, University of Delhi, Delhi.
7. Zahoor Siddiqui, Department of History, School of Correspondence Courses, University of Delhi, Delhi.
8. Ramesh Rao, P.G.D.A.V. College, University of Delhi, Delhi.
9. Vijay Mehta, Advocate, High Court, Jodhpur.
10. N.V. Ruhi, Former Head of Deptt. of Political Science, Saifia Post Graduate Arts, Commerce and Law College, Bhopal.

11. L.S. Herdania, Journalist, Bhopal.
12. Vinny Jain, Lecturer, Agra.
13. Devendra Singh, Trade Unionist, Meerut.
14. Panchanan Saha, Reader, City College, Calcutta.
15. U.S. Venkataraman, Trade Unionist, Artist and Painter, Bangalore.
16. A. Prabhakar Rao, Journalist, Hyderabad.
17. K. Kumar, Times of India.
18. Yogesh Vajpayee, Times of India.
19. Gautam Mehta, Times of India.
20. Kum Kum Chaddha, Hindustan Times.
21. Dinesh Chandra Varshney, Motilal Nehru College, University of Delhi, Delhi.
22. Girish Mishra, Reader, K.M. College, University of Delhi, Delhi.
23. Braj Kumar Pandey.
24. Phani Bora, Communist Leader, Guwahati.
25. Mahesh Buta, Advocate, Jodhpur.
26. Nikhil Dey, Social Worker, Bihar.
27. Aruna Roy, Social Worker, Beawar.
28. Vijay Laxmi Joshi, Indara, Ajmer.

Contents

Preface

This book is the product of collective effort of scholars who came together, despite their differing fields of specialization, on the issue of communal riots in the country from the year 1989-93, i.e. the period beginning with commencement of the Rath Yatra of L.K. Advani to the aftermath of the destruction of Babri Masjid. It is needless to say that this was a significant phase in the development of anti-Congress alternative in Indian politics. The period of less than two years of the government of V. P. Singh witnessed the strange phenomenon of both the BJP and the CPI (M) supporting it from outside. The government itself heralded its plan in the form of announcing the intention to implement on all-India basis the moth eaten and dust covered Mandal Commission Report. This sent shockwaves throughout the country, which faced violent times in response. Macabre acts of violence took place against the announcement marked with sporadic incidents of self immolation. The BJP responded by announcing its intention of undertaking the Rath Yatra to carry the message of Hindutva throughout the length and breadth of the country. This trip of Ram driven in a Toyota Rath was punctuated by communal riots. It appeared that there was nobody to stop this march and consequent orgies.

Most of the contributions in this book are first hand accounts, eyewitness reports, accounts based on reports in the newspapers. These were written soon after the incidents and therefore might not have had an academic style of presentation. We decided to put these accounts in a perspective and therefore introduced a chapter on communal riots in India since the 1960s. This enlarged the scope of the book, not only in terms of the period covered but also in terms of the role played by both Hindus and Muslims. We have not included the issue of the Hindu Sikh divide for which a separate study is needed.

The authors hope the book serves as a documentation of communal riots. Since the time is too recent, official commissions on them are practically non-existent, court proceedings proverbially in the limbo and intent to violence never even truly declared. These accounts of events in the media, and the eyewitnesses, and field reports will serve the purpose of basic information on communal riots that took place. Rioting should not have a place in our body politic since the Constitution enjoins us to eschew that path. And yet they became a part of a bid to capture power, which is the finding of almost all the articles/papers in the book.

This survey covers the happening of major riots in post-Independence India, and underlines their menace in that context particularly the riots during the period 1989-93. It does not, however, cover all the riots during this period. If this work inspires others to engage in compilation and analysis of this significant phenomenon, the task of this volume would be achieved. The contributed articles of the volume are the recording of the happenings during the riots in the wake of the Rath Yatra and the destruction of the Babri Masjid. The opening chapter covers the history of communal riots in independent India. The last contribution is on riots after the destruction of the Babri Masjid.

I thank the scholars who have contributed their articles to this book. I take this opportunity to thank the innumerable persons who have helped me in more ways than one to compile this volume but cannot be mentioned by name. To some among these I would like to especially express my thanks: K. C. Pandey, and Aurobindo Ghosh for helping me procure the reports on riots in Jaipur; Mrs Mehta for the report on Bewar; the Editors of *The Times of India* and *The Hindustan Times*. I also wish to thank Prem Sager Gupta, D. R. Goyal, K. D. Sharma, Anand Gupta and Shikha Gupta. My thanks are due to the Mr. B. P. Garg and Mr. Amit Garg of Gyan Publishing House for bringing out this book in a record short time.

N. L. Gupta

1

Communal Riots : 1964-89

N.L. Gupta

Fascism is the last gasp of conservatism[1], according to John Weiss. He further says, "My own judgement and knowledge led me to suspect that the greatest potential for fascism lies not in the liberal West, but rather in the dialectical polarities now increasing in the non-Western or underdeveloped societies."[2] Lipset and Weiss had con nected fascism with a continuing political tradition from the European past. They recognized the potential of fascism to reappear at some point in future. However, to them it appeared likely that the future of fascism lay in the developing countries.[3] Weiss doubted the prospects for right-wing success in 'liberalized consensus societies'. With the passing away of fascism and Stalinism, the West had enjoyed a period of relative political stability. Lipset affirmed that "the fundamental political problems of the industrial revolution have been solved." He also stated that substantial agreement had been reached on the question of welfare state. As a result, he concluded, "serious ideological controversies have ended at home"; Europe and America had arrived at 'the end of ideology.'[4]

Gilbert Allardyee defines modernization as involving both a process and a consummation. Societies undergoing industrial development are subject to seizure by political extremism. Advanced industrial societies are characterized by political consensus. In this context, fascism could be linked to a crisis period in the modernization process. It is akin to a revolt against modernization.[5] Of course, in developing societies fascism will not take the same form as it assumed in Italy and Germany during the inter-war period. Developing societies like India have their own specificities, and fascism, accordingly, will be specific to the prevailing situations in developing countries.

Jawaharlal Nehru described communalism as the Indian version of fascism.[6] The greater part of communalism is political reaction. Communal leaders inevitably tend to become reactionaries in political and economic matters. He further emphasised that the groups of upper class people try to satisfy their own class interests by making it appear that they stand for the communal demands of religious minorities and majorities. He further said that communalism is more dangerous for the future of India than any armed attack from any foreign country[7] and he urged that there should be no compromise on the basis of communalism. Hindu communalism or Muslim communalism feed each other and are a challenge to the Indian nationhood and nationalism. In other words he linked communalism to the modernist elite and not to the feudal order or the feudal elite. Unfortunately, academic literature on communalism delinks it from the modernist vested interest.

Communalism is a challenge to India's secularism, composite culture and unity in diversity, in fact, its very nationhood. Communalism is an evil which divides men and fragments society, running against national genius and cultural heritage. It poses threat to the unity and integrity of our country. The citizenship of India is a shared citizenship. Danger to even a single citizen whatever community or religion he may belong to, is a danger to all of us, and worse, it demeans all of us. This is a matter of shame and anxiety that Indian nationals must be threatened in their homes and places of business because of their religious affinity by the custodians of some sects. National integration is the basis for India's survival. Communalism is the negation of secularism and democracy. Communal riots in post-Independence India are fascist in nature. Communalism is a political phenomenon and consequently, communal riots are politically motivated. Religion allied with politics tends to generate communal violence and at the same time perpetuates backward leaning or oppressive institutions attached to it. The involvement of saints and sadhus in politics and political movements is not a phenomenon without significance. In 1960s and 1970s, riots were significantly marked by the unhindered rampage and killing of innocent Muslims. The question of their patriotism was constantly raised. Golwalkar declared that the Muslims were guests who cannot stay forever. The question of Muslim loyalty to India was raised. They were variously described as Pakistani spies and agents. In 1970s the Jan Sangh leaders opposed bank nationalization. In Gujarat, Golwalkar, Balraj Madhok, S.S. Bhandari and a host of other Jan Sangh leaders visited various towns and gave a coloured slogan—bank nationalisation was wrong, nationalize Muslims. Horrendous riots subsequently occurred not only in Ahmedabad but in all the major towns of Gujarat. The RSS has been seen as having a vested interest in spreading communal riots in India to communalize the polity, disrupt the growing secula-rization of Indian society and thereby expand its social, political and electoral base. Communal riots in post-Independence India are astutely planned, skilfully organized and deftly executed. The Madan Commission report enquiring into Bhiwandi, Jalgaon and Mahad riots observed : "The organisations which had both directly and indirectly provoked disturbances which took place in Bhiwandi, Khoni, and Nagaon on May 7, 1970 and thereafter is the Rashtriya Utsav Mandal, the majority of whose members belonged to Jan Sangh or were pro-Jan-Sangh and the rest, apart from a few exceptions, belonged to the Shiv Sena."[8] In Jalgaon, similar action was undertaken by Shree Ram Tirth Tarun Mandal and Jalgaon city and district branches Jan Sangh.[9] Stones were generally thrown at the time of night prayers. at Jumma Masjid situated in Maniyar Wada. The communal harmony and amity that prevailed earlier in Jalgaon was shattered by the Jan Sangh on October 1, 1970.[10] The Mahad disturbances were directly provoked by false rumours that the flag on a certain disputed structure was removed by some Muslims after assaulting a police constable on watch duty there, and the people who spread this rumour belonged to the Shiv Sena." The commission further observed that in pursuance of the instructions given by the additional IGP, Mahad, large-scale arrests were made; that several police officers and policemen concerned with effecting these arrests turned a blind eye to what the Hindu rioters were doing and instead concentrated their energies upon the Muslims. It observed that a few innocent Muslims who went to take shelter at the Bhiwandi Taluka police station were arrested instead of being given protection and shelter. There was a nexus between police and the Hindu rioters. In Jalgaon too the only persons who were arrested during the entire course of disturbances were three Muslims. The Commission also held Majlis Tamire-e-Millat responsible for fomenting communal tension.[11] The commission further observed: "There was hardly anything common to these three inquiries except the recurring tale of hatred and violence. It was a lonely, arduous and weary journey through a land of hatred and violence, prejudice and perjury. The encounters on the way were with men without compassion, lusting for the blood of their fellowmen; politicians who trafficked in communal hatred and religious fanaticism; local leaders who sought power by sowing disunity and bitterness; police officers and policemen who were unworthy of their uniform; investigating officers without honour and scruples; men committed to falsehood and wedded to fraud, and dealers in mayhem and murder. Yet the scene has not been all dark and murky, for it has been lit up with other encounters on the way, albeit few, but which shone out "bright as a star when only one is shining in the sky." These were encounters with men who opened out their homes and held out their hands to protect those of the other faith; with officers who, irrespective of the fear of consequences, would not mortgage their conscience to support a lie; and with men who were not afraid to give a call for unity when the others around them were preaching hate."[12]

Ray and Chakravarty in their report on Meerut riots stated : "We have no hesitation in putting the blame squarely on local leaders of the majority communal forces for the riots. The entire episode bore the stamp of organization and advance planning executed with a ruthless disregard for human lives."[13] They observed in relation to Karimganj riots that communal outburst started on the day when communalists organized a massive demonstration of evicted tea garden workers. The demonstration included approximately 1500 Muslim workers. The slogan of community solidarity was raised to break the unity of workers. Subsequent events provoked the utility of communal politics. It was an effective bulwark against the rise of communalism in the area.[14]

J.M. Joshi, a veteran socialist leader, held VHP responsible for communal riots in Pune and Solapur in 1982. According to Moin Shakir, riots in Pune and Solapur were not the result of any political or economic rivalry or competition and were not precipitated by local factors. They were the result of a sustained and calculated campaign by the VHP backed by RSS.

In Hyderabad during the September 1983 riots, 45 persons died and 150 were injured. The riots started on September 7, 1983. The BJP, Arya Samaj, the VHP and the Muslim Majlis-e-ittehadul-Muslimeen were variously responsible in whipping up communal sentiments and fomenting communal tension and violence on the eve of religious festivals or elections. Y.B. Chavan, the then Home Minister of India, said that there was an organized plot behind Ranchi riots in 1967.

In the Tellicherry riots report, the enquiry commission remarked, "I have no doubt that the RSS has taken active part in rousing up anti-Muslim feelings among Hindus of Tellicherry and in preparing the background for disturbances."[15]

The Jitendra Narain Commission regarding Jamshedpur riots in 1979 said, "After giving careful and serious consideration to all the materials that are on record, the commission is of the view that the RSS with its extensive organization in Jamshedpur and which has close links with the BJP and the BMS, had a positive hand in creating a climate which was most propitious for the outbreak of communal disturbances."[16] It specifically blamed these organisations for "authoring, inciting and fomenting the riots." It further said that not a single Hindu could be identified as having been killed or injured by the Bihar Military Police in 22 hours of firing resorted to by the police for quelling the riots. It also said, "This strange phenomenon coupled with the fact that when the Hindu mob had been driven from the disturbed area, a number of Muslims were found dead and the injured corroborated the allegation of collusion of the police with the rioting Hindu mobs."

The Jagmohan Reddy Commission inquiring into the Ahmedabad riots of 1971 observed, "The evidence shows that organized attacks were being made on Muslim properties and lorries were used to carry rioters and weapons, the crowd being led and directed in the instance by a worker of Jan Sangh. Though we have nothing to show that the party as such had taken part or was involved, or that diversionary tactics were being employed to overawe the defenders. One fact emerges clearly: that the entire commissariat was enveloped and many sections including large number of workers were involved, some of them with technical skill."[17] He also observed that "another notable feature which we must make a reference to is the definite part played in various districts which were affected by the workers of the local Jan Sangh and the Hindu Mahasabha organizations or by persons having leanings towards them. There is evidence definitely that they took a leading part in rioting in the districts of Amreli, Banaskantha, Mehsana, Baroda and shows that they were inciting the crowds to riots."[18] The riots in Ahmedabad and other Gujarat towns had a specificity that even the Congressmen had turned communal in their outlook according to the President of the DCC. The DCC of Vadodra did not criticize the riots. On the contrary it blamed the Muslims for the same. Responsible Congressmen criticized Muslims for their communal attitude and suggested that they should go to Pakistan. A highly placed Congress leader of Gujarat, in a public meeting, exhorted the youth in these terms: "There is an anti-national element in the country whose loyalty is towards Pakistan. Police having some limitations cannot trace these elements. Therefore it is your duty to find them out. You should enter their houses, catch hold of them, then do whatever you want to do."[19]

Some sort of planned organization of riots appears to have existed during the Ahmedabad riots. Soon after Jagannath temple clash, rumours appeared to have been systematically spread. By the noon of September 10, hundreds of cyclostyled and printed handbills stating that a cow had been slaughtered, the mahant seriously injured, Muslims had entered the temple and the idol of God had been damaged, were distributed. There was no truth in any of these rumours. In Baroda too rumours were spread about the burning of the Swami Narayan temple. Other pamphlets advocated the Hindus to take action against the Muslims. One pamphlet said : "Hindus get organised, be bold. Take weapons in your hands, and attack the Muslims who are out to destroy the Hindu religion and Hindu temples."

In Aligarh, there was unconcealed cooperation between the RSS, police, and the local district administration. Navman, an active RSS leader who was reported to have engineered the riots secured passes and transport to facilitate the movement of prospective rioters. These riots were replete with instances of RSS and police collaboration aided by certain ministers in the government.

In Biharsharif, the Chief Minister of Bihar had to order the arrest of two and suspension of six District Magistrates. This testifies to the role played by the local police and the administration. The RSS organized mobs and went to the villages to attack Muslims. Subsequently, Yadavs joined the attackers. According to Asghar Ali Engineer, riots in Meerut in 1982, were well planned and lasted for more than four weeks. The pattern of setting fire to the houses and stabbing showed special training.[20] The rioters moved with lists of Muslims, their shops, houses and properties. The list also indicated whether the occupant was a Muslim tenant or a landlord and this was made without any mistake. Only the houses of Muslims were targetted, looted, and burnt. The state machinery moved in such a way that rioters got a free hand. For instance, in the Bombay riots during 1992, which took a toll of up to 2500 lives, were well planned. Bal Thackeray said that the riots were a result of the Shiv Sena activity aimed at teaching the Muslims a lesson. The riots followed a predetermined course of action and only halted when he decided the time as appropriate.[21]

Justice Srikrishna Commission report on Bombay riots indicting Shiv Sena Chief Bal Thackeray and Sena activitists in no uncertain terms, blames them for 'political role' in fomenting communal frenzy and organizing attacks on Muslims. It said, there was no doubt that Shiv Sena and other Shiv Sainiks took lead in organizing attacks on Muslims and their properties under the guidance of several party leaders. The commission said, "Shiv Sena Pramukh Bal Thackeray like a veteran general commanded his loyal Shiv Sainiks to retaliate by organizing attacks against Muslims." It further said that the "Chief Minister wasted four precious days before considering the matter and issuing orders for effective use of Army to control the riots, while the city was guilty of failure to take adequate preventive measures." On the role of the Congress government in the state, the Commission observed "effete political leadership, vacillation for political reasons and conflicting orders issued to the Commissioner of Police resulted in the dilemma to shoot or not to shoot."

The built-in bias of the police force against Muslims became more pronounced with murderous attacks of the constabulary and the officers, which manifested in their reluctance to firmly put down incidence of violence, looting and arson that went on unchecked. However, the report said that considering all aspects, the commission was not inclined to give serious credence to the theory that the disproportionately large number of Muslim deaths in December 1992 was necessarily indicative of an attempt on the part of the police to target and liquidate Muslims because of the communal bias. Recalling the sequence of events prior to the demolition of Babri Masjid in December 1992, the commission noted that after the formal announcement of *kar seva* at Ayodhya, the Hindu parties started recruitment of volunteers in different parts of the city and started Ram Paduka processions. The period saw intense activity on part of the BJP and its allied groups, viz. the

VHP, Bajrang Dal, and the RSS besides Shiv Sena in the form of holding several meetings and carrying out propaganda in favour of construction of Ram Temple at Ayodhya. Muslim organisations like the Students Islamic Action Movement of India (SIMI) and the Bombay Muslim Action Committee carried out propaganda opposing the construction of the temple and calling for Babri Masjid to be left untouched, the commission said.

Some of the speeches made during this period by both sides were likely to incite communal passions. These activities on the part of rival communities were building up an undercurrent of communal tension, the dangerous implications of which were not fully realized by the police and state machinery.

The commission further said, "The Rath Yatra of BJP in support of the campaign for Ram temple at Ayodhya further added to communal tension all over the country and Bombay city was no exception."

"The irresponsible act of Hindutva parties in celebrating and gloating over the demolition of Babri structure was like twisting a knife in the wound and heightened the anguished ire of the Muslims," it said.[22]

The commission indicted the former city police commissioner R.D. Tyagi and 30 other officers for excessive use of force and actively participating in riots, communal provocations and incidents of looting, arson, etc. and strongly recommended strict action against them. Mr Tyagi who joined the Shiv Sena in the run-up to the mid-term Lok Sabha polls was found guilty by the commission of "excessive and unnecessary firing resulting in the death of nine Muslims in the Suleiman Bakery incident."[23]

According to A.G. Noorani, many a riot is a pogrom in disguise. According to Paul R. Brass, "When it can be proved that the police and state authorities more broadly are directly implicated in a 'riot' in which one community provides the principal sole victims, then, of course, one is confronted with pogrom." Riots help in political mobilisation. There is nothing spontaneous about them. They are essentially man made, programmed, whether by fomenting hate or raising issues calculated to arouse mass frenzy, which gives the actual outbreak a colour of spontaneity. He further says, "Although most people everywhere are capable of committing acts of violence under a variety of circumstances, the kind of violence that is committed in 'communal riots' are, I believe, undertaken mostly by 'specialists' who are ready to be called to such occasions, who profit from it and whose activities profit others who may or may not be actually paying for the violence carried out. Such regions have developed what I call 'institutionalized riot system', in which known participants specialize in the conversion of incidents between members of different communities into 'communal riots'. Even here, however, not every incident is allowed to develop into a 'riot'. When full-fledged riots develop, the local politicians and authorities are often either incompetent or they themselves desire the riot to take place, and are willing to place a communal interpretation on the precipitating incidents." He further adds, "I believe that all riots from cities and towns do have a greater or lesser degree of such informal organizational networks.... Here I part company definitely with the 'sequence theorists' of collective action, who imagine a state of tension arising out of grievances, frustrations and discriminations in the relations between the two warring communities which required only the proverbial spark to ignite it. On the contrary, there were regular fire-tenders who maintain the fuel at a combustible level sometimes stroking it, sometimes letting it smoulder. They are the conversion specialists who know how to convert a moment of tension into a riotous event." He says that Hindu-Muslim riots are neither natural nor inevitable. What is new, although there are precedents for it in earlier cases of Hindu-Muslim conflicts, is the "the deliberate inculcation, among the RSS cadres, who provide shock trooper for the entire family of the organization, including the BJP, VHP, Bajrang Dal and others, of a cult of violence aimed at the intimidation of Muslims, their selective killings and the destruction of their property during riots."

The role of the police and administration has not been amicable in communal riots. Rather police officers and men have been generally communalised and biased against Muslims. They fail to bring to book the known preachers of communal hatred and violence. They do not employ all the administrative resources available to them for stopping communal riots. The Hindu communal elements are given a free hand to propagate communal hatred without any objection from the administration, for instance, in the Rourkela riots in 1964. The demolition of a mosque had been allowed to continue for hours in Aligarh with the connivance of officers. In Ranchi, the police even indulged in loot and arson. In 1977 at Varanasi, curfew was imposed only in Muslim localities which were relatively quiet. During curfew, the police broke into the homes of Muslims, arrested all males including a centurion, children and adults and looted and destroyed property worth lakhs. In Moradabad, the PAC troops looted or burnt Muslim shops and houses or helped goondas to do so. In fact Moradabad riots were termed as police versus Muslims and later police in collusion with Hindu communal forces versus Muslims. In Meerut the PAC had gunned down more than 40 unarmed Muslims rounded up from villages near Meerut.

In Varanasi, police took part not only in looting and burning but also in demolishing mosques and temples, as also in Godhra. In Jalgaon 25 children were killed and some of them burnt alive in the presence of the police. Examples of partisan attitude of the police are numerous.

The Jamshedpur Enquiry Commission said that, the administrative failure and provocative behaviour of Hindu chauvinists and resultant panicky reaction by Muslims had led to the disturbances. It is rumoured that not a single Hindu could be identified as having been killed or injured by the Bihar Military Police in the 22 hours of firing resorted to by the police for quelling the riots.

The Bhiwandi Commission held that the authorities had failed to take steps to check communal propaganda, failed to analyse correctly the objectives of the organizers of the Shiv Jayanti procession, and did not take action against the misuse of temples for carrying on communal propaganda after the riots had taken place in Ahmedabad. In 1969 the commission also held that in several instances the police officers and personnel did not prevent Hindu rioters from their acts of rioting and shared communal ideas and actively assisted the Hindu rioters. Some innocent Muslims who went to seek shelter at the Bhiwandi taluka police station were arrested instead of being protected.

Before and during communal riots the role of rumours has been horrendous. Rumours are spread by the word of mouth and in printed and cyclostyled pamphlets. Rumour mongering has been developed into a fine art. In Aurangabad during the 1968 riots, rumour was that the Muslims had attacked the temple but it was not proved that those who had attacked the temple were Muslims. Instead the but entire fury was directed against them and their property. In Ahmedabad in 1969 several handbills were distributed. A call for dharna was given : "Wipe out those who have dishonoured your mothers and sisters, show them that Muslims who have insulted Hindu religion or molested our mothers and sisters will not be able to stay in India." In Jamshedpur in 1979, a pamphlet was distributed which headlined 'An appeal to the religious loving people of Jamshedpur', and said, "Till now we have borne every cruelty peacefully but in the name of peace, Hindus of this area are being crushed.... What is clear is that behind all this are SP, police and some sycophant officers. What is clear is that all constables, havaldars and home guards are ready to support us." In one of the pamphlets distributed by the VHP in Solapur, the people were told that, "There is a well planned conspiracy behind the riots continuously occurring in the country. From Morocco to Malaysia, India is the only country where Muslims are in a minority. Therefore constant efforts are being made to increase the Muslim population. They are dreaming of installing a Muslim government in this country by taking advantage of democratic system in India.... The Centre of Islamic Culture in London is directing all such activities. They plan to make Muslim minority in India into a majority by converting eight crore of Harijans to Islam." In Ahmedabad in1982 communal feelings were aroused in a similar fashion. The Gujarati leaflet distributed by the VHP alleged that the conversion of Harijans to Islam is not on account of their persecution by the upper caste Hindus but is related to large amount of petro-dollars flowing into the country. Another pamphlet stated that a cow had been killed, a Mahant had been seriously injured, and an idol of God had been damaged. There was no truth in either of these statements. Similarly in Baroda, a pamphlet exhorted the Hindus to be bold, take weapons and attack the Muslims who were out to destroy Hindu religion and Hindu temples. Such rumours are spread by groups of Hindu rioters without any consideration to facts and with meticulous efficiency. These influence communal sentiments and induce and intensify riots. Earlier riots used to last for two or three days, but now are spread over weeks and even months. Neither the administration, police, or the electronic media contradict such rumours and statements. It has been argued that riots have taken place in urban areas, particularly medium sized of towns and cities like Ahmedabad, Moradabad, Meerut, Aligarh, and

Bhiwandi.

It is further argued that riots take place in such towns and cities where Muslim population varied from 20 to 40 per cent, and where an affluent Muslim middle-class has come into existence. Rustamji, former member of National Police Commission says, "a riot does not occur in a sleepy little village, nor in a tribal village in M.P. where all live safely in their poverty. It occurs in Moradabad, where metal workers built up a good industry. It occurs in Aligarh where lock workers have made it good, it occurs in Bhiwandi where powerloom industries are prosperous, it occurs in Hatia, Ahmedabad and Hyderabad and Jamshedpur where there are jobs to get, contracts to secure, houses and shops to capture, it occurs in Agra and Ferozabad and in all other towns where economic rivalries are serious and have to be covered with a cloak of communalism."[24]

This is not all true. Communal riots have taken place in metropolitan cities like Bombay and Calcutta too. Riots have taken place in cities like Ahmedabad where 75 per cent of Muslims lived below the poverty line. Riots have taken place where signs of Muslim property were not visible like in Aurangabad (1968), Hyderabad (1965), Pune (1973) and Ahmedabad (1982). In Hyderabad, the Jan Sangh, the Congress and the Majlis-e-Ittehadul Muslimeen (MIM) tried to win and consolidate their political and electoral position through communal riots. In Vadodra, Muslims are very poor and backward. Vadodra riots were the result of rivalry in illicit liquor trade controlled by the local Kahars and Muslims. Antisocial elements both the communities have a field day and became heroes of their respective communities to legitimize themselves. Riots have occurred in rural areas like in Biharsharif, Rourkela and Gonda. They have also taken place in towns of Gujarat where the Muslim population was not very significant percentage-wise nor too prosperous. They have also taken place in working class centres like Jamshedpur, Rourkela, Ahmedabad, Kanpur, Ranchi, Pune, Solapur, etc. In these places the working class unity was disregarded, even the political parties and trade unions were not able to prevent the working class from participating in communal riots. At one place in Ahmedabad, a red flag holding Muslim trade unionist was murdered by Muslim rioters because he tried to protect Hindus. Hindu rioters burnt his dead body because he was a Muslim.[25]

Rafiq Chacha who gave all his life for the cause of workers of Ahmedabad and lived in a mixed locality was murdered because he was a Muslim and his house burnt.[26] While workers participated in communal riots the Tatas provided a platform to the RSS. Riots have taken place where signs of Muslim prosperity were not visible like in Jamshedpur, Rourkela and Ranchi. Similarly Dalits have been involved by Hindu chauvinist forces in riots against Muslims.

Communalism and communal violence lead to schism between communities while Hindus celebrate their victory because they have exacted revenge after seven hundred years. To Muslim communalists every riot is a reminder of the forgotten lesson of the unity of the *Millat.* Unity in diversity becomes the casualty. Communal riots are politically motivated and result in communal political mobilization. Communal riots show a methodical and organized madness. They are pre-planned and are produced by almost identical incidents which arouse religious passions and are followed by the desired similar results conducive to the growth of anti-secular politics. Communalism and communal riots dehumanize man and brutalize society.

II

Rourkela, 1964

The population of Rourkela and its periphery (before

the steel mill was established) was predominantly tribal, along with Muslims. The principal occupation of the population was agriculture. Out of the 2456 displaced families, as a result of acquisition of land for the mill, 400 were rehabilitated in Jhirpani colony and 800 in Jhalda colony on the periphery of the newly developed town. The rest of the families went to resettlement colonies in the interiors. A large number of skilled, semi-skilled and unskilled workers for the steel mill were recruited from outside Rourkela and particularly from Kerala, Tamil Nadu, West Bengal, Punjab, and Bihar.These people could compete better with the local people in urban-oriented occupations. Their tribal and agricultural way of life was influenced rather adversely by industrialization and contact with the outsiders, consequently causing tension, stress and strain. One factor needs to be noted—most of the tribals followed Hindu rituals and ceremonies, even inviting Hindu priests on religious and family ceremonies. They worship Hindu gods and celebrate Hindu festivals. The tribals also had tensions with Muslims to whom they were financially indebted.

The Rourkela riots in 1964 were the continuation of the Hindu-Muslim riots in Jessore in East Pakistan and consequent Hindu-Muslim riots in Calcutta. The immediate cause of Rourkela riots was the passing through it of the Hindu refugee trains to rehabilitation places in Madhya Pradesh. These refugee trains stopped at Rourkela for serving lunch to the refugees Tales of atrocities on Hindus by Muslim population of Jessore in East Pakistan were flashed in lurid details in the Indian press, particularly in the Eastern zone. This provoked the Hindu sentiments and caused the Hindu-Muslim antagonism. During the stoppage of trains at Rourkela, the Hindu refugees narrated the tales of atrocities in great details which caused further provocation and antagonism. The arrangements for food at the railway station were appalling. The contract for supply of food was given to a railway contractor who could at most serve twenty people at a time while the trains carried 600 to 800 persons. This caused resentment and involved the local Hindu population. This led to abnormally long stay of trains at Rourkela when the local Hindu population freely mixed with the refugees which caused greater resentment. Thus the psychological arena of Ea st Pakistan communal disturbances extended to Rourkela.[27]

The trains started moving through Rourkela on 6 March, 1964. The public started offering food to the refugees from 8 March 1964. In course of time the activist of Bharatiya Jan Sangh and the RSS took responsibility of feeding the refugees and this fact was given publicity. On 11 March, the organizers of feeding operations, before securing meals used a loudspeaker on the railway platform condemning Pakistan and its policies and aroused the Hindu sentiments. All this had gone on without any objection from the administration. This process went on unabated for almost one week and the tension too mounted gradually. Throughout this initial period, a few Muslims also joined hands in feeding the refugees at the railway station.[28] On the 14 March, the tension started mounting up due to playing up and on human emotions concerted effort by a group of individuals interested in stepping up emotions on communal lines. The nucleus of people who were interested in aggravating the trouble engineered a well planned propaganda and other kinds of preparations. The main mechanism was spread of rumours. There was also some evidence of 'organizations' supported by men, money and material in inciting communal riots.[29] The extent of the spread of these rumours was indicative of the fact that 84.7 per cent of the Muslims, 93.0 per cent of the Adivasis and 74.9 per cent of the Hindus in Rourkela heard these rumours.[30]

These rumours included : Muslims were coming from outside Rourkela in large numbers to attack Hindus;

local Muslims were preparing arms and ammunition, all Hindus were in danger of being extinguished; Muslims mixed poison in the food given to the refugees; Muslims were operating transmitters to send news to Pakistan; large masses of Muslims amassed a dump of lethal weapons and were preparing to attack Hindus; Muslims poisoned drinking water; Muslims had dumped arms and ammunition in the mosque, all Muslims are Pakistani spies a Muslim was caught red-handed while putting poison in the Central Water Works in the city; Pakistan will soon invade India, etc. The administration took no steps to rebut these rumours.

Due to the fear created by strong rumours of attack by Muslims, the Hindu population started preparing lethal weapons out of iron bars and the like inside the steel mill and also outside. This continued for two to three days without any check and many workers coming out of the plant carried these weapons. Nobody tried to stop this till large-scale killings started.[31]

Between 15 and 19 March about 5000 Muslims and almost an equal number of Hindus, who must have sensed the danger to life left Rourkela. Unfortunately the administration did not comprehend the deteriorating communal situation.

The refugee trains stopped at Rourkela till the night of 16th March after which they started running through after such a request was made by the local railway authorities. On the 17th situation became so tense that despite the through running of trains, the local Muslims sent telegrams and made telephone calls to Bhubaneshwar about the developing dangerous situation stating that they were feeling unsafe, and that they needed protection. The Shanti Sainik sent a telegram to the district magistrate and the chief minister on the 18th saying that the communal riots could break any moment. The chief minister was restrained from coming to Rourkela on the plea that his visit will weaken the hands of the local administration.

At this juncture certain Muslims shouted the slogans-Pakistan is in danger, Pakistan Zindabad to irritate the Hindus. Some Muslim merchants played Pakistan Radio broadcast in a busy market square. These proved a major cause of provocation to Hindus. The old rumours particularly that Muslims have poisoned drinking water, that Muslims are coming in large numbers and that Muslims have dumped arms and ammunitions in the mosque were floated with greater gusto. The adminis-tration took no step to rebut these rumours nor took action against mischievious elements.[32] On 18th March, in the evening a *gwala* was stabbed near the railway station and the news of stabbing spread like wildfire.

Tensions mounted to such an extent that at 10.30 pm the outburst of emotions led to mass killings. Scattered attacks on Muslims started in different parts of the city and surrounding area on the 19th March. The non-Muslims were frightened and infuriated by rumours that 'large masses of Muslims had already started murdering and were advancing towards the town.' There was another rumour that the 'government wanted a retaliation for happenings in East Pakistan.' For three days there was virtually no semblance of administration in the area. Some people went into the interiors in jeeps and carts to spread these rumours.[33]

The disturbances reached a climax on the 20th in Rourkela and the outskirts and continued to spread in the interior areas. The participating crowds consisted mostly of Punjabis, Bengalis, Oriya, and Biharis. Concentrated efforts were made wherever there was concentration of Muslim population, and once these riots broke out, the fury of the mob knew no bounds.[34]

At Jalda resettlement colony, hundreds were butchered and all the Muslims houses burnt. The mob numbering several thousands on 21st had laid siege around the colony and started arson by sprinkling petrol and setting fire—not even babies were spared. Small babies were thrown into the fire. Some wounded survivors were collected together and set on fire. At Jhirpani settlement colony, casualties were comparatively less as Muslims had taken refuge in the nearby engineering college though the property of the entire Muslim community was damaged.

On 20th March, military was asked to take control of the situation. It reached Rourkela on 21st morning but was given the whole responsibility for maintenance of law and order only on 24th of March, after which riots stopped.

In Rourkela the Muslims were the main victims. The rioters were not only Hindus but a number of Adivasis and industrial workers had also joined the fray.

According to the study of Rourkela riots, to a Hindu minded Hindu, riots were an act of reprisal of the earlier manslaughter of East Pakistan. To a secular citizen, much of what happened was the result of the political machinations much of which was deliberate and planned. To others, the worst confusion and bloodshed was due to commissions and inefficient administration the State Government of Orissa which had failed to provide protection to the members of the minority community at a time when emotions were bound to be high among the members of the majority group.[35]

Meerut, 1968

Meerut city is an important town of UP. It is known for the handlooms and scissors industries along with the famous Nauchandi fair. In 1960 its population was about four lakh. Hindus constituted about 65 per cent of the population and Muslims about 30 per cent. A significant number of Hindu migrants were present in the city engaged by and large in industry and trade. The interests of minority community and the displaced persons were competitive. The narrow lanes and by-lanes winding their way through the localities of the majority community passed through minority community areas. Despite the insularity within their physical configuration, there were a number of points of contact between the two compact areas. This lead to neighbouring quarrels sometimes which assumed communal overtones. Once communal riots break out, it becomes difficult to prevent stray cases of arson, loot and even stabbing. Rumours are easily spread but difficult to verify.

Very often, the politics of Meerut moved on communal lines. In 1965, a Congress candidate for the chairmanship of the Municipal Committee of Meerut defeated an independent with the support of the Jan Sangh members and in the victory procession the main slogans were communal. In the fourth general election, the SSP candidate belonging to the Hindu Community won the LS election while his companion for Legislative Assembly seat, a Muslim, was defeated. He got only 27.9 per cent votes.

The RSS and the Jan Sangh are quite popular in Meerut politics. The vice-president of the Meerut Cantonment happened to be the ex-president of the Western UP Chamber of Commerce. The Hindu Mahasabha was also quite active. Its local president brought out a daily newspaper with about 3000 copies circulation. He wrote in his paper unambiguously that India belongs to the majority community and that all efforts to bring about communal harmony were bound to fail. This newspaper increasingly spread hatred and hostility against the minority community. According to the RSS chief of the area, secularism was hypocrisy. Guru Gowalkar and Jagatguru Shankeracharya visited Meerut not long before the riots.[36]

The Meerut city Muslim politics was at that point of time suffering from internecine quarrels and differences.

It was in Meerut that the first significant split took place in the *Jamait-ul-Ullema*. At the all India conference of the *Jamait* in 1964, Maulana Azad Madni was elected general secretary. For the presidentship, however, the name of the Maulana Fakhruddin was proposed by the general secretary but was opposed by the section of the *Jamait*. The compromise arrived at Meerut never worked. The internecine quarrels continued. In 1965 Maulana Atikur Rehman organized and launched the *Majlis-e-Mushawarat* at Bhopal which played a significant role in the defeat of the Congress at different places which the Jamait had been supporting.Thus, while the Hindu communal forces were united against the minority community, the Muslims were divided among themselves. During the conference of Majlis at Meerut, Dr. Faridi made a spirited speech highlighting the problems of the Muslim community. This led to series of articles in the daily newspaper owned by the Hindu Mahasabha leader. Then came the news of Jamait conference and the visit of Sheikh Abdullah.[37]

As soon as the visit of Sheikh Abdullah was announced, a local organization called 'Kashmir Bachao Morcha' was organized by Jan Sangh and RSS leaders of the city. It distributed a highly inflammatory leaflet accusing all those welcoming the Sheikh as traitors. The leader of the local RSS went around the city in a jeep imploring the people of Meerut to prevent the Sheikh from entering Meerut. The Hindu Mahasabha leader published in his newspaper a series of statements from like-minded people about the Sheikh's visit and hinted at the possibility of black flag demonstration. The atmosphere was considerably poisoned by the inflammatory posters, leaflets and editorial.[38]

The Jamait conference was to begin at 6 pm outside the compound of Faiz-am college. At about 4.30 pm, the Kashmir Bachao Morcha began its announced meeting at the Shahid Memorial situated at about 100 yards from the college compound. There were about 200 persons attending the meeting. At about 5.30 pm, the procession started from this point headed by a jeep with black flags and the RSS chief at the mike inside the jeep. It crawled its way to the gate of the college compound. When the jeep tried to enter the compound the two groups clashed. There was stone throwing. The police intervened and saved the situation. This dispersed the procession.[39] The processionists dispersed into lanes and bylanes. Sheikh Abdullah arrived around 6 pm and addressed the conference up to 8 pm.

At about 7 pm, a bus carrying 50 people from nearby villages coming to attend Sheikh's meeting was diverted to proceed through the majority community locality of Thana Sadar. Near the UP roadways depot, in full view of the police station, the bus was stopped by a crowd of about 100/150 persons and the passengers were beaten up and stabbed. Four persons died on the spot. Three others died in hospital.

A tempo rickshaw coming from Waytee was also diverted to Begumpole and into Sadar, where at about 7.30 pm it was stopped and the passengers stabbed. All this evidence shows that miscreants were quite active and had organized themselves for starting communal riots even while the crowd was listening to the speech of Sheikh Abdullah.[40]

Of the 17 persons officially acknowledged to have been killed in the communal riots, 16 belonged to the minority community. The one belonging to the majority community was killed because of a mistaken identity as was the case with two of the injured persons being treated at the hospital. Sharma hospital recorded eight out of nine persons admitted on 28 January belonging to the minority community and only one belonging to the majority community. The next day six persons were admitted who all were Muslims. In the cantonment hospital throughout the period of riots on 28, 29, and 30th January—in all 27 were admitted, 22 being Muslims. There were five cases of stabbing, the victims being the

Muslims. During the riots only two to three shops were reported to have been looted which shows that antisocial elements were not in action and that it was the communal elements who were active with the specific aim of murder.[41]

The two authors said that after a detailed comprehensive survey of the communal riot in Meerut, they had no hesitation in putting the blame squarely on local leaders of the majority communal forces for the riots. They further said that the entire episode bore the stamp of organization and advanced planning executed with ruthless disregard for human lives. They further say that it was amazing that while Dharamvir Anand and Abhay Gupta, president and vice-president of the Cantonment branch of Jan Sangh were arrested, the RSS Chief, who delivered inflammatory speeches and led the procession, was left to roam at large. He confessed that the warrant of arrest against him was withdrawn after he had met the chief minister of UP.[42]

Karimganj, 1968

Karimaganj is a sub-divisional town of Cachar district in Assam situated on the Indo-Pakistan border. The shallow river Koshira about 50 feet wide at this place, divides Karimganj from Pakistan. According to 1961 census, Karimganj town had a population of 28,655 persons. During 1951-61 period, Karimganj population increased by about 50 per cent. The town had a high proportion of migrant Hindu population. Of the permanent residents of the town, 2520 were migrant Hindu refugees while only about 3520 were local born citizens. About 37 per cent of the total population in Karimganj town were non-resident floating population, coming from the surrounding rural areas during the daytime engaging themselves in jobs like handicrafts and rickshawpulling, artisans, and day labourers. In Karimganj subdivision, Hindu-Muslim ratio in 1961 was 56.5 per cent and 43 per cent. In Karimganj town, out of the permanent residents, Hindus comprised 25,092 persons and the Muslims only 3204. The Karimganj police station which covered certain surrounding rural areas comprised of 46 per cent (81,015) Hindus and 52.2 per cent (89,717) Muslims. Muslims were mainly living in surrounding rural areas and were economically more backward and had little role to play in municipal politics of Karimganj town except in small pockets of their concentration like Hadaragram.[43] Riots in Karimganj took place from March 2, 1968 and continued up to March 7, when the Union Home Minister visited the town.

According to Ashwani K. Ray and Suhash Chakravarti, wherever there has been a communal riot, what goads social differences into violent clashes are the political forces of the region operating on specific economic substructure. In other words, political interests act as the catalytic agent to accelerate or decelerate social or religious divisivness. Karimganj had its share in a very substantial measure of this catalyst agent.[44]

Seventysix per cent of Hindu population of Karimganj is engaged in trade and business, bulk of them involved in smuggling. Hindu traders had a grievance that Muslims have an edge over them in the smuggling of goods because of their relations with the Muslim population of the Pakistan border. That created its own kind of tension and these tensions tended to coincide with religious divisions. A substantial number of 'new rich' class grew up because of smuggling trade and included a few Muslims as well. Secondly, the Congress is the only organized party in Karimganj. It was overwhelmingly controlled by Hindus. Thus, state patronage in terms of grants of licenses and purchasing agencies was mainly enjoyed by Hindu traders. Some consumer cooperatives and semi-government organizations were also controlled by the Hindus. There were some Muslims in these organizations but their number was insignificant. Thirdly, some urban propertied Muslims had also engaged in trade which was restarted by Hindu traders. This aspect of local tension found its reflection in trends of the communal rioting in Karimganj where properties rather than persons were the main targets of attack. In fact, the betelnut traders invited the greatest wrath of rioters. Another cause of tension between Hindus and Muslims was the landlord-tenant relationship between Muslims and Hindus respectively. It was particularly true of Hadaragram, a Muslim landlord colony of 80 houses. The prices of land had gone up by about 400 per cent. The Hindu migrant traders who were tenants here resented this when they had sold their properties in East Pakistan at throwaway prices. In this locality not a single house was left unburnt during riots.[45] In the political field, the interests of the two communities found contradictory manifestations. The Hindus of Karimganj stood for recognition of Bengali language as an official language of Assam and the merger of Cachar district with Bengali speaking Tripura. The Muslims opposed both these demands. They stood for Assamese language and opposed the merger with Tripura, lest they be submerged into the overwhelming Hindu majority. They organized a 'shanti parishad' and expressed themselves in favour of Assamese language. In 1958-59, the Muslims of Cachar had organized the 'Assam Sahitya Sabha'. Thus the insecurity of the Muslims, both real and imaginary, under the rule of Hindu refugees led them to a situation where the political role of the communities became opposed to one another.[46]

On September 11, 1967, the day when Communists organized the hunger strike, Maulana Jabil, who was giving evidence before the committee inquiring about the alleged anti-Congress activities of some local Congressmen in 1967 elections, was assaulted in the Congress office which led to some communal clashes and consequent communal tension. The SSP or the PSP did not exist then in Karimganj, nor were the RSS and the

Jan Sangh political identities of any significance.[47] The communal elements were well organized within the two warring factions of the Congress. The Muslim support was divided between these two factions outside the Congress. The migrant Hindus also organised a group called 'progressives'. It supported the claim of Bengali language and represented the interests of Bengali Hindu migrants. The Karimganj Congress could not do so because of Assamese dominated State Congress Committee. So it kept aloof from Bengali language agitation. Owing to this, Muslims supported the Congress. The 'Progressives' won the election of the Legislative Assembly, though by a narrow margin. Muslims overwhelmingly voting for the Congress candidate.[48]

Another factor which had a direct bearing on the communal riots in Karimganj was the local municipal elections due to be held on March 11, 1968 postponed on account of the riots. Of the two contending factions in the municipal election, the 'Nagrik Samiti' consisted of the 'Progressives' and the other 'Paura Kalyan Samiti' was the local outfit supported by the Congress bosses. In the municipal elections, the 'Paura Kalyan Samiti' candidate in the Hadargram locality was a Muslim landlord and the candidate of the 'Kalyan Samiti' was a Hindu trader, both otherwise rivals in the betelnut trade. This also added to the communal tension.

On March 1, 1968, a cow belonging to a Muslim of Hadargram trespassed into a Hindu house. When the cow was being taken by a Hindu boy out of the compound, he was beaten up by a Muslim resident of the house of the owner of the cow. The cow was snatched away. The resultant fracas was avoided. Meanwhile the news got around about the "Muslim arrogance", and some traders of the 'Nagrik Samiti' approached the Hindu lad. The next morning on March 2, the lad accompanied by friends put up difficult demands for settlement. The elders arbitrated that he be paid Rs 200 as against his demand of Rs 365. This was agreed upon. It was around 10 am At this stage, a batch of about 20 or 25 men led by one Gandhi, a 'Nagrik Samiti' candidate for Municipal elections entered the scene. They announced that the arbitration was fake and gave a call for vengeance for such act of "Muslim arrogance". Suddenly the atmosphere became tense with abuses followed by shouts and some stone throwing. The boys of the Bipan Pal High School immediately came out and attacked the Karimganj High Madarsa injuring a number of students and teachers. The life of the Maulvi was saved by the Hindu neighbours.

In Hadaragram where the trouble originated, the group of original miscreants was immediately joined by local traders. The rampage began around 10.15 am mainly directed against Muslim properties, godowns and houses. The entire locality was soon set on fire, coupled with looting of Muslim homes. None of the 80 Muslim houses in that area, was spared. The trouble spread to adjacent Chorakuli where there were about 17 Muslim houses belonging to the propertied class, in the midst of a Hindu locality. All these Muslim houses were gutted. The looting and arson spread to the trading centre where again selectively all Muslim shops were attacked in areas like Chorbazar, Jabiganj, Masjid Road, etc. But the target of the rioters' fury was the Ajmal Hotel. Only one Hindu shop by mistaken identity was looted. As soon as its Hindu identity was established, looting was stopped. The rioters prevented the fire brigade from functioning. From the next day, riots spread to rural areas and continued till March 7, when the Union Home Minister visited Karimganj. In some of the rural areas of Karimganj, Muslim retaliation had been as severe, particularly in areas like Girishganj Bazar, Sarar Pak, and Raghurtuk Bazar. Hindus were beaten and some Hindu shops gutted.[49] The casualties were on 1.3.68. Hindu injured; on 2.3.68, 10 Hindus and 30 Muslims; on 3.3.68, one Muslim; on 4.3.68, 6 Hindus, 2 Muslims; on 5.3.68, 20 Hindus, 1 Muslim; on 6.3.68, 4

Hindus; on 2.3.68, 7 Muslims and one Hindu died in Hadaragram and adjacent areas. The approximate loss of property was: Hadaragram-89 Muslims and one Hindu, Charakoli 19 Muslims, Bahswar 6 Muslims, Raghurtuk Bazar 26 Hindus, Baraigram 2 Muslims, Girishganj Bazar 14 Hindus, no Muslim, Jasaharia 4 Hindus, Bilbari 7 Hindus, Chhararpur Bazar 12 Hindu, Paldhar 16 Hindus Gulalkhand 5 Muslims, no Hindu, Birgram 10 Muslims, Kurikhala 15 Muslims, Chhivahala 4 Muslims, no Hindu.[50]

Aurangabad, 1968

Aurangabad had no history of communal riots since Independence. In fact it was around 1964-65 that communal organizations began to come up in Aurangabad. The *Jamiat-e-Islami* did not have any active branches till about 1964. It was during these 4/5 years that communal organizations began to exploit all India communal issues and tensions to make inroads in the otherwise peaceful atmosphere.

The fourth General Elections was the first big opportunity for the Jan Sangh to approach the masses on a purely communal platform and they utilized it to the hilt. The Jan Sangh could do it especially because the opposing Congress candidate in Aurangabad was a Muslim and there was no effective progressive opposition. The fact that in the 1962 elections, the Muslim electorate had overwhelmingly voted for the Muslim Congress candidate in preference to a respected opposition candidate was exploited by the Jan Sangh. The 1967 elections marked a definite shift of a section of Aurangabad people; especially in the influential trading community and certain other well-defined social groups towards a communal platform.[51]

The Jan Sangh sought to consolidate the advances thus made by holding a State conference at Aurangabad in December, 1967. It was addressed by Deen Dayal

Upadhyaya and Atal Bihari Vajpayee. Their speeches did not stimulate communal passions. But there were other speeches at another rally held during the session in which Muslims were named openly as country's enemy number one along with the Congress and Communists. Both before and after the 1967 elections, the local Jan Sangh press continuously made appeals to communal passions.[52] The Muslim intelligence, however, saw the events in the all India context. It viewed the rise of Hindu communal forces as a threat to the existence of the Muslim community and felt a sense of insecurity and itself developed a communal approach. The *Jamiat-e-Islami* built up an effective base among this section of the middle-class.[53]

During the six months before the riots took place, following the Jan Sangh conference, several events took place which heightened the communal tension. First came the municipal elections in which the Congress lost majority, particularly in municipal minority wards. The opposition included diverse elements like the Jan Sangh. Though the opposition was divided before the elections, it managed to form a combination to oust the Congress and evolve a formula by which presidentship and other posts could come to all by rotation. The first president was a Muslim with progressive views. His election was not liked by communalists and by a section of Congressmen. A press campaign to discredit the new presidentiship of the municipality was carried on.[54]

Next in order came the conference of *Tameer-i-Millat*. Its leaders from Hyderabad launched a tirade against Hindu communalists giving graphic description of communal riots elsewhere in India and rousing the Muslims to defend themselves with arms. Mr. Khabilullah Hussaini in his presidential address gave a slogan to the Muslim youth, "prepare yourself and start action". He exhorted the Muslims throughout the country to organize themselves and arm themselves with whatever weapons they could get. In the city the entire local press played up the issue and fanned communal fires. The atmosphere was seized upon by certain rabid elements to pour oil on troubled waters by inviting V.R. Patil, a Hindu Mahasabha leader from Solapur. His speech was one long hymn of hate and ridicule of the Muslims. He made an open declaration that given the power he would raze every mosque and drive every Muslim from Maharashtra.[55]

The actual riot took place on 8 June, 1968. The excuse for the riot was an accidental injury to a cow by a Muslim baker's boy while trying to chase it away from the shop. It was a wound inflicted with a knife. The cow was taken to the veterinary hospital. The boy was also taken into police custody. All this was over by 3 pm.[56]

The communal elements spread the rumour that the cow was killed. A loudspeaker van went to inform their friends in distant localities that the trouble spot was at Shahaganj. The whole activity was carried out by known Hindu chauvinist youths. At 3 pm a scant meeting was held. After the meeting, systematic efforts were made to mobilize communal groups all over the city at one place and go on a rampage. The course of action shows a planned method. A riotous group hit the baker's shop and its owner. The leadership of the crowd was provided by RSS-Jan Sangh workers, their sympathizers, were students, and trading class youth. This was almost clearly admitted, when the local Jan Sangh presidents said at the citizens' meeting, held soon after the riots in the presence of the chief minister who had come to Aurangabad to study the situation that, what had happened (the riots) had to happen and it was good that it had happened. There were some instances on that fateful night in which the complicity of the Jan Sangh was clearly seen. A group of college students with known sympathy for the Jan Sangh went in a batch and attacked a leading Muslim businessman's house and ransacked it. A group of persons attacked a furniture shop belonging to a Muslim and burnt it to ashes. It was led by Subhash Pahade, a known Jan Sangh worker. He was caught redhanded actively engaged in the riots and was arrested. A Jan Sangh councillor threatened a social worker who was trying to quench the fire which had consumed a Muslim 'gadi' shop. Along with these elements there were some Congress elements from the trading community who took a leading part in loot and arson.[57]

The riots, though started as a blatant organized aggression of Hindu communalists, did not remain a one sided affair. The Hindu communalists had their day for about one and a half hours. Soon the Muslims began retaliation at 7.30 pm and set fire to Hindu shops situated mainly on the junction of Hindu and Muslim localities. The retaliation was determined and the loss of property of both the communities was great. Thus the responsibility for starting the actual riots by attacking, backing openly looting the property belonging to the Muslims rests squarely on the Hindu communal elements. The Muslims retaliated with grim determination later. The riots were thus not spontaneous but planned and prepared by systematic propaganda preceding the riots and by actually mobilizing communal elements and taking initiative on the day of riots.[58]

It is also important to observe that the riots remained confined to the main bazaar roads. No incidents took place in lanes and bylanes, nor were the houses burnt. Only shops were the targets. There were hardly any attacks on person except for one incident of stabbing of a Hindu. The fury of the riots abated in a few hours and not a trace of it was left on daily life of the people within forty-eight hours.

Ahmedabad, 1969

The blood bath during Ahmedabad riots (September 18 to 23, 1969) was so naked that Y.B. Chavan, the then Union Home Minister, on his visit to Ahmedabad on September 24, 1969 said that violence on September 21 and 22 was on a large-scale and that the trouble was the first of its kind in magnitude since Independence. He further said that, "the communal parties were functioning in the state and they are also active there". He further said that the two aspects were important in communal trouble. One was the adequacy of advance intelligence and the other prompt action by the local officials.[59] The Gujarat government miserably failed on these counts. News of mass killings, massacre and killing of women and children on the one hand and police inactivity or inadequate police action on the other, made the Muslims declare that if the minority did not receive adequate protection, they will ask all Muslims with their children and wives to come out without any arms and go to the localities occupied by the Hindu communities and offer their lives with their children and women.[60] It was on the intervention of the Prime Minister Indira Gandhi that the Army was called by the State Government but it was not given full powers instead was asked to assist the civil authorities. Again the Prime Minister intervened and the Army took full charge of the city on September 23, 1969 and the riots stopped soon after. She also sent a three member MPs team consisting of Chanderjeet Yadav, Randhir Singh and Azad Madani. In fact after the findings, the Prime Minister visited Ahmedabad herself. During the riots, according to conservative estimates, 2000 lives were lost. Majority of deaths were due to stabbing and arson. The loss of property, production and wages was estimated at Rs 100 crores. The damage to organized industry was estimated to be Rs 33.25 crores by the Gujarat Chamber of Commerce, Rs 5 crores worth wages were lost by workers. Loss of private property in the form of household articles of families who had lost everything and many of whom had lost bread earners as well could be more than 5 crores. The textile mills lost a sizeable number of orders of Puja and Diwali holidays. Burning of mosques and durgahs was also on a big scale. Fortynine mosques were attacked out of which eleven were completely demolished and the rest were damaged on a big scale. According to veteran journalist Subrata Banerjee a dargah of Khokar Shah, a pilgrimage both for Hindus and Muslims was razed to the grounds and a six inch mound of clay was placed there with a garland and it became a Hindu shrine on that site. Many such dargahs were replaced overnight by shrines dedicated to Hanuman. Some of these were designated "Hulladea" Hanuman (riot Hanuman shrine).[61] Fire destroyed 3969 dwellings and shops and 2317 more were physically destroyed. About 600 families lost their belongings and shelter.[62] On September 21, attacks were made on passenger trains near Naroda station. 17 persons were killed. There was hardly a shop of Muslims in Hindu and mixed areas which was not burnt or destroyed. Almost all the small seven printing works of which Ahmedabad craftsmen are famous were destroyed. In Khokhra- Mehmdarand-Amraivadi, the massacre was so ghastly that not a single member of the minority community was left alive.[63]

The basic cause of Ahmedabad riots was raising the communal tension to a pitch by communal parties particularly the RSS and the Jan Sangh, and the immediate cause was the incident at the Jagannath temple. In 1967 general elections, the Jan Sangh attempted to emerge as a powerful contender for power in Gujarat. It failed miserably. The only stronghold it then had was Rajkot. Since elections, top leaders had been visiting the state regularly and by 1969 had whole time leaders in every taluka because the party then had been concentrating mainly on students and youth.

In January 1969, the RSS had a four-day camp at Ahmedabad. About 1800 volunteers attended that camp. Guru Golwalkar, the then RSS chief attended and addressed the camp on all the four days. He is reported to have said at the camp that Muslims were guests in

India and that guests do not stay for all time and that Muslims be made to realize this. It was also reported that detailed instructions were given as to how a Hindu youth should behave in the eventuality of a communal riot.[64]

In the month of March 1969, there were two minor incidents. At Naghori ward in Shahpur ward, there was a scuffle between Muslims and Vaghlis over some minor incident. It was expected to foster anti-Muslim sentiments. Another incident occurred when a police officer upturned a pushcart carrying a collection of old books among which reportedly were copies of Quran. The local Muslims protested and attacked the police station. The police officer was obliged to apologize even though he contested the facts. This incident was also given a communal turn by Hindu communalists because the police officer concerned was a Hindu.[65] In April 1969, Municipal Corporation elections were held. The Jan Sangh contested 55 seats and won two. During the elections it tried to communalize the situation and whip up anti-Muslim feelings.

Golwalkar toured Gujarat-Saurashtra once again and carried forward the anti-Muslim sentiments. Another Jan Sangh leader S.S. Bhandari visited various towns of Gujarat to organize the students wing of the Jan Sangh. In the third week of July nationalization of 14 banks took place. The deputy Prime Minister Morarji Desai resigned. There was new political alignment in the country. The Syndicate Congress began to cooperate with the Jan Sangh and the Swatantra Party. Gujarat State Government was with the Syndicate. Hence its relations with Jan Sangh became very cordial.

On Independence Day at Bhavnagar one minor but significant incident took place. Some police officers went to Sandhiwad, a Muslim locality, and tried to compel the Muslim shopkeepers to close their shops. The shopkeepers replied that they had opened the shops as it was Independence Day. The police officials replied, "Your Independence Day can be in Pakistan and not in India." They forced them to close their shops. All political parties demanded the transfer of the said police officials. The demand was accepted, but this reflected the trend in the state police.[66]

On August 31, there was a one lakh strong Al Aqsa protest demonstration against Israel organised by the Muslims in Ahmedabad as was done in many other places in India. In the demonstration there was one slogan: Anyone clashing with Islam will be annihilated. Whatever the textual relevance, the impressive turnout of the Muslims made the slogan acquire a sinister meaning for the non-Muslims and a communal overtone. Only a few days later, on September 4, 1969 another incident occurred. A Muslim police officer was alleged to have kicked a copy of Ramayana at Ram Lila celebration. He was trying to enforce the order that loud-speakers could not be used after 24 hours. There was some opposition to it and he tried to stop the use of loudspeakers. During this he is alleged to have kicked or insulted a copy of Ramayana. Since the sub-inspector was a Muslim, the whole incident was given a communal colour and an inquiry and suspension of the officer was demanded. The Hindu Dharma Raksha Samiti organised a fast in support of the demand. Bal Krishna Maharaja and Sevakram Thakay went on fast. On September 14, 1969 Ratan Lal Gupta with 57 other Jan Sangh volunteers announced their fast. From September 4 to 14, a vigorous anti-Muslim campaign was carried on. Nanaji Deshmukh, the treasurer of Jan Sangh, visited Ahmedabad on September 13 during the fast and Balraj Madhok, another all-India Jan Sangh leader visited Baroda on the same day and gave "Quit India" slogan for Muslims. The "Quit India" posters were pasted at various places including Muslim houses and mosques. Balraj Madhok visited Ahmedabad on September 14, 1969. Speaking at Rifle and Military Training Association, he is reported to have said that banks were unnecessarily nationalized, instead Muslims should be nationalized. He further said that attack by Pakistan on India through Rajasthan was imminent and that in that event Muslims in Gujarat cannot be relied upon. He suggested that the Indian Muslims be shifted to Pakistan.

The Gujarat government asked the Muslim officer to apologize and suspended him pending an enquiry. The Jan Sangh, the RSS, the Hindu Dharma Raksha Samiti, and Hindu Mahasabha organized a victory procession on September 14, 1969. The main slogan during the procession was, "*Gaddar har Musalman, Bhejo use Pakistan.*" Jagannath Joshi, the general secretary of Jan Sangh, addressed a private meeting of Jan Sangh activists on September 19 at W.K. Hall.[67] All these events had heightened the pitch of communal temper.

The Jagannath temple provided the spark of communal riots. The temple is situated outside the Jamalpur gate to the north of which lies a predominantly Muslim area. The temple has a big cowshed and a *gaushala*. Every morning these cows are taken out for grazing and brought back at about 3 pm. Near the temple is situated the *Takia* of Mohammed Shah Bukhari. Every year *Urs* is held here and large number of Muslim men, women and children gather here to pay respect. On September 18, 1969 at about 3.30 pm cows were returning to the temple. Something happened which started a stampede and some push carts were overturned. Women and children started screaming. There was a quarrel between the sadhus and the hawkers. The quarrel lasted about 20 minutes. After going back the sadhus started throwing stones from the terrace. The people on the road counterattacked and threw stones with the result that three glasspanes above the main gate were broken and idols were damaged. But immediately the rumour was spread that 300 Muslims armed with acid bulbs attacked the temple, seriously wounding several sadhus. On hearing this rumour, the Muslim leaders and the police reached the spot. At 5 pm, the *Urs* procession with *Nishans* passed near the temple. Everything was calm and the procession passed peacefully. Yet within a short time a lone dairy shop owned by a Muslim was destroyed 10 kilometres away in a Jan Sangh stronghold. But nothing happened in the locality where the temple was situated which is a predominantly Muslim area. Hindus and Muslims lived in peace throughout the period of riots. The Muslim leaders went to the temple to apologize on behalf of the community. They wanted the police to find out if the Mahant would be willing to meet them. At about 11 pm, a Muslim owned laundry shop was set on fire and the fire brigade was prevented from extinguishing the fire. The shop was situated about 100 steps away from the police station. The police took no action. The crowd attacked a mosquc in thc arca and set fire to it. Late at night another Muslim laundry shop was set on fire at Sarangpur police gate. In Raipur, a bastion of Jan Sangh and in Khadia some other Muslim shops were burnt and looted.

Next morning September 19, 1969, a meeting of leaders of all political parties and prominent persons was organized at Karanj police station. The meeting decided to issue two statements, one joint statement appealing mainly for peace and the other expressing apology signed by Muslim leaders. At the meeting in the temple a sadhu, Kamta Prasad said that sadhus were prepared to sacrifice their life but the act at the temple must be avenged, that they were not prepared to accept any apology and that they would exact revenge. The Muslim leaders left the temple. On the same day, Hindu Dharma Raksha Samiti had a public meeting where provocative and aggressive speeches were made.

By this time the city was in the grip of communal riots and Muslim houses, shops, mosques and dargahs were attacked in a planned and systematic manner.[68]

The Muslim leaders approached the inspector general of police of Gujarat State and the police commissioner in the Karanj police station. The only reply they received from both of them was that they were waiting for the government orders. The Muslim leaders went to see the chief minister to request him to take action, to impose curfew all over the city and to give instructions to the police to shoot at sight. The chief minister told them that the needful will be done.[69]

By the night of September 19th the city was burning. It became impossible for the fire brigade to cope with the task and even if they went to some place, they were prevented by the rioters. At 11 pm the curfew was imposed within the city walls only. The curfew was imposed for 36 hours after the temple incident and after more than 24 hours of burning and looting Muslim shops, houses, mosques and dargahs.[70] By the night of September 20 the situation turned worse. Murders and massacres on large-scale were going on in various localities outside the walled city. There was no curfew there. On September 20, the Union Home Minister and the Prime Minister made anxious enquiries from the Gujarat Government about the situation in Ahmedabad. It was after these inquiries that the curfew was extended all over the city and the army was called to assist the civil authorities. The army on its own could not take action due to lack of power. On September 21, there were mass killings on large-scale and the police failed to check the attacks. Women were molested and girls were kidnapped. According to *The Times of India*, in the suburban areas the crowds had a field day meeting no resistance from either the police or the people. In Khokhra-Mehmdarand-Amraivati the massacre was so ghastly that not a single member of the minority community was left alive. The *Gujarat Samachar* reported on September 20, that "armed arsonists went berserk, setting fire to shops and houses belonging to the minority community. Huge columns of smoke spiralling high gave a picture of city on fire."

On September 21 attacks were extended to the passenger trains and seventeen passengers were killed. On September 22 daily papers reported heavy toll of life. The papers also reported that communal frenzy spread to Baroda, Wadiad, Palampur, Kadi, Grohra and Viyan gani. The riots also spread to Mehsana, Chudusma, Mausa, Palnni, Talod, Pranty, Gondal, Amreli, Junnahgarh, Kamla Mold, Akdol, Sarsa, Karamsad and Chinoda.[71] On September 24, 1969 seven Jan Sangh and Hindu Mahasabha leaders including the Secretary of Gujarat Parishad Committee of Jan Sangh were arrested. The veteran leader of Gujarat, Inderlal Yagnik, MP was on fast in protest of the communal frenzy, massacre, arson and loot. The three members team sent to Ahmedabad by the Prime Minister described the riots as unprecedented. Randhir Singh said that the hooligan attacks seemed to be well-planned and the arsonists had singled out the houses of the minority community. Ajit Bhattacharjee, Editor, in his article noted, "Eyewitnesses told of fleets of cars shuttling up and down carrying rioters and petrol tins."[72] The rioters carried a list whether Muslims were the owner of the property or tenants or whether there was a Hindu partner with the Muslim trader. Scientific methods were applied: first rumours, burning, looting, stray stabbing and then mass killings. Availability of petrol, kerosene oil and latest weapons also suggest this. All these point to one thing—that the whole thing was pre-planned. The then Governor of Gujarat stated categorically that he was convinced that behind these riots in Gujarat was an organized groups. Ajit Bhattacharya said that clearly these riots could not have been acts of spontaneous anger. Subrata Banerjee, another veteran journalist said, "I have come back from Ahmedabad with the impression that what happened can very justifiably be compared to the anti-Jewish pogrom in Hitler's Germany or the Negro-lynching in the deep South of

USA." Badshah Khan (Frontier Gandhi) after his visit to Ahmedabad said, "I have visited Gujarat and after seeing the destruction with my own eyes I have come to the conclusion that all this happened under a well organized plan."[73]

The planned nature of the riots is also apparent from the rumours and pamphlets that were circulated on September 19, and onwards. By noon of 19 September, hundreds of printed and cyclostyled handbills stating that a cow had been killed, the Mahant seriously 'injured' and that the idol of god had been damaged were instigated. There was no truth in any of these. *Sevak* evening daily reported on 20th September, 1969 that several women—obviously Hindu from description—had been stripped and raped publicly. This was contradicted next day but the mischief was done. The AIR Ahmedabad announced that Municipal Dairy milk had been poisoned though after few hours it was officially contradicted.[74] Some of the pamphlets distributed during the riots were:

1. *Hindus Be Alert:* Heinous attack on Jagannath Temple is a severe challenge to the Hindu community. Hindu community should unite and create the capacity to retaliate and join the programme of Hindu Dharma Raksha Samiti in large numbers. From tomorrow onwards come out in support of all programmes and take pledge today to cut out all economic and social relations with the community that has attacked our religion.

2. *Let Hindu People Be Awake:* There is no way out but to carry forward this movement to the feud that either Muslims be driven out to Pakistan or be annihilated. Present religious volunteers are far greater than all the national leaders produced so far. So this movement must continue. Gandhiji drove out English through non-violence. Simi-

larly by hook or by crook Muslims should be driven to Pakistan or annihilate them totally. It is the sacred duty of all Hindus to see that no Muslim remains in India.

3. *Hindu Religion Loving People Be Ready*: Hindus be ready and oppose Muslims. Drive out Muslims from the city. Hindus organize yourselves. Be alert. Appeals in the press as also the apologies are all deception. So be ready to defend your religion as well as your sisters and mothers. Alert! Alert! Alert!.
4. *Public Warning:* By seriously attacking the Hindu temple and by inhumanly torturing the Hindu families, you had not only harmed peace and pride of Gujarat but also damaged social and economic employment. You have got the befitting rebuff, yet you are continuing stray attacks. You had not yet gathered your senses, it seems. So you are hereby publicly warned to stop here if at all you want security of your community, otherwise your total destruction is decided. All the responsibility of adverse results will be on your shoulders. We will not hesitate to stake our lives in defence of Hindu religion and our country *i.e.* Bharat. long live religion, we are Hindu religion loving brothers and sisters.[75]

While the middle-class people took the lead, the working class and scavengers were mobilized on a large-scale and neither the political parties nor the trade unions could stop it. On September 26, a peace march was led by the Governor of Gujarat. Despite his six days of fast, 77 year old Indulal Yagnik joined the peace March along with George Fernandes while no Congressmen joined the march despite appeals. During the march, the Governor addressed people and told the people belonging to the minority community that they must make a solemn pledge to ensure that no one need to fear danger in living with the other community.

III

Bhiwandi, 1970

Bhiwandi is taluka headquarters of Bhiwandi taluka in the Thane district and is situated about 53 kms from Mumbai. The Bhiwandi-Nizampur Municipal council is a 'B' class municipality. It has the largest population of all the taluka towns in the Thane district, about 65 per cent of the population being Muslims and 35 per cent Hindus during 1970.[76] Bhiwandi is a town of power looms owned both by Muslims and Hindus. Very often their factories are situated in the same building.

In the communal riots starting on May 7, 1970 in the wake of Ahmedabad riots in 1969, 78 persons were killed in which 17 were Hindus, 50 were Muslims and 2 were unidentified persons in the communal disturbances, while 9 Muslims were killed in police firing. According to the District police, the total loss suffered by the Hindus was Rs 70,39,560 while that suffered by the Muslims was Rs 82,80,603.[77] The disturbances took a heavy toll. A number of families lost their livelihood and many others found themselves without a roof over their heads. In all 17,422 persons, members of 3,447 families were affected. There were also thousands in the relief camps.[78] The organisation which has directly and indirectly provoked Bhiwandi disturbances which took place in Bhiwandi, Khoni and Nagaon, the two suburbs of Bhiwandi on May 7, 1970 and thereafter was the Rashtriya Utsav Mandal. The majority of the members of this organisation belonged to the Jan Sangh, or, were its supporters. It had brought the communal tension in Bhiwandi to a pitch.[80] The Shiv Sena was responsible to a great extent after Bal Thackeray made a communal speech about Bhiwandi and its Muslim inhabitants at a Shiv Sena meeting held in Thane on May 30, 1969 in the course of which he referred to

Bhiwandi as a second Pakistan and said that such shameful incidents were taking place in Bhiwandi that he was ashamed to speak about them in the presence of ladies.[81] The Hindu Mahasabha was responsible to the extent that its All India President Pandit Brij Narayan- Brajesh addressed public meetings at various places in Thane district including Bhiwandi from 7 to 11 March, 1970 and made communal speeches.[82] The Tameer-E-Millet organised meetings at which its all India and Maharashtra state leaders made communal speeches particularly after 1969 Ahmedabad riots.[88] They exhorted the Muslims to rely upon themselves and not to take to the authorities for protection. The attacks at the MIM meetings against the Hindu communal parties and the counter attacks by communal-minded Hindu parties against the MIM brought about a constant state of unrest in the minds of certain sections of both communities in Bhiwandi and as a result of their efforts the MIM did not make much headway in Bhiwandi.[89]

According to the Commission, the cause of the communal disturbances in Bhiwandi was a basic or underlying cause of all communal disturbances namely communal tension. The Commission finds that basic or underlying causes in the communal tension were created by misbehaviour or processionists in the Shiv Jayanti processions taken out from 1964 to 1969. The situation was compounded by the following: the insistence of certain sections of Hindus to take Shiv Jayanti procession past the Nizampura Jumma Mosque combined with the refusal of Muslims to agree to this, the communal activities of certain political parties, organisations and individuals and the Municipal politics. The immediate cause was the deliberate misbehaviour of the processionists in the Shiv Jayanti procession which was taken out in Bhiwandi on May 7, 1970.[90]

Prior to 1964, Shiv Sena Jayanti was celebrated in Bhiwandi mostly privately and on a small-scale. It was in 1964 that for the first time a public celebration of

Shiv Jayanti took place. A Shiv Jayanti Utsav Samiti was formed by some youngsters. The Samiti totally excluded the Muslims. Even though the organisers of the procession had agreed to a route which avoided four mosques, in the course of the procession the PSP group wanted to change the route and take a road which went past the Quarter gate Mosque. The police intervention stopped it. However, the behaviour of a section of Hindu processionists particularly the RSS and the PSP sections was calculated to provoke and humiliate the Muslims. Provocation and anti-Muslim slogans were shouted and "gulal" was thrown in great excess. A communal incident took place in that year resulting in a near riot. It was averted by the intervention of police officials and leaders of both the communities. This incident took place near the Nazarana talkies and was the result of a quarrel between some Hindu and Muslim youths over the sale of cinema tickets. The next day about 150 Hindu youths armed with sticks went to the Muslim locality of Madarchalla where they were confronted by a group of Muslim youths similarly armed. No actual clash however took place.

The 1965 Shiv Jayanti procession was the very first procession, other than purely Muslim processions which went past the Nizampura Jumma Mosque. No incident occurred. However, another important event in communal political history of Bhiwandi was arrest of 18 Muslim leaders after Pakistan attack on India in September 1965. The detention of some of these leaders was unjustifiable and efforts were soon made to get their release. Even the Chief Minister in his public speech admitted that detention was unjustified.

The 1966 Shiv Jayanti procession was again characterized by excessive throwing of 'gulal' and for its unduly long halts at two Muslim localities shouting slogans and playing games. The 1967 celebrations like 1964 celebrations, were organised by the young elements forming a Shiv Jayanti Utsav Samiti. Not only Muslim leaders but also older and more experienced Hindu leaders were excluded from the Samiti. The intentions of the organisation was clear from the fact that they spent Rs 1000 on purchase of 'Gulal' to be thrown at the time of procession. The processionists shouted abusive and anti-Muslim slogans and led to the first communal riots as the procession went past the said mosque. The younger Hindu elements, most of whom were either members of the Jan Sangh, or, were pro-Jan Sangh, not only insisted in the meetings of the peace committee and the Shiv Jayanti Utsav Samiti that the procession should go past the Nizampura Jumma masjid. Further they demanded that there should be no restrictions whatsoever on the throwing of 'gulal'or the shouting of slogans. The year 1967 thus witnessed the first communal riot in Bhiwandi. The riot took place as the Shiv Jayanti procession was passing by the Nizampur Jumma Mosque. Another event took place on the occasion of Id-e-Milad celebrations. The Muslims insisted to take out the procession through traditional route which passed through the Hindu localities. The Muslims were not allowed to do this so they resented this order and cancelled the procession altogether. At the time of 1968 Shiv Jayanti procession abusive, provocative and anti-Muslim slogans were shouted. The whole atmosphere was vitiated by a group of Hindu youths even though the Muslims participated in the procession, showered flowers and sprinkled rose water, it, served *sharbat* to the processionists and erected decorative arches.[91] Another incident of 1968 which led to communal tension was the holding of Jan Sangh District convention on March 10, 1968 which coincided with Bakr-Id. The Jan Sangh groups coming from various parts went past the Quarter Gate Mosque shouting the slogan "Jan Sangh Vijay Aso". After the prayers, Muslims shouted the slogan "Nare Takbir, Allah ho Akbar". The police intervened and avoided the communal clash. In September 1968, there were 3 incidents of minor assault on Muslims and two cases of rioting in which some Hindus were beaten. In 1968 for the first time Navratri procession was organised by Dr Vyas, the President of Jan Sangh of Bhiwandi.

In April 1969 these extremist Hindu leaders walked out of Shiv Jayanti Utsav Samiti and resigned from it with the result that by their absence the procession that year became a model of what such a procession should be. As a result of these withdrawals from the Samiti in April 1969 a new organisation Rashtriya Utsav Mandal (RUM) was formed by Dr B.P. Vyas, President of Bhiwandi branch of Jan Sangh and a group of nineteen Hindus who had walked out of Shiv Jayanti Samiti. Out of these nineteen persons, fifteen belonged to Jan Sangh or were pro-Jan Sangh, one belonged to Shiv Sena and the remaining three did not belong to any particular party. Right from its inception, the RUM followed a communal line. It held weekly prayer meetings in which communal speeches were made. Accordingly the RUM played a leading role in the communal history of Bhiwandi and was responsible for bringing the communal tension to a pitch.[92] It also spread its activities and influence in villages around Bhiwandi. In all matters likely to create communal tension, the RUM adopted a militant and aggressive attitude and set itself up as the champion of what it considered to be the rights of Hindus against Muslims and to teach the Muslims their place, to teach them a lesson. Thus from the very beginning, the nature of RUM activities were not only communal but aggressively communal.[93] The RUM celebrated Shiv Rajyabhishek Din, the Gandhi Jayanti and Guru Nanak Jayanti and observed the death anniversaries of Tilak, Veer Savarkar, Shahaji Raju and Sambhaji. A number of public meetings were held in villages around Bhiwandi to induce the villagers to join the Shiv Jayanti procession. After the Ahmedabad disturbances, the RUM carried on intensive communal propaganda inflaming the minds of the Hindus against the Muslims.[94] The speech of P.B. Bhave on May 5,1920 exhorted the audience to kill the enemy and to punish traitors as Shivaji had done. He vividly described the pulling down of Hindu temples by Aurangzeb and Shivaji attacking mosques and *dargahs* in Bhiwandi and looting nobles of Surat. Bhave's speech was thus the culminating point of tension which was building up in Bhiwandi. The stage was now set for conflagration.[95]

According to the Commission two other events that attacked the communal line of Bhiwandi were the General elections and the Municipal elections. In the General elections as a result of the support of majority of Muslims, the PWP candidate Bhatachandra alias Bhai Patel was elected to the Maharashtra legislative assembly with a large majority. The municipal elections which took place in August 1967 were characterized by voting on communal lines. Most of the Muslims who were elected were from Bhiwandi. Seva Samiti candidates and several Muslims who had stood as independents lost to the Samiti candidates. The Hindu candidates who had taken a leading role in Shiv Jayanti Utsav Samiti of 1967 were elected from Hindu localities.

About 10,000 persons participated in the Shiv Jayanti procession on May 7,1970. About 5000 persons from surrounding villages participated in the procession. They came from their villages on foot and carried lathis with Bhagwa flag tied to them. In some cases people came in bullock carts. It was for the first time that villagers participated in the procession. The villagers shouted abusive and provocative anti-Muslim slogans as they passed through mixed localities. Their behaviour was aggressive and militant. The villagers who came by Bhiwandi-shehal road stoned some Muslim houses and factories on Panjarapole. Those who came by Bhiwandi-Karivali Road threw 'gulal' on the Moti Masjid and the Hydere Mosque. The Police did not take any action against slogan shouting or throwing of gulal on the mosque.[96]

The processionists who assembled at the starting point were rowdy and boisterous. Several of them were shouting unapproved slogans. These slogans included, *"Gali Gali mein shor hai, sab Mussalman chor hai"*, *"Jo hamse takarayega, woh mitti mein mil jayega"*, *"Mussalman murdaba"*, etc. According to the commission, two processionists shouting these slogans were arrested but soon after intervention of Hindu leaders they were released. According to the Commission from the time the two Hindu slogan shouters were released, the police lost control over the situation. The procession that started again was rowdy and indisciplined and the processionists behaved in a provocative, defiant, aggressive and militant manner. There was excessive throwing of 'gulal'. The 'gulal' among others fell on Muslims and the Muslim leaders in the procession. It also fell on passersby and bystanders in the Muslim localities and on buildings including Sandagar Mohalla Jumma Mosque. As the procession entered the Muslim locality of Madarchalla, it started breaking up into groups. The gap between groups widened as the procession moved along. The processionists deliberately halted at different places on the route to indulge in the shouting of provocative and abusive anti-Muslim slogans and deliberately flouted the time table fixed by Shiv Jayanti Utsav Samiti so as to pass by the mosques during the prayer time. In the Bhusar Mohalla at Old Thane Road 'gulal' was excessively thrown not only on one another but on bystanders who were Muslims. Near old fish market, altercation took place between Muslim bystanders and processionists. Some of the Muslims started throwing stones on the processionists. The processionist immediately started pelting stones at the Muslims and their houses, shops and factories and attacked the Muslims standing on the road with *lathis* and a free fight took place between the processionists and the Muslims. Muslims used stones, brick-bats, soda water bottles, *lathis* and acid bulbs. Then it was free for all. Arson, loot, murder took place unstopped. The rioting was so violent and large-scale that the police had to open firing on 18 occasions on 7 May, 1990 and 14 occasions on 8 May, 1970. Once each on 9 May,12 and 23.[97] The Commission pointed out that there were no simultaneous attacks on the Shiv Jayanti procession and the Hindus and their properties in any locality. The disturbances in different localities started at different times. Several of these disturbances were started by the Hindus. Muslims did not start them.[98] The Commission held that the evidence proved that no conspiracy was entered into by any Muslims to attack the Shiv Jayanti procession. They did not attack the Hindus and their properties in any other locality.[99] It further held that so far as the processionists were concerned, at the instance and instigation of the RUM, a majority of the processionists had been carrying lathis to which Bhagwa flag and banners were tied. This helped them to circumvent the ban on carrying of weapons and this prior preparation for the disturbances was made by the processionists.[100]

Jalgaon, 1970

Jalgaon is a district headquarter of the Jalgaon district. According to 1961 census, the total population of Jalgaon was 80,361 out of which 65,370 were Hindus and 10,601 were Muslims and 4390 belonged to other communities. Thus the percentage of Muslim population in 1961 was 13.1. The city of Jalgaon is divided in two parts, namely old Jalgaon and new Jalgaon. There were only a few Muslim houses situated in new Jalgaon; majority of the Muslim localities being situated in old Jalgaon particularly in central old Jalgaon. These Muslim localities are surrounded on all sides and separated from one another by Hindu localities and form small islands in their midst. The locations that suffered in the disturbances were Muslim localities in old Jalgaon, the Muslim localities in new Jalgaon remaining completely unaffected.[101]

According to the Madan Commission Enquiry a prominent part that played in the communal history of Jalgaon was the Shree Ram Tarun Mandal (RTM). It was formed in 1966 or 1967 by P.K. Jase, secretary of the Jalgaon District of the Jan Sangh. The RTM had an ostensible object of celebrating *utsav*. It however also conducted a gymnasium which was situated about 300 feet from the Jumma Mosque in old Jalgaon. There was close identity of interests and objects between the Jalgaon city Jan Sangh and the RTM. The RTM was established, controlled and managed by the Jalgaon city Jan Sangh and the district Jan Sangh followed their policies. It was in reality merely an organisation to carry out the policies of the Jalgaon city Jan Sangh and Jalgaon district Jan Sangh.[102]

Before October 1969, the relations between the two communities in Jalgaon were harmonious. No communal disturbances had taken place in Jalgaon before May 8, 1970. Both Hindus and Muslims took part in each others religious festivals. Hindus offered coconuts at the Lalshah main dargah and members of both communities took part in the annual celebrations of the *Urs*. Two Hindus were being cooped *and* made president, vice-president and secretaries on the commi-ttee appointed for these celebrations on Kartiki Ekadashi day when the 'Rath' kept in the Rath Chowk was taken out in a procession, the Muslims honoured the 'Rath' by offering 'pan supari' both at the Maniyar wada Jumma Mosque and Bhilpura Mosque. Hindus and Muslims participated in the Moharram procession and took out '*savaries*'. No incident had occurred at the time of any festival, whether Hindu or Muslim, nor at the time of Shiv Jayanti processions though these processions passed through Muslim localities.[103]

The communal harmony and amity that prevailed in Jalgaon was shattered by the Jan Sangh on October 1, 1969. The deteriorating communal situation in the country culminating in communal disturbances in

Ahmedabad and other cities of Gujarat and the rumours that were circulated with respect thereto made their impact in Jalgaon as in other places. The starting point was the board put up by Jan Sangh at Rath Chowk charging Pakistan with having a hand in Ahmedabad riots. In the communal atmosphere created by Ahmedabad riots this enflamed the communal feelings of Hindus against Muslims particularly in old Jalgaon. The immediate result was the pelting of stones in the evening of October 2, 1969 on the Maniyar Wada Jumma Mosque and the assaulting of some Muslims and the roaming about of gangs of Hindu boys who went assaulting Muslim children and abusing Muslims. On the other hand at the private meetings held at Jamaat-e-Islami exploited the situation created by Ahmedabad riots; it called upon the Muslims to unite in order to protect themselves. The Nasik and Jalgaon districts conference of the Maharashtra Pradesh Jamaat-e-Islami held on February 6 and 7, 1970 widened the gulf between the two communities. 1970 was a peak period of communal tension in Jalgaon. Holi and Moharram fell in that month and from the very first day of that month the tempo of communal incidents quickened. On March 1, some Hindu boys removed sheep fence, poultry pens, firewood, etc, from Muslim houses in Koli path for throwing them into the Holi fire. When Muslims caught hold of three of these boys, other 25 to 30 boys beat them and rescued the three boys. Another Muslim was also assaulted and beaten. There were repeated incidents of stone throwing on the Maniyar Wada Jumma Mosque. These incidents of stone throwing took place throughout the month. Some stones were also thrown on a few occasions on some Hindu houses and the Laxmi Narayan Temple. On April 13, 1970 Shiv Sena held a meeting at which P.V. Jog, a Shiv Sena leader from Pune made communal and provocative speech. On April 16, at another meeting, the Shiv Sena chief Bal Thackeray and Datta Salvi made communal and provocative speeches. This meeting was followed by incidents of stone-throwing on Muslim houses. A quarrel over cards which took place in the end of April 1970 was given a communal colour. The president of the RTM and the joint secretary of the Jalgaon city Jan Sangh came to the police station to get released a Hindu involved in the dispute. The 'kirtans' given by Afak Buwa about four months prior to the disturbances and by Sadashiv Shirwalkar on the night of May 7, 1970 were both provocative and incited Hindu feelings against Muslims. The two boards displayed by the Jan Sangh and the RTM on March 9, 1970 at public places contained messages of a communal nature.[104] The Jalgaon disturbances started with a quarrel at about 2.45 pm on May 8, 1970 near a pan-shop at Rath Chowk. This was between a Muslim and some Hindus in the course of which the Muslim was assaulted. He fled to his house and the Hindus chased him. After some time a number of Hindus came there and started stoning his house and the houses of other Muslims and some Muslims were assaulted and injured. The disturbances then spread to other areas of Maniyar Wada. Arson to Muslim properties took place in Maniyar Wada and a municipal fire engine was obstructed by the Hindu rioters. The Muslim shops outside the Jumma Mosque were broken open and looted. From Maniyar Wada, the disturbances spread to Rath Chowk where also arson to Muslim properties took place and again a fire brigade was obstructed by Hindu rioters. Some other localities were affected where Muslim houses were burnt. The Madira mosque situated in Islampura was also attacked. There were obstructions to fire brigades in other places also. The disturbances were put down at about 9.30 pm and no further incident took place thereafter.[105]

In all 43 persns died. Of these one was a Hindu. Out of 42 Muslims that died 6 were men, 11 women, 11 male children and 14 female children. In all 47 injured persons were treated as indoor patients and 49 as out door patients. Out of 47 indoor patients, 10 had bullet injuries received in the course of police firings: out of these ten, nine were Hindus and one a Muslim boy about 12 years of age. Arson was committed to 112 Muslim properties, out of which 87 were completely gutted. In addition, 28 other Muslim properties suffered other damage and 250 Muslim properties were looted. Six Hindu properties were affected during the disturbances, out of which three were completely gutted, one partially burnt, one suffered some damage. Damage that was caused to the Hindu houses was the result of fires spreading from the Muslims houses which had been set on fire. The total loss suffered by the Muslims was Rs 33,90,997 and by the Hindu Rs 83,725.[106]

In the opinion of the Commission, the nature of the work done by the special investigation squad at Jalgaon was three-fold: destructive, preservative, and creative. The destructive aspect was to render worthless the evidence against the Hindus accused in many important cases. The preservative aspect was that no credible evidence came or remained on the record which might establish an allegation made during the disturbances. The creative aspect was to invent a cause for the disturbances which would provide the Hindu rioters with a "moral justification" for rioting. For this purpose the squad invented the following three false stories:

1. That some Muslims outraged the modesty of 8 Hindu women;
2. That rioting at Maniyar Wada was started by Muslims; and
3. That the rioting at Bhilpura and Islampura was also started by Muslims.

All the accused in these three cases were acquitted.[107]

Chailiasa, 1970

Chailiasa is the district headquarters of Singhbhum. It was inhabited (1970) by about thirty thousand people of which eight thousand were Muslims. A considerable number of East Bengal refugees also lived in the town. Chailiasa has been free of communal riots till 1970. It was quiet even when Jamshedpur and other places were enveloped by communal riots.

A few months before the riots erupted on April 15, 1970, there was tension in the social atmosphere of Chailiasa town. There was tension in the air over the Ram Navmi procession whether it would start or not start off from the Urdu library into a lane to pass in front of a mosque in the interior of Bari Bazar. This dispute came into existence only in 1970 as a consequence of the Moharrum procession passing by the side of a temple and stopping there for some time and beating on the drums while Kirtan was going on inside the temple. This procession had to deviate from its route through which it was scheduled to pass. Since then there was a talk of trial of strength between RSS and Jammat-e-Islami youths. A top RSS leader Bhavju attended and addressed a specially organised rally at the local Gandhi Maidan on April 7, 1970 just one week before the riots. For days together, rumours were afloat that serious trouble would take place during Ram Navami. Many Muslim families had moved on to "safe zones". On April 13th, a meeting of the dormant peace committee was called and it was decided that leaders of the peace committee will head the Ram Navami procession.[108]

On April 15, 1970, the 10,000 strong Ram Navami procession started from Baba Mandir. Crackers were burst at the Mandir and in the Sadar Bazaar area. The organisers of the procession went round the market and asked Hindu shopkeepers to shut down their shutters. The Muslim shopkeepers followed suit. They moved in the jeep owned by Gopal Sharma, an activist of Jan Sangh. In fact he was himself driving. Slogans like, "*Maro Musalman ko, Jai Bajrang Bali*" were being shouted in the procession. Volunteers controlling the procession were armed with lethal weapons.

When one half of the procession had passed, the 'point of danger' *i.e.* Barkandaztoli, some of the processionists tried to divert the procession through the mosque. At that moment some crackers were burst. Police claims that these crackers came from the Muslim populated residential area. Another version was that crackers were burst by processionists. A general melee followed and within minutes the police arrived in force and shooting began, followed by loot and arson.[109]

In the first two hours, the riot was an affair between Hindus and Muslims in which some 45 persons were injured and some lost their lives. Then curfew followed. Soon the lower rank policemen took the field and resumed the riot on their own, a riot more ferocious, devastating and brutal. The communal riot was turned into a war waged by the policemen against the minority. The cause of this burning was a rumour spread like wild fire that a constable was murdered by the Muslims. All the burning, looting, and assaults took place just near the two police stations. Petrol was used on large-scale and shops were looted less and set on fire more. Electricity went off and telephone lines too went dead. The official figure of dead was 23 while non-official estimates put it at 32. Only two Hindus were killed. Two persons were closed inside a bora (sack) and were burnt alive. Four more women were burnt beyond recognition. Two Muslims coming from Orissa in their car were burnt alive along with the vehicle. Two persons were hiding in the tailor's shop. The shop was closed from outside and set on fire. One Mohammed Mustafa was dragged from a bus and beaten to death. Mohammed Hanif, grand old man of Chailiasa, who every year offered pan and cold drinks to all who took part in the Ram Navami procession, was shot while standing in front of his garage and his body reportedly burnt with petrol.[110] Such examples abound.

There was huge loss of property. In all 67 properties—shops, houses, buses, cars, rickshaws, etc, were burnt—or looted. Only 15 shops were looted, the rest were burnt. This included 54 Muslim properties and 13 Hindu properties.[111]

The police not only failed to protect the Muslims but did not take any steps to prevent violence. No police posse was posted at any sensitive place and most of the acts took place near police stations indicating police inaction. At Chailiasa, the Muslims openly alleged that the assaults on them were led by the lower ranks of the police. The darkness at Chailiasa was deepened by contrast of such radiant examples of secularism by members of communities as handing over of a five year old Hindu boy after four days of tender care by Muslims of Barkandaztoli. Three South Indian Hindus were given shelter by a Muslim family of the same locality for days together.

Nonari and Sajni, 1972

In Nonari, about 107 houses of Muslims were looted and 76 were set on fire. Standing crops in the fields as well as fodder were either destroyed or taken away and cattle formed part of the looting. The village is rich and the total loss is estimated at Rs one crore. One person was killed, which Muslims claimed to be of their community but the authorities discounted it. In Sajni, about 100 houses of Muslims were looted as 43 were set on fire. As the village was congested, two houses of Hindus too caught fire and were burnt in the process.[112]

Azamgarh district in which these two villages are situated had been riot free during the tense partition days, but not so after independence particularly since mid-sixties. Since then, large-scale flare ups in Mall and a large number of incidents took place in different villages. Unlike other places, all these scuffles took place between Harijans and Muslims.

In Azamgarh, most of the ex-zamindars as well as rich and middle-class peasants were Muslims. The Hindu landlord could be counted on finger tips. On the other hand, small peasants and landless workers were Harijans so there was an antagonism between Harijans and Muslims. A section of Hindu landlords also used Harijans to settle their scores with Muslim counterparts. Another feature of the villages of Azamgarh was that most persons belonging to the middle and lower class families had gone to Malaysia for finding work and sent lots of money and purchased land. A new class of nouveau rich came into existence. As far as the harijans in fifties and early sixties, they were paid very low wages—as low as 30 to 40 paisa or 750 grams of food grains. In early seventies, their wages improved to two or three rupees or two kilograms of food grains. Another feature of the area was that land disputes occurred fairly often and resulted in not only court cases but also in murder, dacoity and loot.

Due to growing socio-economic aspirations, adult franchise, elections of Gram Panchayats and economic consequences of various Harijan welfare plans, the Harijans took keen interest in politics and organised themselves in a strong group in Nonari. The group leader was Sitaram, a Bhar. He formed Harijan Kalyan Parishad and led many anti-landlord and anti-Muslim movements. The Harijan under his leadership even boycotted work on the fields of landlords for which the latter had either to work themselves or bring labourers from outside. All this led to a bitter feud between the Muslims and Harijans and the hostility often resulted in armed clashes. Sitaram was once jailed on a complaint by a Muslim landlord.

On November 14, a meeting of the Harijan Kalyan Parishad was held in Nonari. The Muslims attacked the house of Sitaram in the night of November 14, Sitaram and his brother Jaitun, a student of Pushpanagar Intermediate college were murdered.[113]

In the morning of 15th November, a crowd started gathering near the village. Some students of Pushapanagar college rushed to the village. The crowd swelled to about 10,000 in no time. Many of them came from nearby villages. By 8 am, information was received by the Saraimir police station and by 9.30 am, police party consisting of five constables, eight Jawans of PAC and the incharge of the police station reached the spot. The Muslim inhabitants fled the village leaving behind women, children and old men in the two well-built houses of the village. Loot and arson which started in the morning continued till evening when the PAC arrived and bought the situation under control.[114]

Sajni's was a different case. It was a small village of 125 houses, mostly of mud and clay and 100 of them belonging to Muslims. In contrast to Nonari, Muslims were not very rich at least they could be called middle-class peasants. Of the 25 Hindu families, all but one belonged to Harijan caste and were families of landless workers.

In the evening of December 10, a few Muslim boys of the village tried to molest a Hindu Brahmin girl of another village. The girl was, however, saved by a Hindu boy of Saini, who was beaten up by hooligans. The village Panchayat reprimanded the boys and their guardians. On December 11, the police came to investigate into the matter. The communal elements exploited the situation and the rumour was spread that a Brahmin girl was raped.[115]

In the morning of December 12, a crowd started gathering near the village. It swelled to about five thousand. Six constables and a sub-inspector arrived on the spot. This small force was inadequate but the Muslims along with Thakur Ram Bachan Singh, a Hindu landlord and other Hindus fought against the crowd. One of the Muslims, Vakil Ahmad had a gun and it helped to keep the attackers at bay. The tug of war went on upto 2.30 pm when the PAC arrived. The PAC asked the villagers to go back to the village from the border from where they were resisting the attackers and confiscated Vakil Ahmed's gun. Came upon its heels was the loot and arson. Whoever had tried to resist them, was beaten up by the PAC. This went on upto 5 pm, when the circle officer arrived on the spot and brought the situation under control.[116] The communal element of both the communities had a field day.

Aligarh, 1978

Aligarh riots started on October 5,1978. Curfew was imposed from dawn to dusk for about six weeks. By official admission, about 30 persons were killed in riots with Muslims for the most part at the receiving end.

When following the murder of a known goonda on October 5, the riots broke out resulting during that phase in about a dozen deaths, most of them from PAC bullets, and almost all of them Muslims, the President of the city unit of the Janta Party who was an activist of the RSS and the Jan Sangh was openly accused of being involved in the riots. In these riots the involvement of the RSS had been alleged both by Hindus and Muslims. The president of the Janta Party unit was released almost immediately after the arrest under pressure from the State's Chief Minister. Certain features of these riots were : all accounts of the riots agreed that the majority of the deaths took place because of firing by the PAC; it was only after the BSF was called in and it took out flag march, that confidence was restored. Amidst all this the Aligarh Muslim University remained an island of peace.[117]

A study team consisting of M.C. Menon and

Samanta Bannerjee was appointed by the PUCL to make a on the spot study of these riots. It carried out its study on October 21-22 in Aligarh and met and interviewed many people of different professions, parties including Congress, Janta party, Jan Sangh and the RSS. Its observations are given below.

The communal disturbances in Aligarh were caused by a series of tension-ridden events since June 1978. The situation reached a climax on October 5 when Hindu communalists ran berserk. The PAC too betrayed the Hindu communal sentiments by shooting and killing innocent and unarmed Muslims.

The immediate cause that started the riots on October 5 was the death of a Hindu wrestler Bhore from stab wounds. According to Krishan Kumar Navamany, president of the city unit of Janta Party, Bhore could identify three of the five assailants, all of them being Muslims. The team after meeting various people came to the conclusion that both sides comprised gangsters, and rough-necks drawn from Hindus and Muslims. Every one agreed that Bhorey was an anti-social elements. During the emergency Bhorey had belonged to the Congress but with coming in of Janta Party government, he joined Janta Party. It further concluded that Bhorey's death was the result of inter-gang warfare. In Aligarh every cinema house proprietor maintained a gang of ruffians on his pay-roll to shave off disturbances over the sale of tickets. Bhore was on the pay-roll of the owner of Seema talkies. On October 5, he was assaultd outside the cinema hall by a group of rough toughs. The reason was rivalry over the area of influence and clientele of the cinema houses. That the rivalry between the gangs had no communal colour was corroborated by many people including political leaders, academicians and members of local population.[118]

The team found that communal tension in Aligarh had been building up for quite some time, particularly over the issue of Aligarh Muslim University Bill which was introduced in Parliament and which proposed to reiterate the minority character of the University. A campaign against the Bill had been going on since June. A meeting was held in August that was presided over by Shiv Hari Shankar, a Jan Sangh leader and an advocate. Provocative speeches were made at the meeting. The speakers had warned that if the Bill was passed, "Aligarh would be made into another Marath Wada". The reference being to the anti-Scheduled Caste riots sparked off by the upper caste people of Marathwada region of Maharashtra against the naming of the University, there after B.R. Ambedekar. The two Hindu members of AMU's teaching staff, who also figured prominently in disturbances on October 5, had been agitating for quite some time for setting up another univeristy at Aligarh which they said would be secular in character. K.K. Navaman was emphatic about the discriminatory character of AMU. Another cause of tension was the location of 10 to 15 Muslim houses in Manak Chowk, the worst affected area during October 5 riots. The Hindus had been trying to oust the Muslims from the area for quite some time. Manak Chowk is a stronghold of the RSS. Navaman also had his house in Manak Chowk area. These Muslims were the main target of attack on October 5. According to Navaman, one Vishnu Dutt who had been the referee at a wrestling match on September 12 was assaulted by Muslims on September 15. On September 16, one Kacher Mal, a Hindu had been assaulted and died on September 18. There were two different versions of his death. While Navaman thought that he had been a victim of Muslim communalism, others felt that it had been a sequel to family quarrel. Kacher Mal was murdered on September 18, Bhorey on October 5 at 3.30 pm, and Rattam Lal and Ganesh Lall at 3.45 p m the same day. Bhorey was declared dead in the District Hospital. His associates 'snatched' the dead body from official custody in spite of the presence of the SP (city), ADM (city) and city Magistrate and personnel of the PAC at the hospital. Those who had 'snatched' the dead body consisted of people earlier detained by the police. They were released, under pressure of gherao. This was imposed by the erstwhile RSS and Jan Sangh men led by Navaman.[119] The team wondered how the whole episode could have happened. More so, in the presence of the PAC and other senior officials, particularly in view of the tension in the city since September 12. Even postmortem was not done before the body was 'snatched'. The body of Bhorey was taken out in a procession along the areas prone to communal riots. It was allowed to be carried towards Abdul Karim Chowk and Upar kot instead of proceeding to the cremation ground or the house of Bhorey's family. The processionists shouted provocative slogans "blood for blood", "they have made it a Pakistan". The body was placed in the middle of the road leading to Upar-Kot. The processionists looted Muslim shops. In fact some Muslims were assaulted in the compound of the hospital itself in the presence of top officials. The Muslim resorted to brick batting from the Upar Kot area. The PAC resorted to firing indiscriminately. Though it was ordered to fire in the air to disperse the mob, it deliberately fired at the Muslim houses.

The Congress leader, Devendra Pal Singh, gave an account to the team of the happenings at that moment. He said that Bene Isreal lane was a market area where only Muslims had lived and is about 0.5 kms from Abdul Karim Chowk, no Hindu communalist was there making trouble on October 5, and that it was free of provocation, that in spite of this PAC men fired on the Muslims. Two persons died. Another Muslim was killed in the same area as a result of firing. 12 persons were killed in Manak Chowk. According to a witness on scene, RSS elements had tried to take possession of the Muslim houses about two weeks earlier. Even though the alleged culprits were identified by the local people they were not arrested by the police. Almost every Muslim house in Manak Chowk carried a tale of tragedy-killing or loot or arson. The carnage started at 5.30 pm on October 5, an hour after curfew was imposed and continued till midnight. In spite of the repeated appeals to the police, no help came. Added to the assault by Hindu communalists was the indiscriminate firing by the PAC.[120] The curfew was often turned into a smokescreen from behind which the hoodlums operated with impunity. Even a cigarette shop opposite the police station was burnt during curfew hours.

From available reports, the team could make out that the concentration of attack on Manak Chowk had nothing to do with the main procession carrying Bhorey's body. The attack had been pre-planned and had been a part of a threatened plan to oust the few Muslim houses that remained in the *Mohalla*. The riots again broke out in the tourist week of November. According to the statement of S.D. Patel on behalf of the government in the Rajya Sabha, the riots of November 6, 1978 were a consequence of rumours spreading over a stabbing incident between two persons belonging to the minority community. On 8 November there were several incidents of stabbing and firing by members of the public. Police had to open fire. Sixteen persons lost life in these incidents and 32 were injured. Thirty-four houses were affected by arson and looting and property worth 1.75 lakh was destroyed. According to him on October 5, 1978, eleven persons had lost their lives and 34 were injured. Property worth 3.5 lakh was lost. Fifty-six shops and houses were set on fire and looted.[121] The Commissioner of Police is the person responsible for the second wave of riots of November, said Mr Inderdeep Sinha, MP in Rajya Sabha. Against the orders of the District Magistrate, the Commissioner lifted the curfew. For some time there was confusion in the city. One police van went on propagating "There is curfew". That was under the instructions of the DM. Another van was going about saying,"There is no curfew, you can do whatever you like." That was under the instructions of the Commissioner. It transferred the DM who belonged to the Scheduled Caste and the SSP Prashad who belonged to the backward community.[122] The DM was told by the Commissioner, "You son of a chamar, you want to save the Muslims."[123] According to Harkishan Singh Surjeet, member of the Rajya Sabha, the Aligarh riots on October five were an organised attack on the minority community-nothing else. He further said that there was not a single instance when a Muslim used any arm or attacked anyone. He again said that the PAC made the Muslims and their houses as targets of attack and that not a single Hindu house was the target of police bullets. Only the houses of the minority community suffered, their children were killed.[124] Mr Kuldeep Nayar, an eminent editor wrote, "There have been confusing reports of what caused the Aigarh riots. But all are agreed on two points: one, the Muslims were the worst sufferers and secondly, the PAC did little to protect them. Both have an ominous connotation."[125] Communalization of life in the city reached such a height that if a boy went to purchase something from a shop, the shopkeeper asked whether he was a Hindu or a Muslim. If he was a Muslim the shopkeeper would not sell.[126]

Jamshedpur, 1979

The mega industrial city of Jamshedpur saw communal riots in 1964 along with Calcutta and Rourkela in the wake of communal riots in East Pakistan and migration of Hindus from there to India. About 1979, Jameshedpur riots, the Jitender Narain Commission of inquiry said, "After giving careful and serious consideration to all the materials that are on record, the Commission is of the view that the RSS with its extensive organisation in Jamshedpur and which has close links the BJP and the BMS had a positive hand in creating a climate which was most propitious for the outbreak of communal disturbances."[127]

According to M.J. Akbar, Jamshedpur is the communalists dream for a hundred different reasons. There were memories of 1964 riots when the Muslims were butchered by Hindus incited by tales of true and imagined torture of Hindus in Pakistan. Then too adivasis were fed lies and used by Hindu leaders against Muslims. Muslims in the city form one of the richest communities in the country. They have jobs, more than half of the employees of TISCO for instance were then Muslims. Muslims had also entered trade while some Muslim goondas had a profitable role to play in the illicit liquor business and money lending markets. Muslims with any economic stake were the first target of Hindu communalists. But the vital reason that provoked the Jamshedpur riots was caste and local politics. After the Janta victory in 1977, law and order in the state virtually collapsed as the lame duck ministry had lost interest in governing. Things did not improve much under the Janta government in the state. Amongst the people ignored by the SP was the local Janata (RSS) MLA Dinanath Pandey who played a key role in engineering the riots. According to one source, the Janata politicians working with the RSS and others including Muslim Jamaat-e-Islami had decided to provoke communal riots as early as October, 1978. Their aim was to discredit the city administration and have the officials transferred. By the end of March, 1979 everybody in Jamshedpur knew that a communal riot was in the offing. In any case by the end of March both the communities had begun stock piling their weapons of offence and defence.[128]

When Balasaheb Deoras came to visit Jamshedpur on 1 April 1979, talk of Ram Navami procession was already polluting the air. Among other things Deoras told the audience that it was very sad that in their own country Hindus were not allowed to take out their religious processions, and that though the number of mosques was increasing in India, no Muslim country allowed a Hindu temple to be constructed. Mr Deoras received a pen from the local Jamaat-e-Islami leader Shamim Ahmed Madri as a token of friendship and the pen was significant for Madri because he had brought it from Saudi Arabia.[129]

On April 5, 1979 the administration had refused the use of Road no 14 and 15 which marked the boundaries of Sabir Nagar, a Muslim Basti situated at about 200 yards away from Dimanbasti, an adivasi colony. On road no 14 was a thatched mosque built by the residents of Sabir Nagar. In the premises of the mosque, a madarsa was also being run. The roads number 14 and 15 are just mid tracks while road number 15 goes upto Dimanbasti. Road no. 14 stops short on the other side of the fields.[130]

The immediate though not real cause of the 1979 riots was the question of the Ram Navami procession passing through road no. 14. The Muslims objected to this route on the plea that there was a mosque on the road and thus they insisted that the road no. 15 be used. A compromise was reached that the procession would take road no. 15 and would divert to road no. 14 through a connecting mid track. It was also decided that Muslims would accompany the procession to see to safety. But that was not to happen.

The 'jhanda' from Dimanbasti had begun only in 1978 and in that year it used road no. 15 when the administration had disallowed the use of road no. 14. On April 5,1979 the administration again refused the use of road no. 14. Some processions were begun but were stopped by Hindu leaders who insisted that until the Dimanbasti dispute was settled Ram Navami would not be celebrated. In protest against the administration, the Hindus forced the closure of shops and cinema hall. The administration made arrests. On April 7, 1979 the Sri Ram Navami Kendriya Akhara Samiti issued a pamphlet which was utterly communal. The pamphlet was headlined, "An appeal to Religion Loving Public of Jamshedpur" and shoulder headline said *Dharam ki jai ho and Adharam ka nash ho.* The appeal said:

> Till now the people have borne the cruelty peacefully, but in the name of peace, the Hindus of the area are being crushed. In Dhakidih the police destroyed the image of Hanuman, in Jugsalai the police reined lathis and tear gas, in Mango the Hindus have been reduced to minority. It is clear that behind this are the SP and some sycophant officers of his. What is clear is that all the constables, havaldars, homeguards, etc, are ready to support us. The reasons why you could not take out your procession on the Dashmi remain and as long as this corrupt and anti-Hindu SP stays here, images will continue to be destroyed. But in this struggle we must remember our culture and our self respect. Keeping this in mind, the Sri Ram Navami Akhara Kendriya Samiti has decided that all the akharas will come at two in the afternoon on 11th April which is Hanuman Jayanti. Only the Mango (thatis Dimanbasti) Akhara will come out at eleven in the morning and pass through road no. 14. According to our decision every one will come here first, bring out this akhara and then disperse to their localities to bring out their processions. We want to tell the governor of Bihar, the Chief Minister, the District officials and all the policemen and officials that if any untoward incident takes place during these peaceful processions, then the full responsibility for that rests on the shoulders of the administration. So the administration must make arrangements for the safety with impartiality. This was an open provocation and it sent the temperature of the city Soaring high.[131] Meanwhile on 11th April, in the morning, Hindus began assembling at Dimanbasti carrying weapons in their hands officially for the games.

At eight in the morning, the 'Jhanda' left the Dimanbasti. Only about 25 people from Dimanbasti itself accompanied the akhara, the rest were outsiders. The Procession went through the designated route and with a lot of noise but no violence. In fact there was virtually no damage to Sabirnagar-Dimanbasti area, apart from a couple of burnt huts.

There was sigh of relief, but soon the trouble started. The next point where trouble could start was in Mango, less than a kilometre from the road where the procession would go through a Muslim area. The procession proceeded very slowly. This was clearly an effort to delay the procession till 11 am when Hindus from all over the city were scheduled to join the procession as per the pamphlet. The number of processionists went on growing and at least 15,000 people gathered. In the lanes of Mango particularly in Agadbasti and Azamnagar, the Muslims began to gather, some afraid of the violent mood of the processionists and some with mischief in their minds. Both sides were prepared for the battle. The tension had taken its toll on the nerves. A little after ten, the procession stopped opposite the mosque. It was at this point that the Jan Sangh MLA Dinanath Pandey played his trump card. He said that the procession would not move till the Hindu leaders who had been previously arrested were released. The officials pleaded that they cannot release them even if they so wanted without legalities gone through. But Mr Pandey did not budge. Provocative speeches were made. At 11.40. am the inevitable happened. A stone was thrown. A bomb exploded. The rest was murder.[132]

The Muslims of Mango were prepared for the violence: they had obviously been instigated by the communalists and they held their own in the ensuing battle. They also attacked the Hindu areas of Deaguttu until they were repulsed by the police. The Muslims were aggressors here. Anil Prasad Srivastava, a Tata apprentice died. The parents of a child called Kailash were butchered, a temple was attacked. Arrows and guns were finally used by both sides. At the same time, as if on cue, mobs of Hindus began attacking. Muslim areas. And this time the police joined the mob and destroyed Muslim homes. The Bihar military police wrote their names in the history of shame. They were not a peace keeping force but became the armed wing of the RSS.[133] The army was called. By 11 at night it had received orders to enforce law and order and immediately they made an impact. In order to discredit the armed forces at least two hands of goondas disguised themselves in army uniforms in order to continue in havoc. They were arrested later. The saddest incident in the tragedy took place during the evacuation of an ambulance load of refugees. After 12 hours of violence on April 11, sometime after 1 at night, the administration was able to arrange for vehicles to pick up Muslims stranded in schools and the Mosque in Bhaluliasa. Tata Medical hospitals ambulance, buses, trucks and sundry other vehicles were pressed into service. Ambulance no. BRX 6112 was part of the second convoy and was carrying about 60 people. It was driven by an Adivasi and was in the middle of the convoy which was being escorted at the head and the back by police jeeps. The two police guards were actually inside the ambulance in order to provide protection in case of any mishap. The ambulance was driven a short distance into a lane and then the driver and the policeman decamped. On cue, a mob attacked the ambulance and set fire to it. In a similar crime a bus with six Muslims was burnt. All died.[134]

TISCO began relief work as soon as the refugee camps were set up, supplying 40,000 meals a day. The price that the city had to pay for four days of madness was enormous. Nearly 1600 pucca houses had to be completely rebuilt. People's faith had been wounded. One hundred and thirty-eight houses were demolished in Bhaluliasa. Harijan Basti was attacked by Muslims.

Harijans had damaged a Muslim graveyard. Adivasis let loose their deadly arrows. They were mobilised by RSS elements on false rumours. Slogans of revenge rent the air. Their was a passionate anger. There was betrayal.[135]

IV

Moradabad, 1980

Moradabad is known for its brassware, small-scale industry. Muslims constitute about 60 per cent of the population of the city.

On the 13th August 1980, Moradabad saw the most bloody orgy of violence. It was Id day. More than 50,000 Muslims with their children had assembled in the idgah to say prayers. It was a day of festivities after Ramzan month. Shamianas were set up at different places to greet the namazis. By the side of the Idgah was a mosque and just opposite the Idgah across the main road are shops owned by Punjabi Hindus and nearby a Punjabi colony. The day of rejoicing and festivities was turned into a black day.

This day was not a day of Hindu-Muslim communal riots but a calculated, cold blooded massacre of Muslims by a rabid communal police force which tried to cover up its genocide by making it out to be a Hindu-Muslim riot. Moradabad was a case of police brutality—pure and simple. Hundreds died including many children in the massacre and the stampede, and hundreds were injured, for many of them death came slowly. Moradabad was not communal on 13th August but the police made it communal later.[136]

It was during the Id prayers that a pig wandered into the namaz. The Muslims asked the policemen on duty, "How come the pig wandered into the namaz?" The policemen replied that it was not their duty to stop a pig from wandering in the namaz. The police opened fire. Then came-brickbating from the crowd, firing by the police, police officer injured scores of namazis shot dead. All took place within five minutes of the prayers drawing to a close. A stampede followed police firing in which more than 50 persons lost their lives.[137] Many rushed to the mosque. But the police later actually entered the mosque and fired in the courtyard of the mosque. One Dr Naseem Ahmad told M.J. Akbar that he helped to recover 24 bodies including those of their teen children from the mosque courtyard.[138]

The furious crowd coming out of the Idgah roughed up policemen in different localities on its way. In the evening, a Muslim mob attacked the Gulshahid police chowki killing two policemen, burning the chowki and stealing two guns. This shows that violence on that day was not communal at all. The mob could have attacked many Punjabi Hindus shops, houses and factories situated near the Idgah. They did not do so. Their fury was against the men in police uniform or the hated PAC.

According to M.J. Akbar it was simply a case of the force meant to preserve law and order becoming thoroughly irresponsible. According to Shamsul Islam, the general secretary of the Cong (I), there was no government. Prime Minister Indira Gandhi herself admitted that the administration was in bad shape.[139] The disturbances in the city were long drawn out, with fresh outbreaks beginning on September 10 and October 20. Hundreds were dragged out of their homes, beaten up and locked up except on the last occasion the curfew was imposed only against the Muslims. Hindus were free to come and go at will.[140]

The police tried to divert the attention from the police force and turn the whole thing into a Hindu-Muslim communal riot and it succeeded. Policemen went around taunting Hindus to attack Muslims and at least in one instance the PAC allowed students of the K.G.K. college to launch an organised assault on the Muslims of Pul Parar colony. Students of the same college were reported to have had a mob to Ram Talaiya, a village across the railway line and burnt alive 15 men, women and children.[141]

Usual rumours were floated and pamphlets distributed enflaming communal sentiments. Water supply was poisoned by Muslims. Shiva temple next to cremation ground was demolished and its priest killed in retaliation. Muslims living in the 'line-par' area lost their lives and a Mosque in the area was demolished. The rumour on August 14 was that a certain PAC platoon had been wiped out by Muslims, persuaded other PAC jawans to kill ten men who had been brought to Kotwali by beating them to death with sticks Muslim MLA was distributing arms from a white Maruti car; that the Muslims were planning to turn the city into a fortress in order to lay the basis of another Pakistan, they have a dream of creating a Muslim state within UP, constituting of Western districts... so they are creating the same conditions of panic and disorder for bending the knees of Hindus as they did in 1945, 1946 and 1947.[142]

Hindu goondas enjoyed immunity. They took Muslims off the buses coming into the city bus stand and killed them in broad daylight on Grand Trunk Road. The evidence of the frenzy among Hindus being whipped up by the police was overwhelming.[143] Thus first it was the killing of Muslims by the police and the PAC and later it became police in collusion with Hindu communalists against Muslims. In these riots about 1500 to 2000 persons perished.

The events of Moradabad bear witness to the regression of a society and of its political administrative and judicial organs to a depth where one may no longer speak of the norms of a minimally civilised community.[144]

Biharsharif, 1981

Biharsharif is headquarters of Nalanda district situated 50 miles from Patna. According to 1971 census its population was 1,30,000 of which 48 per cent consisted of Muslims. The major component of Hindu population is Yadavs who are mainly agriculturists.They cultivated very profitable crop of potatoes which led to construction of quite a few cold storages in Biharsharif. The trading community consisted of 'sonis' and 'telis'. Some Muslims also entered trade and had their markets, cold storages and shares in cinema houses. Biharsharif is known for bidi industry. About 15,000 workers mostly Muslims were employed. Bidi factories were generally owned by Muslims. Bidis were manufactured not only in Biharsharif town but also in the surrounding villages. The workers were highly unionized and were under the influence of the Communist Party of India. While in the first three general elections the town was represented in the legislative assembly by Muslim candidates, in the 4th General Elections a communist became a member of the Assembly. In the next election in 1972 in the wake of break-up of Pakistan and emergence of Bangladesh, Jan Sangh won the seat. In the next election in 1977 the communists won the elections again both for Lok Sabha and the Legislative Assembly. Thus there were communal tensions in the political field. The RSS and Jan Sangh had their main base among 'telis'.

Biharsharif having such large Muslim population had many cemetries spread over the town. The Yadavs had an eye on them. With increasing population of the town ànd migration of people from rural areas to town had led to soaring of land prices.

According to Dinanath Singh of *Indian Nation*, a daily from Patna, these lands of the graveyards have been shown as *gairmazura land.* There were disputes regarding almost all of them and cases were pending in courts for years together. While the Muslims wanted these graveyards to be demarcated and fenced, the Yadavs claimed them as fields or 'Khalihans'. At some of the places, the Yadavs had raised huts. There were 23 such points in the town where men were living since long in a state of strife and mutual distrust.[145]

Towards the end of 1980, a dispute over a piece of cemetery land was going on between the Yadavs and the Muslims at Gagandivan. Land belonged to the Muslims but Yadavs were claiming it as their own. The Yadavs on one night constructed a temple on the land and covered it with cow-dung. The Muslims discovered it a month later and a pitched battle was fought between the Yadavs and Muslims with bombs and bullets. There were no serious casualities and the police brought the situation under control.[146]

On 30th April 1981, a brawl between Yadavs and Muslims took place in a toddy shop. Yadavs who wanted to sabotage the authorities attempt to demarcate and fence the cemetery lands came in conflict with the Muslims. The RSS was waiting in the wings to start the massacre. After the brawl in the toddy shop at about 3 pm, the police miserably failed to comprehend and bring the situation under control. Soon after the brawl, the city was bristling with rumours. Killing and looting started. By 7 pm shops in far-off places were being burnt and looted. The first victim to die was a retired police constable Qumrul Hasan about 2 kilometres away from the place of the brawl.[147]

Next day a mob attacked Alinagar where 12 Muslim houses in which 120 persons lived were burnt. One man, 14 women and children were killed. Raj Kishore, the city head of the RSS and Pannalal another RSS activist led the mob. The Bihar military police abetted the goondas in burning and looting properties and killing people. In Biharsharif the actual loss of life was not more than 20 but in nearby villages the killings were on mass scale. The sober estimate was total deaths 150, though the official estimate was 52. The RSS organised mobs from the town to attack the villages. According to local CPI MLA, the RSS activists visited rural areas in jeeps and on scooters and spread the rumour that 200 Yadavs were killed by the Muslims, CPI MP, a Yadav was killed, a Koire leader was murdered, Muslims had brought wagonload of bombs from outside. The worst happened in Gulm village. On 22nd May a mob equipped with bombs, rifles and other lethal weapons attacked the village at about 5 or 6 in the morning and kept killing, burning and looting till it was dark. The police did not arrive. Paswans and Yadavs joined the attacks.[148]

The district authorities and the police failed to maintain peace and control the riots. The Chief Minister, Dr Jagannath Mishra issued orders for arrest of two district magistrates and suspension of six others. Later under the pressure of the IAS lobby, the orders for arrest were withdrawn. According to him five leaders of the RSS were also arrested among others. Collective fines were imposed on villages where riots took place which were opposed by the RSS and the Jan Sangh.

In Biharsharif riots, the RSS not only divided Hindu and Muslim communities on communal lines but also took communal virus to the rural areas. In Biharsharif, both political and economic factors intermixed in creating communal tension and consequent riots.

Bhagalpur, 1989

The Ramjanam Bhoomi- Babri Masjid controversy took a heavy toll of human life. More than 800 persons died. The rural areas numbering 200 were affected by riots. 3,932 houses were burnt to ashes; 891 shops were looted or gutted. 3000 powerlooms were gutted. 876 Muslims and 50 Hindus were killed. 106 persons were missing. About 260 were seriously injured or disabled. 1100 Hindus and 900 Muslims were arrested. About 50,000 persons were deprived of livelihood. Also 37 mosques, 7 madarsa's, 8 tombs were destroyed. More than 300 Hindu houses were gutted.[149] Huge mobs attacked villages even in remote areas. Communal aggressiveness in the villages was not only a fall out of the events in the bigger city but had spread quite widely in villages even before violence rocked the main city and Bhagalpur. In this the role of the Ramjanam Bhoomi issues and its highly communal use could not be over emphasized.[150]

The Ramshila pujan procession started from Tartarpur area because it was not a religious festival procession but a political procession. The processionists shouted provocative slogans: *Hindi-Hindu-Hindustan, Muslim Jao Kabristan, Jai Maakali, Karo Tartarpur Khali, Babar ki santano Hindustan chodo, etc.* Even Bihar military police and some other policemen also joined in slogan shouting. The procession was led by two notorious anti-social elements Kameshwar Yadav and Mahadev Singh who were rivals of another anti-social Mohammed Ansari. When verbal discussion was going on whether the procession should either enter Tartarpur, some bombs were thrown on the procession probably by Ansari and his men. It caused great turmoil in the procession. There was police firing. Four persons (two Hindus and two Muslims) died. The nearby colleges were affected. Around 20 students were killed. Rumours of exaggerated deaths at the hands of Muslims spread like wild fire even in the villages. Mobs spread into different localities and set ablaze Muslim shops. Places of worship were special targets. obviously such a massacre could not have taken place without police connivance. It was alleged that the whole thing happened in the very presence of the police. The leaders of Bihar

Policemens Association alleged that the entire incident took place at the behest of some political leaders.[151] The madness continued for three days starting on October 24, 1989.

According to Ashgar Ali Engineer, Bhagalpur had all the elements required for fuelling a communal riot-communal rivalries, political rivalries and criminal rivalries. The Ram Janam bhoomi controversy was the spark required to ignite the situation.[152]

References

1. John Weiss: "Fascism as the Extremism of the Right" in Gilbert Allardyce (ed): *The Place of Fascism in European History*, Prentice-Hall Inc., New Jersey 1971, p. 122.
2. *Ibid*, p. 125.
3. Gilbert Allardyce, *Ibid*, p. 120.
4. *Ibid*, p. 21
5. *Ibid*, p. 21
6. N.L. Gupta (ed) *Nehru on Communalism*, Sampradayikta Virodhi Committee, New Delhi, 1965, p. 123
7. *Ibid*, p. 123
8. *Madan Commission Report*. Volume VI-Parts VI and VII, p. 82
9. *Ibid*, p. 92
10. *Ibid*, p. 97
11. *Ibid*, pp. 97-98
12. *Ibid*, p. 179-80
13. Ashwani K Ray and Subhash Chakravarti, *Meerut Riots-A Case Study*, svc New Delhi, p. 13.
14. Ashwani K Ray and Subhash Chakravarti, *Karimganj Riots-A Political Study*, svc, New Delhi, pp. 16-17.
15. ManiShankar, "An Analytical view of Communal Violence". In Ashgar Ali Engineer (ed) *Communal Riots in Post Independence India*, Sangam Books Pvt. Ltd. Hyderabad, 1984, p. 85.
16. *Ibid*,

17. Ghanshyam Shah, "The 1969 Communal Riots in Ahmedabad: A Case study" in Ashgar Ali Engineer, *op. cit.* p. 192.
18. Manishanker *op. cit* p. 95.
19. Ghanshyam Shah : *op. cit*, p. 198.
20. Ashgar Ali Engineer: An Analytical Study of Meerut Riots in Ashgar Ali Engineer, *op.cit.*p. 272.
21. Jim Masselos: "The Bombay riots of January 1993: The politics of urban conflagaration". In John McGuire, Peter Reeves and Howard Brasted, *Politics of Violence From Ayodhya to Behrampada*, Sage Publications India Pvt. Ltd. New Delhi, 1996, p. 117.
22. The *Tribune*, August 7, 1998.
24. Manishankar, *op. cit.* p.94.
25. *Ahmedabad Riots-X-rayed, nd, np.* p.2.
26. *Ibid*, p.1.
27. B.B. Chatterjee, P.N. Singh, G.R.S. Rao: *Riots in Rourkela-a Psychological Study, Popular Book Services*, New Delhi-1967 p.30.
28. *Ibid*,
29. *Ibid*, p. 31.
30. *Ibid*, p. 32.
31. *Ibid*, p. 33
32. *Ibid*, p. 34.
33. *Ibid*, p. 35
34. *Ibid*, p. 35
35. *Ibid*, p. 128
36. Ashwani Kumar Ray and Subhash Chakravarti *op. cit.* SVÇ pp. 3-4.
37. *Ibid*, pp. 5 and 6.
38. *Ibid*, p. 7.
39. *Ibid*, p. 8.
40. *Ibid*, p. 10.
41. *Ibid*, pp. 11-12.
42. *Ibid*, pp. 13-14.
43. Ashwani Ray and Subhash Chakravarty, *Karimganj Riots op. cit.* pp.1 to 6.

44. *Ibid*, p. 2.
45. *Ibid*, pp. 9-12.
46. *Ibid*, pp. 13-15.
47. *Ibid*, p. 17.
48. *Ibid*, pp. 15-22.
49. *Ibid*, pp. 24-27.
50. *Ibid*, pp. 29-30.
51. *Aurangabad Riots- An Analytical Study*, svc, New Delhi p.6.
52. *Ibid*.
53. *Ibid*.
54. *Ibid*, p. 7.
55. *Ibid*, p. 8.
56. *Ibid*, p. 9.
57. *Ibid*,
61. *Ibid*, p. 37-38.
62. Ghanshyam Shah: "The 1969 Communal Riots in Ahmedabad : A case study". In Ashgar Ali Engineer (ed). *op. cit.*, Sangam Books India Pvt. Ltd.; Hyderabad, p. 191.
63. Research worker, p. 20.
64. *Ibid*, p. 4.
65. *Ibid*.
66. *Ibid*, p. 6.
67. *Ibid*, pp. 8-9, 14.
68. *Ibid*, pp. 12-14.
69. *Ibid*, p. 14.
70. *Ibid*, p. 16.
71. *Ibid*, p. 16.
72. *Ibid*, p. 27.
73. *Ibid*, p. 40.
74. *Ibid*, p. 43.
75. *Ibid*, pp. 17-19.
76. *Madan Commission*, Vol. VI-parts VI and VII p.21.
77. *Ibid*, p. 76.
78. *Ibid*, pp. 88-89.

79. *Ibid*, p. 82.
80. *Ibid*, p. 80.
81. *Ibid*, p. 81.
82. *Ibid*, p. 81.
88. *Ibid*.
89. *Ibid*, p. 38.
90. *Ibid*, pp. 73/74.
91. *Ibid*, p. 22-23.
92. *Ibid*, p. 27.
93. *Ibid*, p. 41.
94. *Ibid*, pp. 42-43.
95. *Ibid*, p. 59.
96. *Ibid*, pp. 59-60.
97. *Ibid*, pp. 77-82.
98. *Ibid*, p. 72.
99. *Ibid*, p. 70.
100. *Ibid*, p. 73.
101. The Madan Commission Report p. 92.
102. *Ibid*, pp. 92-93.
103. *Ibid*, pp. 95-97.
104. *Ibid*, pp. 97-100.
105. *Ibid*, p. 110.
106. *Ibid*, p. 111.
107. *Ibid*, p. 118.
108. Singh, NK, *Chailiasa Riots, An On the Spot Study*, svc, New Delhi; 1970, p.4.
109. *Ibid*, pp. 7-9.
111. *Ibid*, pp. 10-11.
112. *A Tail of Two Villages:* Sampradyikta Virodhi Committee, New Delhi, p.1.
113. *Ibid*, p. 6.
114. *Ibid*, p. 6-7.
115. *Ibid*, p. 10.
116. *Ibid*, p. 10.
117. *Economic & Political Weekly*, November 18, 1978, pp. 1869-70.

118. *Ibid*, p. 1882.
119. *Ibid*, pp. 1882-1883.
120. *Ibid*, p. 1884.
121. Secular Democracy, November 11, 1978 p. 21.
122. *Ibid*, p. 12.
123. *Ibid*, p. 20.
124. *Ibid*, p. 16.
125. *Ibid*, p. 11.
126. *Ibid*, p. 13.
127. Mani Shankar; "An Analytical view of communal violence". In Ashgar Ali Engineer (ed) *Communal Riots in Post Independence India*, Hyderabad, 1984, p.95.
128. M.J. Akbar, *Riots after Riots*, pp. 21-24.
129. *Ibid*, p. 25.
130. *Ibid*, p. 21.
131. *Ibid*, p. 26.
132. *Ibid*, pp. 27-28.
133. *Ibid*, p. 28.
134. *Ibid*, pp. 29-30.
135. *Ibid*, p. 31.
136. M.J. Akbar : *Riot after Riot*, Penguin Books, New Delhi 1988, p. 33.
137. Satish Sabarwal and Mashirul Hasan : Moradabad Riots, 1980: Causes and meanings. In Ashgar Ali Engineer (ed) *Communal Riots in Post Independence India*, Sangam Books Pvt. Ltd., Hyderabad, 1984, p. 223.
138. M.J. Akbar: opt. cit., p.37.
139. *Ibid*, p. 28.
140. Satish Sabarwal and Mushirul Hahan, opt. cit., p. 224.
141. *Ibid*, p. 224.
142. *Ibid*, pp. 214, 218, 244-45.
143. *Ibid*, p. 225.
144. *Ibid*, p. 226.
145. Ashgar Ali Engineer: "Biharsharif Carnage: A field Inquiry". In Ashgar Ali Engineer (ed) *Communal Riots in Post Independence India*, Sangam Books India Pvt. Ltd., Hydera-

bad, 1984, pp. 239-40.

146. *Ibid*, p. 240.

147. *Ibid*, p. 242.

148. *Ibid*, pp. 243-44.

149. Ashgar Ali Engineer: "Grim Tragedy of Bhagalpur riots". In *Economic & Political Weekly*, Feb 10, 1990, p. 305 and 307.

150. Bharat Dogra : Bhagalpur : "Communal violence spreads to villages". In EPW, January 20, 1990.

151. Ashgar Ali Engineer, op. cit., p. 306.

152. *Ibid*, p. 305.

2

Communal Riots Caused in the Wake of Rath Yatra : 1990-91

N. L. Gupta

The Home Ministry Report of 1990-91 states: "The communal situation remained surcharged for most part of the year due to Ram Janam Bhoomi-Babri Masjid issue. Several parts of Andhra Pradesh, Bihar, Gujarat, Maharashtra, Orissa, Uttar Pradesh and West Bengal witnessed communal riots resulting in considerable loss of lives and property."

"The Ram Janam Bhoomi-Babri Masjid dispute remained a difficult issue for some time and had been the major factor responsible for disturbing the communal amity in the country during the year. The mobilization campaign for the *kar seva* for the proposed Ram Janam Bhoomi temple at Ayodhya on 30th October, 1990, vitiated the communal atmosphere lowering the threshold of mutual tolerance and inflamed communal passions. Serious law and order problems developed at Ayodhya and communal riots occurred in many parts of the country."

Subodh Kant Sahay, the Minister of State for Home Affairs in the Union Governments of V.P. Singh and Chandra Shekhar referring to the ongoing developments in Ayodhya had said according to the *Times of India* (TOI) of October 26, 1991 that the situation would not have been so aggravated if the Rath Yatra of L.K. Advani had been stopped at Somnath itself.

The Andhra Pradesh Chief Minister Janardhan Reddy, had blamed VHPs *kar seva* programme at Ayodhya for stoking communal passions that led to communal carnage in Hyderabad. (*TOI*, 22.12.90) The Gujarat Chief Minister had also blamed BJP and Janata Dal for encouraging violence in Gujarat during 1990. (*TOI*, 18.12.90)

Dr Harish Khare, resident editor of *The Times of India* wrote, "It may be recalled that it was in Gujarat that the party (BJP) first experimented with the Hindu platform. It was here that BJP took liberties with law and order in last October/November. It was here that the BJP registered its most impressive gains so much so that when Mr. Advani wanted a safe sanctuary, he came to Gandhinagar. (*TOI*, 2.11.90)

A. Rastogi, Home Secretary of the Government of Uttar Pradesh had said before the 10th general elections that activities of VHP/BJP after October 30 and November 2, 1990 incidents in Ayodhya worsened the communal situation. Another senior officer of the UP government had said that communal tension would not be removed till the elections were over. (*TOI*, 10.1.91)

The Lok Sabha after a long debate on communal riots taking place in the wake of Ram Janam Bhoomi Rath Yatra in September and October 1990, passed a resolution on October 5, 1990 which read:

> This house reiterates its commitment to the ideal of a democratic secular state, to harmony in our society and to amity between all sections of our people.

Rising above all other considerations, it is our commitment to harmony and to accord in the nation, that persuades us to unanimously appeal to the people of our country not to dilute this tenet enshrined in our Constitution. Any and all issues that have a potential for divisive and communal discord amongst our citizens can be resolved through discussion and discourse and not by forcible means or by offending the sentiments of any community."

The main instrument for mobilization campaign and for engineering communal riots throughout the major states started in September, 1990. The BJP executive at its meeting in Palampur in June 1989 had passed a resolution on Ram Janam Bhoomi-Babri Masjid demanding the government to hand over the "Ram Janamsthan' i.e. the entire Babri Masjid-Ram Janam Bhoomi disputed complex to the Hindus, which meant the BJP-VHP combine through negotiations or legislation. L.K. Advani said that the resolution was a political one and had to be translated into votes. He decided in August 1990 to take out his socalled Ram Rath Yatra to achieve this objective of translating Palampur resolution into votes to achieve power at the Centre in the next elections which he had planned to force in December, 1990. He also decided in August not to continue support to V.P. Singh Government. The experience of 1989 elections after 5 lakh *Shila poojans*, 5 day *Dharam Yatra* led by 2000 saints and *Dharam Acharyas* covering 5000 colonies, *Ramjyoti Yatra* led from the major religious centres before Diwali in 1989, the *Padyatra* of 1000 kms from Kanyakumari to Madras for socalled liberation of temples from government control, various other religious processions and yagyas did not yield the desired results in terms of votes and seats in the Lok Sabha in 1989 and later in State Legislatures in February/March 1990. With all this and the direct or indirect alliance or seat adjustments with the National Front and Left parties under all opposition unity platform in

1989, it could secure only 11 per cent votes and 85 seats in the Lok Sabha. In 1977 elections, the predecessor of the BJP—the Jan Sangh faction of the short-lived Janata Party—had won 98 seats. After all, in the Uttar Pradesh it could win only 8 Lok Sabha seats, none in Southern states, won majority in two states—Himachal Pradesh and Madhya Pradesh. It had to form coalition government in Rajasthan with Janata Dal support and joined the Chimanbhai Patel Ministry as a junior partner in Gujarat. Hence there was a need for more drastic action to come to power at the Centre. The RSS-BJP combine, thus, went over to their old and tested experience of communalising the polity and engineering communal riots to win over the Parliamentary and State Legislature seats. Hence evolved the concept of the Ram Rath Yatra—a yatra of violence, hatred and brutality. The RSS-Bharatiya Jan Sangh—BJP sponsored riots have been apart from being political riots, fascist pogroms and electoral riots. The history of riots after 1960 in various places amply indicate it. The political resolution passed at Palampur was sought to be translated into votes and capturing of parliamentary and legislature seats and to win political power through communal riots.

L.K. Advani planned to go in for mid-term elections in December 1990 and thus started his socalled Ram Rath Yatra to raise the communal temper, engineer communal riots and brutalize civil society challenging the nation, state, national integrity and unity based on the ideals enshrined in the Constitution, in fact, challenging the most basic foundation of Indian society—secularism and secularization of socio-political cultural life. It was a challenge to all those patriots and secularists who stand for the ideals of humanism, freedom, unity and integrity and to the concept of the individual being the unit of civil society and the Indian nation-state.

The RSS had set the agenda before its parliamentary wing—the BJP—to capture power at the Centre. Its

General Secretary H.V. Seshadri said that the Hindu mind was becoming firmer in its conviction that the long awaited (around sixtyfive years) historic moment had arrived when the RSS could achieve the pinnacle of glory in every aspect including political and that the time of reckoning of all anti-Hindu forces was fast nearing. He said the RSS was set up with the aim of creating a 'Hindu Rashtra', and it should not remain merely a dream. There could be no other way other than the establishment of Hindu Rashtra to transform the destiny of India, that the Hindu power has taken the Avtar as well in the form of Advani's Rath Yatra.

The RSS-BJP started the aggressive communal and fundamentalist cult of their own to achieve their political end of capturing power at the Centre. They put India under a seige and unleashed communal terrorism on an unprecedented scale inside the country endangering the vary fabric of the Indian nationhood and the Indian nation state.

The "moment of destiny" seems to have come for the RSS because V.P. Singh agreed in negotiations with the RSS leadership before the Ninth General Elections in 1989 in Bombay that the Babri Mosque did not exist, that in reality it was a temple. This understanding with V.P. Singh was confirmed by H.V. Seshadri when he said that the Prime Minister V.P. Singh had previously recognized the reality. L.K. Advani in his speech in Parliament speaking on the confidence motion on 8th December, 1990 confirmed that the secret negotiations between the Prime Minister V.P. Singh and the RSS in Bombay were true. Emboldened by this assurance and the electoral alliance entered into with the Janata Dal, hopes of capturing power at the Centre were natural. *The Organiser* said that V.P. Singh could finally climb down on the issue of handing over the mosque complex to the BJP-VHP since he had been making compromises at every step to save his chair, despite all the bravado he had sometimes indulged in, to avoid confrontation. He was dependent upon BJP for remaining in power and to win next elections whenever they came. The BJP had assured of its support to him in the case of wranglings in the Janata Dal for Prime Ministership. When asked if the BJP could support a JD leader other than V.P Singh for Prime Minstership, L.K. Advani said that the 1989 electoral mandate was for V.P. Singh.

H.V. Seshadri said that as the Prime Minister had himself privately conceded the reality of the situation the only just and honourable course for the government would be to issue an ordinance to place the entire area of the disputed site of Babri Masjid-Ram Janam Bhoomi complex at the disposal of Hindus, that is BJP and VHP. The beginning was made, the ordinance was issued to acquire the entire area—disputed and undisputed, an agreement was reached with Advani before he was to start for Dhanbad to continue his socalled *Yatra*; V.P. Singh agreed on October 20, 1990 to join Advani for *kar seva* at Ayodhya on the 30th October. The RSS-BJPdescribed the ordinance as good and thought that placing the entire disputed and undisputed land of Babri Masjid-Ram Janam Bhoomi complex at their disposal even with the understanding that the mosque complex would not be tampered with till the Supreme Court decision whether there was ever Ram Temple at that spot, would have completely demoralized the Muslims.

The RSS-BJP would not depend upon the agreement with the Prime Minister alone and would not take any chance with a weak Prime Minister. With a weak, government at the Centre they decided to mount an aggressive campaign. In 1988 itself they had started militant 'Hindu' campaign and had engineered communal riots as well as they did on the eve of 1989 General election though not on the scale as in 1990-91. On the ideological level it was said that Hindu Rashtra was the same as Bharat Rashtra. Atal Behari Vajpayee said that the state should be neither anti-religious nor non-religious but should be *Sarva Dharma Sambhav* and the RSS Chief Murli Deoras said that pride in Hindutva and Sarva Dharma Sambhav go together. He further said that Hindu Rashtra and Bharat Rashtra were the same. Seshadri said the question was not merely of the construction of the temple, rather what was important was the retention of the identity of the Hindu community. He further said that the performance of *Shilanyas* for the Ram Mandir was the *Shilanyas* for the resurrected Hindu *Rashtra* itself, that Hindu power was the *Rashtra* power, that Hindu power had taken a political avtar in L.K. Advani's Rath Yatra. Seshadri further said that *Dharam Yudh* had the potentiality of changing the destiny of Bharat, that Sadhus and Dharamacharyas participated in thousands to uphold the Dharma rights of the entire Hindu society. Seshadri further said that religious men would naturally help the BJP in its election campaign in the 10th Lok Sabha elections. Jayabhan Singh, an RSS man and the chief organizer of *Ram Shila Poojan Samaroh* in MP said that "everyone who is born in India has to be a Hindu."

The Organiser said the Shilanyas climaxed struggle for the release of the soul of India under Muslim, British and Congress rule—the later representing the hybrid brand of earlier two imperialisms, and according to Seshadri, the struggle was not merely for the sake of a Mandir in place of a Masjid but liberating the soul of Bharat from 'psuedo-secularism' and 'rank communalism', that the act of hoisting the saffron flag on the Babri mosque tower on 30th October, 1990 was the supreme symbol. It was another victorious step in the culmination of the relentless struggle by the 'Hindu nation' against the Islamic aggression of the past 1000 years, and that is a polarization between Babar's progeny and the descendants of Ram. The RSS Pratinidhi Sabha resolved that the flag atop the mosque fulfilled the centuries' old aspirations of Hindus; as if it could undo the history of the Delhi sultanate and the Mughal rule or the British imperialist rule. Of course, the RSS never talks of the slavery under the British rule. After all it was an ally of British imperialism throughout the freedom struggle.

L.K. Advani said that the Indian Constitution divides the country into two parts on religious basis. The RSS gave a call to all political parties to desist from dangerous policy of pampering the separatist Christians and Muslims. It said tribals could be safe only as constituents of Hindu society. Nanaji Deshmukh said that Indian politics had been put to ransom by organized Muslim block votes and K.R. Malkani gave a call to "nationalize" Muslim vote banks. It is just in line with the old politics of RSS to 'nationalize' Muslims. L.K Advani said that Muslims could not be defended by the paramilitary forces or by the state and that they could be secure only in a Hindu society and a Hindu Raj. The RSS prepared one crore inland letters and distributed them free of cost. On the cover was published a map of Akhand Bharat which included the whole of the subcontinent, Burma, Sri Lanka and Thailand with Bhagua flag in the middle and the legend on the map saying "Organise Hindus and make strong India."

B.K. Kelkar called upon the BJP to reconstruct India on the basis of Hindu rennaissance to give a Hindu thrust qualitatively to Indian politics because social transformation had failed as they ignored Hindu psyche. Hindutva and Hindu consciousness was the only powerful and unbreakable link. According to Seshadri, the future of the BJP depends upon how consistently and commitedly it will continue to adhere its policies with the Hindu content and that Hindu Rashtra is the same as *Sanatan Dharma* and rises or declines with it. Another ideologue said that Shivaji personified the concept of Hindu nationhood and hence, every Hindu should become a Shivaji.

It is to achieve these aims set forth by the communal and fundamentalist ideologies of the RSS that the BJP and VHP set on their task of destroying the composite culture, secular edifice and socio-cultural Indian ethos that has been created during the freedom struggle and under the Gandhi-Nehru model in independent India. Jai Dubhashi a member of BJP National Executive Committee called Advani's Rath as a symbolic gesture against Nehruism. He called Nehru a symbol of terror and tyranny of the ilk of Hitler and Stalin, a symbol of what is wrong rather than what is not right. They indulged in communal violence, rather inhuman bestiality and brutality, killing Muslims, their women, children being the main targets, to terrorize them, to force them to capitulate, to humiliate and demoralize them, and to win over their votes out of terror. V.P. Vanprasthi, an RSS activist said that Muslims should be asked to fill up a proforma indicating their belief in a single nation India or two nations theory and this formality must be repeated every 20 years.

In 1988, VHP took out 'Dharam Yatra' involving sadhus and dharamacharyas for 5 days. It said every temple was a symbol of nationalism. Then Jyoti Yatras were taken out. After that along with Advani's Rath Yatra, 400 yatras in different parts of the country were taken out. Earlier 1000 kilometre long Padyatra from Kanyakumari to Madras to liberate the Ayodhya temple from Government control was taken out. *The Organiser* deplored that Hindu religious heads had been deprived of their temple and *Muth* properties. The BJP working committee said that the government control on temples was unjust, unfair and discriminatory. It said these sources should be mobilized for Hindu causes which means for RSS-BJP purposes. L.K. Advani said they collected eight crore of rupees for construction of the Ram temple. And the process of communalisation climaxed with Advani's Rath Yatra which started from outside the Somnath temple because Morarji Desai did not allow its entry into the Somnath Temple premises and prohibited the employees from garlanding Advani. All the same wherever this yatra of hatred and hostility with Advani's provocative speeches, provocative slogan shouting,exhibition of Lathis, swords, *trishuls* and other weapons passed it left violence, murder and arson in its trail. Then followed the *Kalas Yatra* round. The communal violence was organized in so many states right from Assam to West Bengal, Bihar, UP, Rajasthan, MP, Delhi, Gujarat, Maharashtra, Andhra Pradesh, Karnataka and on a very wide scale particularly in the Hindu belt. Even in Rajasthan, the military had to help police in 17 places. It resulted in death of more than a thousand people and unnumbered casualties, arson, burning and looting. The bestiality and brutality was horrendous. Communal violence was preplanned and well organised. It was done to consolidate the Hindu 'vote bank'. The violence this time was more widespread than even in 1989 before the 9th general elections, in fact more than ever in independent India. The stake being capture of power, nothing was left to chance. Ten lakh Bajrang Dal volunteers with *Trishuls* were pressed into service. It was the fundamentalism of RSS-BJP and to call it Hindu fundamentalism will be a misnomer.

Communal riots in the wake of L.K. Advani's Yatra created civil war conditions as the organising secretary of the Giriraj VHP Kishore had forecast. The riots occurred wherever the Rath Yatra passed through. These riots were political, fascist pogroms was led by RSS—BJP men against Muslims to consolidate 'Hindu' vote bank as advocated by the RSS and its parliamentary wing—the BJP to capture power at the Centre.

The communal riots were more horrendous, barbaric, heinous and brutal this time than ever before since independence; and all this bestiality was spread in the name of Lord Ram. These riots were widespread over almost all states right from Assam to West Bengal, Bihar, Orissa, Uttar Pradesh, Madhya Pradesh,

Rajasthan, Andhra Pradesh, Karnataka, Gujarat, Maharashtra and Delhi, with major concentration in UP, MP, Rajasthan, Gujarat and Andhra Pradesh—the Hindi belt and also where the BJP was in Government, amongst these UP, Gujarat and Rajasthan being the main targets.

In UP, communal riots took place on the widest possible scale. Curfew was imposed in 49 districts. According to a highly placed official in the UP administration, 66 out of 85 constituencies were communally sensitive. What happened in UP reminds one of the religious wars in France.

"A fresh edict of toleration had hardly been issued when civil war was precipitated by a horrible crime. Some armed retainers of the Duke of Guise, coming upon a Huguenot congregation at Vassy in Champagne, attacked them and murdered 300 people. A wild cry of fury rose from all the Calvinists; throughout the whole land where there were riots. At Toulouse, for example, fighting in the streets lasted for four days and 400 persons perished. It was one of the worst years in the history of France. A veritable reign of terror prevailed everywhere, and while the crops were destroyed famine stalked throughout the land. Bands of robbers and ravishers under the names of Christian parties but savages at heart, put the whole people to ransom and to sack. Indeed, the wars of Religion were like hell; the tongue can describe them better than the imagination can conceive them. The whole sweet and pleasant land of France, from the Burgundian to the Spanish frontier, was widowed and desolated, her pride humbled by her own sons and her Golden Lilies trampled in the bloody mire."

In UP though, it was a one-sided affair. The rioters armed with tridents, swords, daggers, iron rods, petrol bombs and cans were moving freely indulging in arson, loot, killings and burning of innocent men, women and children, and terrorising the minority community, widowing and desecrating the holy land of UP.

In Gujarat, according to Ashraf Sayeed reporting in *The Times of India* of 27 April 1991: The communal violence spread with precision from Surat to Vadodra to Ankleshwar within five days like wildfire. The puzzling aspect of the rioting has been the clockwise precision of incidents. Surat witnessed communal carnage on Saturday/Sunday; Vadodra on Monday/Tuesday; Ankleshwar on Wednesday/Thursday.

From April to December 1990, the state witnessed nearly 1400 communal incidents in which 224 people died and 775 people were injured. From January to April 1991, 120 riots took place in which 38 persons were killed and 170 wounded. In the past communal forces had gained tremendously in the Lok Sabha and the subsequent assembly elections by keeping the communal pot stirring. Riots were confined to places where the Congress pitted its candidates against the BJP whether it was Surat, Baroda or Barauch district. According to S.M. Shukla (*The Times of India*) three factors led to communal carnage in Panchmahal district within 3 days from October 31, 1990—intensive propaganda of Ayodhya Ram Rath Yatra in rural areas, rumours, and whispering campaign to arouse communal frenzy.

The major towns affected in UP by communal violence were Agra, Lucknow, Jhansi, Bulandshahr, Meerut, Kanpur, Varanasi, Ghaziabad, Hapur, Aligarh, Muzaffarnagar, Gorakhpur, Azamgarh, Mirzapur, Khurja, Bijnaur, Saharanpur, Farukhabad, Fatehgarh, Etah, Allahabad, Rampur, Bareilly, Sultanpur, Basti, Colonelganj, Deoria, Hardoi, and Almora, Bajpur, Modinagar towns in Nainital district. Curfew had to be imposed in 49 districts of UP; in Rajasthan in Jaipur, Jodhpur, Sawai Madhopur, Beawar, Pali, Churu, Kota, Sriganganagar, Ajmer, Nagaur, Udaipur; in Madhya Pradesh in Indore, Mhow, Dewas, Raipur; in Gujarat in

Ahmedabad, Baroda, Deesa, Madasa, Dhanera, Barauch, Halol, Padia, Jainjodhpur, Dehgam, Godhra, Surat, Banaskantha, Palampur, Jamnagar, Panchmahal, etc.; in Karnataka in Bidar, Tumkur district, Kolar, Bulbagat, Somarpet, Ramnagram, Chaunapatha and Karesim Hasonaballi in Bangalore District, Dudeslaballapur in Kamkapura taluk, Kalanji village in Dakshina Kannada district, Devangeva, and in Mangalore; in Andhra Pradesh in Secunderabad, Hyderabad and nearby areas; in Bihar in Samastipur, Darbhanga, Ranchi, Mussalahpur, Mungher, Bhagalpur; in Assam in Barakvalley; In Haryana in Faridabad; In Orissa in Bhadrak in Balasore district and spread to villages even at 25 kilometres distance; in Kerala in Mattancherry area in Trichur district; in Maharashtra in Nagpur, Kamtee, Central and North West Bombay, etc.

The riots paid BJP dividends in Lok Sabha and Assembly elections held in June 1991. For example, in UP, BJP won Lucknow, Agra, Kanpur, Rampur, Jhansi, Varanasi, Hapur, Aligarh, Muzaffarnagar, Gorakhpur, Mirzapur, Basti, Sultanpur, Bareilly, Almora, Nainital, Bijnour, Etawah, Gorakhpur, Gonda and adjoining constituencies like Hamirpur in Jhansi district, Chandauli in Varanasi district, Maharajganj in Gorakhpur district Balrampur near Gonda, and Anola in Basti district. It won both the Lok Sabha seats in Barak valley in Assam and Secunderabad seat and Majlis Ittehad-ul-Muslimeen (MIM) another communal organization, won Hyderabad seat on equal and complete division between Hindu and Muslim communalists. In Gujarat it won Ahmedabad, Gandhinagar, Baroda, Surat, Banaskantha, Godhra, Broach, Jamnagar, Kapadvanj, Saharkanth, Surendranagar in Ahmedabad district, Mandni (ST) in Surat district, etc. In Karnataka it won Bidar (SC), Bangalore south, Tumkur and Mangalore. Riots occurred in these constituencies. In Rajasthan it won Churu, Kota, Madhupur, Jaipur, Pali, Ajmer, among others where riots took place. In Bihar it won Ranchi among others. The myth that riots do not take place in BJP governed states of which it often boasted was also shattered. The riots in Rajasthan, Gujarat and Madhya Pradesh were most widespread after UP and in Rajasthan the Army had to be called in 17 places to quell the riots. 200 persons belonging to the minority community who were detained under the Terrorist and Disruptive Activities Act in 1989 in Rajasthan continue to languish in various jails in spite of several concerned citizens and politicians bringing to the notice of the State and Central government about the illegality of the whole affair. They were arrested in 1989 while TADA was issued by the Rajasthan Government only in March 1990. Apparently the detention is illegal; nothing had been done to alleviate their misery.

The home minister Digvijay Singh admitted in the State Assembly that 228 persons were detained under TADA and that out of these there were 178 persons against whom no charges were established, nor any explosives or weapons recovered from them. The army was called in UP and Rajasthan repeatedly. Religious places were destroyed on a vast scale and sacrilege committed. The other features of these riots were continued for 3 months in succession, the longest period ever. The riots broke out and re-occurred several times in the same place; earlier riots would not take place in the same place once they were quelled. The riots saw pitched battles between mobs belonging to different communities and between mobs and police. The mobs used countrymade bombs and pistols in such confrontations. The other weapons used were daggers, swords, tridents, butcher's knives, licensed firearms, apart from use of petrol for arson and burning alive of human beings. Police found 160 petrol bombs and 50 litre petrol cans from the house of Mukesh Bhati, a Bajrang Dal activist in Hyderabad. Families were driven out of their homes and burnt alive. Elders were burnt or murdered in front of their children. Even the tutor of a

16-year-old child murdered his parents before the child's sight. Muslim families were pulled out of trains and killed by *kar sevaks* between Varanasi and Jafrabad, Children aged 5, 6 or 10 years were even not spared and were killed or Children of were thrown out of running trains. The Jammu Tawi train was set ablaze at Ahmedabad. In Indore the riot occurred when the supporters of RSS, VHP and BJP took out a victory parade and distributed sweets. The story is similar elsewhere too. In Aligarh, a family with a child of 12 years—was pulled out of a train and killed. In Khurja, 10 persons of a family including a one and half year old child and a 70 year old woman were burnt alive. In Jahangirpuri, 13 persons of a family including children of 4 and 5 years of age were burnt alive. In Hyderabad in one house three elderly people of a family who were having dinner were hacked to death, while two children saved their lives by hiding under a cot, two others ran out, while their parents were being hacked by the assailants. The two horrified children who hid themselves under the cot watched this horrendous act of savagary from underneath the cot. The two other children who had slipped away, managed to slip unside the home of a member of the other community. They were dragged out and their bellies ripped open. A nine year old deaf and dumb boy was attacked with swords. A petty businessman, his sister, wife and two children were killed by a mob, their bodies thrown into the flames of their burning house. The sister's hands were chopped off with swords, wife draggged out of kitchen and a sword pierced into her abdomen, house was set on fire and bodies were thrown in the surging fire. Woman, girls and children became main targets and that too during the Year of the Girl-child. The rioters seemed to revel in torturing their victims and choosing the most brutal ways of murdering innocents: In the name of building Hindu character, the minds of youngmen had been brutalized. A large number of persons participated at mass level in these crimes which also resulted in pitched battles and arson and looting. Women also got involved in committing communal violence and so did the tribals, which is quite a new phenomenon. Communal clashes took place even during the curfew hours and the police could not check. Either the force was inadequate or in some cases as in Rajasthan, it was incapacitated for some time in view of the ruling party instigating communal riots. Army had to be called on an unprecedented scale in every state even in BJP ruled states like Rajasthan. In Rajasthan it was called at seventeen places. At places the PAC became a gang of organized killers. It killed innocent people while in the process of doing their daily chores in Aligarh. Religious shrines of the minority community became special targets of destruction for the first time on such a scale. Masked men on motorcycles and scooters went on a frenzy of shooting in crowded places. So was electronic media used to start rumours of communal killings following and consequently communal riots taking place. Cassettes were played in cars in a on loudspeakers creating panic, other than spreading rumours and resulting in riots. Audio cassettes with sounds of religious slogans shouted by crowds, footsteps of a mob on the move and sounds of women and children shrieking, screaming and wailing were used to create riot-like situations. False rumours became a major source of starting riots. Wherever Uma Bharati and Sadhvi Rithambhara went and delivered speeches, riots ensued.

The main provocating slogans were : 1) *Bachha Bachha Ram Ka, Janambhoomi Ke Kam Ka;* 2) *Tel Lagau Dabur Ka, Nam Mitao Babar Ka:* 3) *Hindi, Hindu, Hindustan, Kahan Se Aye Musalman;* 4) *Musalmanon Ke Liye Do Sthan Pakistan Ya Kabristan;* 5) *Maro Inko Jaanse, Nahin To Bhejo Pakistan;* 6) *Babar Ki Santan Ko Ek Dhaka Aur Do;* 7) *Babri Auladon Ko Ham Bardasht Nahin Karenge;* 8) *Ho Ram Ke Mukhalif Aur Bharatiya Bhi Ho; Sambhav Nahin Kabhi Bhi, Keh Do Bajake Danka;*

9) *Jab Ek Ek Ali Ki Chhaati Par Das Barjrangabali Chadh Jayenge, Tab Pata Chal Jayega Ki Yeh Sthan Ram Janambhoomi hai Ya Babri Masjid Ka,* etc. Leaving out BJP ruled states, in every state the RSS, BJP and VHP leaders, office bearers, MPs and MLA and corporators were arrested. For example, in Assam, Kailashpati Misra, Vice President of the BJP, K. Purkaysetha, Vice-President of Assam BJP, and Bansilal Soni, RSS incharge of north East India were arrested at Hailakandi. Several VHP, Bajrang Dal and Jagran Morcha activists along with 30 workers were arrested in connection with communal riots in Gonda district. Shiv Prakash Shukla, the BJP MLA from Gorakhpur and HMS MLA O.P. Paswan were detained under NSA.

It Hazaribagh, Bihar, the entry of the local BJP M.P. Yadunath Pandey, the VHP general secretary Ashok Singhal into the Hazaribagh sub-division was banned from September 20th till October 30th, 1990 to avoid communal rioting. The District President of the VHP, Mahavirlal Vishwakarma, its Secretary Gangadhar Dubey and the district chief of the RSS Brajmohan Kesari and other leaders and activists were arrested on 19th September among others. The BJP MLA. Shiv Prakash Shukla from Gorakhpur and Hindu Mahasabha MLA O.P. Paswan were detained under the National Security Act. Two BJP MLAs Kantibhai Kachoria from Deesa town in Eakaskantha and Vithalbhai Shah from Delgam town in Ahmedabad district were arrested for instigating people for rioting. A large number of BJP workers were detained under TADA in Gujarat for their involvement in riots.

In Andhra Pradesh 300 BJP workers were arrested according to the BJP secretary. The State BJP president Venkaiah Naidu, the State Secretary B. Dattalreya were taken into preventive custody. The Hyderabad city BJP president Bal Reddy MLA, Ravinder Reddy MLA, A. Narendra, former BJP MLA, were also arrested under the A.P. Prevention of Dangerous Activities and

Communal Offenders Act of 1984. The police found 130 petrol bombs and 50 litre petrol cans from the house of Mukesh Bhati, a Hyderabad Bajrang Dal leader. Forty-three BJP, VHP and Bajrang Dal leaders were arrested in Meerut. In Cuttack, Jushna Rai, president of city BJP, and N.K. Mohanthy, president of BJP youth wing among other activists were arrested. In Saharanpur, 5 local BJP leaders were taken into custody under NSA for fanning the riots. Sadhvi Rithambara's entry was prohibited in Gujarat and cassettes of her speeches were banned in Delhi for two months. In Baroda BJP workers were detained under TADA for their involvement in communal riots.

Conditions were created to cow down and demoralize the Muslim community. L.K. Advani said the police or the state cannot save Muslims. Only Hindus, i.e. RSS-BJP could save them. Ashok Singhal threatened them and said either they cooperate with 'Hindus'(i.e. RSS-BJP, VHP) or face situation like Colonelganj where 32 villages mainly inhabited by Muslims were burnt in 48 hours and 42 people killed or burnt alive in seven hours. He further said that politicians could not save Muslims. If anybody could save them it was Hindus; they should cooperate with them and they could protect them; Acharya Giriraj Kishore, joint secretary VHP said, "If the minority will continue to be guided by the fundamentalists who are not allowing them to join the mainstream—they will not be allowed to sleep in peace." He advised the Bajrang Dal volunteers to use weapons. He would prefer civil war. The vice president of the BJP, Malkani said that the Muslim vote bank should be 'nationalised.' According to Ashok Singhal 10 lakh Bajrang Dal volunteers had been trained, naturally, in the use of trishule, swords and other lethal weapons. The saffron army in Bihar was equipped even with licensed and unlicensed firearms too. This time the civil war was unleashed by RSS-BJP in the form of communal terror. The civil war thus unleashed in the form of communal terrorism was an election game. At the same time it was a challenge not only to Muslim minority but also to the nation-states and to all secular forces in the country, to those who stand for integrity and unity of India. Seshadri referring to October 30, 1990 events particularly the *kar sevaks* going atop the Babri Masjid and hoisting the saffron flag there said that the entire plan of October 30th was chalked out precisely with this end in view; to give sufficient time to an adversary to prepare himself and then to challenge in an open trial of strength, for the struggle is not merely for the sake of a Mandir in place of a so-called Masjid; on the other hand it represents the struggle...to throw out the shackles of pseudo-secularism and rank communalists, who have held it subjugated (Bharat) all these past decades since Independence.

3

Communal Riots in Jaipur

K.B. Garg, H.C.Bharatiya, S.S.Oberoi and K.C. Pande

In November 1989, on the occasion of the victory procession of the BJP candidate in the Lok Sabha elections, when in the history of Jaipur, for the first time, communal riots took place, provocation and ugly slogans were shouted such as: *Bachha Ram Ka Aur Sab Haram Ka : Musalman Ke Do sthan, Pakistan aur Kabristan.* (Everyone is for Ram, and everyone else is a bastard; Muslims have two places to go to—Pakistan or the graveyard).

"The Supreme Court cannot judge only the Ram Janam Bhoomi, we are not prepared to accept the decision of the Supreme Court in religious matters." Such were the views of L.K. Advani, leader of a party which has expressed its faith in the Indian Constitution. L.K. Advani's Rath Yatra started on September 25 from Somnath temple. The BJP leaders delivered inflammatory speeches in a public meeting organised by the party on 10 December, 1990 at Chhoti Chaupar.

The chief minister, Bhairon Singh Shekhawat, threw

a challenge to Mufti Mohammad Sayeed, the the home Minister of India to stop the Rath Yatra if it was within his power to do. The BJP had given a call for Bharat Bandh just after the arrest of Advani on the morning of 23rd October. The government in Rajasthan was busy in making the *bandh* a success. Shekhawat on his return from Delhi, called a meeting at the BJP headquarters to plan ways and means of making the *bandh* a success. By that time the government order to close all educational institutions had already been passed.

(Rashtradoot, Oct 24, 1990).

Report of BJP Meeting at Chhoti Chaupar

The General Secretary of the BJP, Ghanshyam Tiwari, addressing a meeting at Chhoti Chaupar challenged the Muslims "They should understand that they cannot have hostility towards Hindus as there can be no hostility towards a crocodile while living in a sea." (*Nav- bharat Times*, October 24, 1990).

Around 3 pm, groups of young people went around the markets forcing the closure of the shops on October 23, 1990 (*Dainik Navjyoti*, Oct 24, 1990). It is in this background that the shameful communal riots of Oct 24, 1990 can be viewed.

Commmunal Riots on Oct. 24, 1990

Just to spread anarchy and create an atmosphere of fear and terror, old tyres were collected at more than 10 places in the city and set afire. At around 9 am about 200 people under the leadership of a BJP legislator went round Chandpati market shouting inciting slogans to spread terror. When the police pointed out that this might lead to communal riots the police was reassured that they would not allow such a flare-up and that demonstrators would not visit the minority dominated *bazars* and living quarters. They especially assured that they would not visit areas like Ramganj Bazar.

Soon after miscreants started arson and looting in the shops owned by the minority community in the same bazar. Later on, they penetrated into the minority *mohallas* in groups of hundreds shouting inciting slogans. One such group went straight towards Ramganj. Simultaneously, other groups converged on this area—some from Ghatgate side and forced the minority community to close their shops and immediately communal riots occurred in Manak Chowk and Ramganj areas. When the police approached the same BJP legislator, he expressed his inability to control the rioters. Due to lack of rifles and tear gas shells the police was a mute witness to the riots. At this time, a rumour had also circulated that ten Hindus were forcibly kept in a mosque. A huge mob collected in front of the mosque and started pelting stones. In the meantime the police reached the spot to the quell rioters in which a police constable died of a gunshot. Nobody knew who fired the shot, but this acted as fuel to the fire. The police, later on, clarified that the constable did not get killed because of police firing. After this incident, the old city and many areas outside the walled city were engulfed in riots. The facts clearly indict the BJP directly for starting these riots. Actually L.K. Advani laid the foundation of these communal riots with the advent of his Yatra on September 25, 1990. The State Chief Minister on October 12 by challenging the Home Minister and on October 23 by planning a strategy for a successful *bandh* had given clear indication of his own and his government's intentions. BJP and the Shekhwat government bear a definite and total responsibility for the outbreak of these communal riots. The terrible tolls of deaths and stabbing cases clearly show that the RSS, VHP, Shiv Sena and Bajrang Dal played a full-blooded role in these riots. Some instances have come to light where some people sent their families away on October 23, 1990 saying that there was a possibility of riots occurring in their areas though the city was peaceful till then. These people had prior knowledge of riots and later on the police arrested them on serious charges. All these facts testify to the fact that the riots were well-planned and premeditated with careful scrutiny of the strategy to be followed. Another fact which comes to light is that the administration had either forgotton the lessons of the riots of 1989 or they had just chosen to forget it. Otherwise the riots could be quelled right at the beginning.

Start of the rioting

Communal riots descended on Jaipur like a calamity. Stabbing, murder, looting and arson made the whole walled city break out in a terrifying cry. Some outlying colonies could also not escape these riots. The rioters in streets and *mohallas* duping the police and creating havoc made it amply clear that it was all pre-planned. The loss of life and property in these riots shall always remain a black spot in the horrifying memory of these events. The police at places had to resort to firing besides using teargas shells. Consequently, many people were wounded. Curfew was clamped at 11 O'clock yet rioting could not be controlled. The army had to be called in. Only then could the situation be controlled to some extent.

The pattern of rioting was almost the same in all the areas. It began by stone pelting and using lathi and other weapons for attack; then looting, arson and violence prevailed. The attitude of militant organizations of the majority community and the BJP is undoubtedly dangerous and shameful. Unfortunately, such an attitude on the part of minority community could also be witnessed at places. The treatment meted out to 'Kolis' in 'Koli Mohalla' by the minority community was definitely equally barbaric, deceitful and shameful. Except for 'Dakoto-ki-basti', 'Shastri Nagar', and of course, the Koli Mohalla, most of the atrocities were committed in the areas inhabited by the minority community. On the night of 24th of October, 1990 in Rishivigalav Nagar the atrocities committed on the minority community surpassed all limits. Police was embroiled in strange kind of problems and could not be effective. Due to policemen being shot dead or wounded, the police under provocation resorted to excessive use of force. The minority community has a special complaint that the Rajasthan Armed Constabulory and the police in particular vented their ire on them. In these communal riots the role of the BJP and some of the legislators is not only highly shameful but deserves to be condemned by all.

Anti-social elements also had a heyday besides the rioters. Getting shops or houses vacated by the minority community tenants, settling old scores or rumour-mongering was at its peak. Some newspapers also come into this category including a leading newspaper of Rajasthan. Stock brokers were busy betting on the number of Hindus or Muslims died—eclipsing the fact from their mind that all the dead were Indian human beings—be they Muslims or Hindus. Not even one of the dead belonged to any well-to-do family or was an income-tax payer or a political or religious leader.

After the Riots

The need of the hour was relief work. Even here, the voluntary organizations did much better than the administration. But it is regrettable that some of these organizations have been and are working only for one community. Thus, the riot affected people did get relief but this in no way helped to mitigate the divisive feelings. Instead it promoted ill-will between the two communities. The pattern of behaviour and working psychology of these organizations was the same as that prevailed in SMS Hospital where, before interment of the dead bodies in the mortuary the fly buttons of the corpses were opened to ascertain whether the dead body was of a Hindu or a circumcised Muslim. This was another shameful aspect of these riots. The major work of rehabilitation of the victims of these riots is still pending. Considering the partisan attitude adopted and its consequence that occurs, one is filled with sorrow and remorse. One wonders where would all this lead to? Even the government is following its discriminatory policy in relief work. First to receive the relief cheques were the members of the majority community and the lion's share of the relief amount was received by two close associates of a BJP legislator. Their houses had been only slightly damaged.

Terror and fear is embedded in hearts of the riot victims. They shiver to think of going back to their own houses. Rumour-mongering is, even today, having a heyday, resulting in widespread incidents of panic, slogan mongering and stone pelting though on a smaller scale. In the night less cassettes of screams and shouts continue to be played to spread terror in the hearts of the people. Those who are bold enough to think of returning to their homes are being dissuaded and disheartened and told that they should not be eager to return to face death again. An attempt was made by peace-loving citizens and the administration for the rehabilitation of the victims in their own homes. In 'Koli Basti' this was carried out to a large extent. Yet the situation remains far from normal there. It was expected of the majority community in each '*basti*' to instil a feeling of assurance and safety to the minority members and bring them back to their homes but it remains a dream to this day. The betters bet on the date, time and place of the next riots. To win these bets rumour-mongering and sham quarrels are indulged in for spreading terror and insecurity in the hearts of the people.

Besides the damage to life and property the mutual confidence between the two communities has become the biggest casualty. The remaining bitterness has resulted in polarization of the two communities to a large extent. To combat this process does not seem to be all that easy. The complexity of the situation can be further assessed from the fact that people responsible for riots were of these very *mohallas* though they prefer ignorance now to avoid being branded and say that outsiders caused these riots. In the FIR lodged, many such names of residents of the same *mohalla* figure, though no action has been taken against them. Even when such elements were taken into custody they were later on released either on bail under Article 151 or were released on the recommendation of the BJP legislators. Whatever the state administration may prefer and try to take some steps in this regard, the state government neither professes nor desires to normalize the situation. The leaders of the ruling party are extremely busy in either arranging welcome meetings for the *'Kar-Sevaks'* or devoting the dead *kar-sevak* to the rank of martyrs. So the possibility in such an atmosphere to tie back the slander threats of trust and confidence does not exist.

Communal elements are becoming really experts at concocting tales of woe. This was amply illustrated by the statements of two people whom we met during the process of our inquiry. We visited the house of an antisocial person arrested by the police. His wife narrated a harrowing tale of victimization of her adolescent daughter and young children. This really moved us. But a little later while talking to her elder son we came to know that it was nothing but a concocted tale. The reality was that the family person had no grown-up daughter. The man had sent his family to his in-laws a day earlier saying that there was some possibility of riots. In another *mohalla* we visited, we were told that one particular family had removed their belongings earlier. Photos were shown to us to confirm this. But on inquiry we came to know that the photo showing removal of household goods were of some other day. They had been victims of riots on 24th October itself.

Two contradictory currents are blowing these days. Riot victims, on the one hand, are trying to sell their property in other areas where a different community holds majority in order to purchase house in the locality where people of their own community are mainly settled. If this trend strengthens it will have farreaching consequences. If cities are divided on communal lines how can the whole country remain united? On the other hand, secular forces are trying to get organised to face this challenge. This step is desirable as well as essential. But this task is very difficult. Peace committees and secular forces do become active when the danger arises but before the situation comes under control they get inactive and disintegrated. On the other hand communal forces are getting organized, strengthened and expanding. It is yet to be seen whether secular forces will be able to function at all. The Congress, the JD and other so-called secular forces are so much engrossed in the struggle for power that none of them put in a demand for judicial enquiry for quite some time. Whatever the reason, this silence on their part is definitely going to harm the country.

Some points to ponder

These riots have put forth some moot points for thought and need prompt consideration:

1. The majority community has been complaining that the minorities have stayed away from the mainstream of national life due to a fundamentalist leadership; and they are being progressively divorced from the national mainstream. But, at the same time, the attitude and the treatment meted out to them by the majority community which has been responsible for this reaction has not been taken into account. The majority community by putting the responsibility for their own actions on the minority community are further pushing them into the clutches of fundamentalist leaderships. The minority community ascribes this to its

sense of better insecurity and a feeling that by following a fundamentalist leadership they would be able to solve the problem of insecurity by themselves. They think this is the only solution for them. Both communities lay the blame at each other, behave towards each other in such a way that the foundation of aberrations and distortions in their mutual relationship gets strengthened. In this way they are unwittingly declaring the rights and duties enshrined in the Indian Constitution null and void. In addition, this direction is rendering a large section of the secular population belonging to different communities almost feeble and futile. While this is the only section of society which may have the capacity of facing this problem squarely if this section gets disheartened and disbanded, the Constitution, the nation and even the population of the country may not be capable of confronting and controlling this menace.

When someone affected belonging to this section gets angry for any sundry reason, he burns the national flag or the Indian Constitution. The legislators even proclaim themselves to be communal and challenge the others to take whatever action they can. Even a top leader declares that the decision of the Supreme Court is not binding on him in religious matters. Such elements are at the helm of affairs in some states and are wishfully burning 'Ram-Jyoti' so that in the near future they may occupy the seat of power in the Central Government. How are these leaders in any way different than the terrorists operating in different parts of the country in their effort to disintegrate the nation.

When a State Chief Minister challenges the Home Minister of the Government of India to stop the Rath Yatra, it seems as if they were engaged in a wrestling match. When the Central Government goes on bowing down to such challenges, the days of democracy seems to be numbered in this country.

Is the time not ripe for safeguarding and enforcing

the Constitution rigorously and to root out the communal elements—be they political or cultural and whether they belong to the majority or the minority community? Are the spineless Central Governments capable of ridding the country of this pestilence and danger? The fact is that unless the public forces them to do so, it shall never be done. To lay the blame on governments, administration, political leaders and parties is of no avail. The question is of asking oneself whether the time has not come to stand up and do something to drain out the poison of communalism from the system.

The question of secularism needs also to be reviewed. The situation existing today is that there are as many views on secularism as many parties or individuals are there. The foremost point to be noted as regards secularism is that religion has no role to play either in politics or administration. But the interpretation put on today is that all religions have a right to interfere in politics. This is the basis of all ills. Hence, till the problem of religious interference in politics whatever be its colour is not ended, this problem cannot be eradicated. Another point is that this should not be the operational philosophy of the majority community only. All religious groups should abide by it. Though this principle puts an additional onus on the majority community so that the minorities may become fearless and follow the path of secularism without any hesitation, these recent communal riots have brought the fact to light that most of minority communities leadership thinks that the road to secularism is only a one-way traffic so that benefits may accrue to them but they need do nothing in return. This existing situation is not desirable nor correct, hence, needs a change.

Religious places have become cause of communal tension and riots like the incurable cancer. This fact needs to be realized and accepted. Religions and places of worship should be brought within the ambit of judicial courts forcefully and actively. No one can declare these matters to be beyond the rule of law and justice in a democracy. If they do so, communal riots are the outcomes of the whims of such people. As and when religion and religious matters crop up and interfere in politics, proper legal and constitutional safeguards should be arranged. There is a definite mention of secularism in the Preamble of our Constitution but we have rendered it meaningless by giving it twists and turns in our interpretations. Constitutional interpretation of secularism should be undertaken promptly so that it may become clear that interference in matters of state policy in the name of religion and caste is prohibited and illegal. The Constitution is supreme in the country. This has not only to be said openly but to be implemented emphatically. Constructions of new places of religious worship for next fifty years should be banned so that the mounting frenzy of constructing a religious place is checked. Loudspeakers at religious and other places should be banned. Do we need so many places of worship and, that too with loudspeakers ? Our purpose should be pursuit not propaganda of religion.

If we look at the recent riots in Jaipur, we may find that, though communal organisations and the high caste leaders of BJP were in the forefront of inciting this communal frenzy the riots also took place amongst the Muslims and the lower castes and they had to pay a heavy price for that. Communal sentiments were incited to start these riots but the economic factors underlying these cannot be ruled out. Property and its ownership has become a major cause of tension. These riots illustrate the point that inhabitants in one given locality, be they of one community or the other, if in majority in that locality try to get the properties of the minority residing there vacated through fear or coercion. Professional antisocial elements and property brokers have played a notoriously clearcut role in the shady and cheap property deals of such kind. There have been ample proof that the tenants of minority community of a property belonging to a majority community landlord have witnessed their belongings being not only thrown out but set afire so that the possibility of their return is ruled out and the property remains safe. Now the tenants are not allowed to come back to these premises. These antisocial elements owing to political patrona carry on their nefarious trade with impunity in normal times but communal riots provide a golden opportunity to acquire these. To check such acts, some legal measures are needed so that the rights of the tenants are safeguarded.

With other poverty-stricken people, the need to uplift economically and socially, both should be planned and subsequent measures must be followed up.

The call of "Hindu Rashtra" given out by Advani and other leaders is a call for danger. This should be realized by the majority community. First, the very idea of a Hindu Rashtra is neither correct nor possible with so many minority communities living in secular India. If one supposes for a moment, that Hindu Rashtra comes into existence which state or states or part of the country would it constitute? With the demand for Khalistan in Punjab, would it be able to include Sikhs in Hindu Rashtra? Hindus in Assam are another factor to consider with their demand for secession from India. The clamping of emergency is a vital proof of this. Nagaland and Mizoram being mainly Christianity professing regions are already waging a separatist struggle. Will Advani be capable of bringing them under a Hindu Rashtra and DMK in Tamil Nadu is depicting Ravana a God instead of Ram. Will Advani forecast for how long would they constitute Hindu Rashtra ? A burning example of history is that a state based on religion is not viable. Islamic Pakistan has already broken into two and the process of disintegration still continues. Has Advani got the capability of belying historical facts?

4

Communal Terror in Jaipur

Dalip S. Swamy, Zahoor Siddiqui, Ramesh Rao and Salar Khan

The People's Rights Organization constituted a team consisting of Professor Dalip S. Swamy, Zahoor Siddiqui, Ramesh Rao and Salar Khan to investigate the nature and causes of communal riots in Jaipur. The team visited Jaipur on 6th December, 1990 and met more than 50 persons, including the family members of the victims, social workers, professionals, students, university teachers, administrative and police officers. The following report is based on the information available from the grassroots even though the information from top police officers has also been duly considered.

Jaipur is a metropolitan city inhabited by 1.4 million ethnically different people with 0.4 million comprising the Muslims. Its forts, palaces and a flourishing business of gems and jewellery attract national and international tourists. Until 1988 the city prided itself on its communal harmony and amity. Even in 1947 and 1984 when communal madness gripped Delhi and other parts of the country, nothing had happened in Jaipur.

The social sanity was, however, fractured on 27th November, 1989 when a victory procession of a BJP MP led to an outbreak of Hindu-Muslim riots in the city. The riot took a toll of six lives, injured 300 persons, 139 shops and 109 houses were burnt down. No sooner did the social wound of the November riots heal than another riot, with a much greater ferocity occurred within a year, on 24th October, 1990 after the arrest of L.K. Advani in Bihar. It was truly a fascist assault on the Muslims, in which the State was covertly abetting the rioters and in some cases its organs, especially the Rajasthan Armed Constabulary (RAC) played the role of a partisan, communal surrogate fascist force.

The magnitude of the second riot was severe by all standards. On 24th October, 23 mobs armed with lethal weapons attacked 56 localities. As a result, 52 persons were killed, of them five were killed in police firing and eight in RAC firing, more than 144 seriously injured, 229 houses and 163 shops were looted and set on fire, 8 mosques and 2 *dargahs* were destroyed and property worth Rs 5 crores looted or destroyed. The administration arrested 450 persons and imposed curfew which continued for 22 days. Even a month after the riots, cassettes with provocative messages — *maro, kato, pakado, bachao* — were being played at public places in several parts of the city and people staked millions of rupees, speculating whether another riot would take place or aborted on 6th December. The city continues to remain in social trauma. On 15th November a rumour, based on two cows fighting in a street in Ramganj, was enough to create a panic such that shopkeepers in Ramganj as well as in neighbouring localities closed their shops and people fled to their houses. The social discord is now so deep that it will take years of dedicated social work to restore harmony.

A TV mechanic, Abdul Wahab reported that the riot is an instrument for securing electoral advantage. After the riots of November 1989, the BJP emerged as the dominant party in the Assembly. He alleged that BJP had even bribed Ahmed Baksh, who contested elections on the IUML ticket from Johari Bazaar, paying Rs 40,000 even though he is an outsider from Kota. Ahmed secured about 8000 Muslim votes, traditionally expected to be cast in favour of Congress (I) candidate, which were sufficient to ensure the victory of BJP candidate, Kali Charan Saraf in the Assembly elections last year. Emboldened by the sequence of riot-election victory, Kali Charan Saraf whipped up communal passions on 23rd October. On the next day his followers from the local Bajrang Dal created trouble in Ramganj Chaupar.

Abdul Wahab characterized both Congress and BJP as communally surcharged. The difference was that while the former openly preaches Hindu communalism and attacks Muslims openly, the latter does not preach communalism, nevertheless it does stab them in the back.

Hate Campaign

The October riots occurred in Jaipur because of the hate campaign organised by the BJP since the Rath Yatra started from Somnath. This campaign was intensified over a fortnight prior to the arrest of L.K. Advani on 23rd October in Bihar. On 12th October when Advani's Rath was in Jaipur, a prominent BJP leader, Chaturvedi announced that he would resign from the ministry to participate in *kar seva* in Ayodhya. Addressing a public meeting on that day, the Chief Minister, Bhairon Singh Sekhawat challenged the central Home Minister, Mufti Mohammed Sayeed to stop the Rath Yatra in Jaipur (if he had the guts to do so). The General Secretary of BJP, Ghanshyam Tiwari, who lost in the 1989 Assembly elections, challenged the Muslims : *pani mein rah kar magar se bair nahin hota. Agar bhai chara dikhana hai to Ayodhya sonpani hogi.* He also reiterated his statement (one that he had made in the Assembly) that he still remains communal.

On Diwali day (18th October) an idol of Hanuman in a Shiv temple was allegedly destroyed in Brahmpuri. Several BJP leaders, including Girdhari Lal Bhargav, Ramesh Bhardwaj and Ujala Arora reached the spot and pacified the crowd gathered there. Later the police enquiry revealed that there was no disturbance but some persons were playing cards which infuriated the residents. The police arrested Yakub, Mohan and Jamalluddin, who were playing cards in that temple. A local daily *Rajdoot* reported that such incidents occurred in other Hindu temples too which created tension in the city.

On 21st October, Chief Minister Bhairon Singh Sekhawat also asked the BJP high command to permit him to resign so that he could participate in *kar seva.* The President of BJP, Ram Das Aggarwal informed the press reporters that several ministers had indeed submitted their resignation letters to him for participating in *kar seva.* The *Rajasthan Patrika* reported that all ministers expressed their desire to resign from the government.

Tension in the city over the places of worship and the hate campaign evidently indicated the possibility of a communal flare up. And the administration was also aware of the vulnerable communal situation in the city, because the intelligence agencies had informed the administration of the possibility of a communal flare-up. More so, because such warnings were carried by several local newspapers.

The hate campaign reached its climax by 23rd October. After Advani's arrest in Bihar, a public meeting was organized at Chhoti Chaupar, a prominent park in front of Kotwali under the chairmanship of Ram Das Aggarwal. A section of the Press reported that some persons on their way to the public meeting disturbed many shops in Maniyaron Ka Rasta, Hawa Mahal, and so on, and also attacked a mosque. But the police was able to repel the hooligans. The meeting was addressed by many BJP leaders, including Bhairon Singh Shekhawat who declared his support to the Bharat Bandh on 24th October. Many speakers used provocative language, whipping up communal passions. After the meeting the returning crowd again disturbed peace in those very places where they had created disturbance earlier in the day. But they again failed as the police pickets were already posted there.

Under this background of surcharged atmosphere, of heightened emotions and passions, the BJP convened an urgent meeting in Bharatiya Bhawan at about midnight to chalk out an "action plan" for making the Bharat Bandh a success on the next day.

Rumours-mongering

On 24th October *Dainik Nav Jyoti*, a Hindi daily reported that, "according to reliable sources police is instructed not to prevent the youth trying to close shops and markets". At about 5 am a *mazar* (tomb) adjacent to the Chief Secretary's residence was attacked. This was perhaps a warning or a signal that even the Chicf Secretary's area was pregnable. At 8.30 a.m. tyres were set ablaze simultaneously at about a dozen prominent crossings and mainroads—on the crossing near the Governor's residence, Ajmeri Road. Civil Lines, behind the Chief Minister's residence. A senior police officer reported that the city was dotted with smoke and mobs were moving by 10.30 a.m.

As the mobs were forming, because of the smoke in several places, rumours circulated. Growing density of smoke made it easy to believe that 'Muslims have set Hindu houses on fire in many localities'.

A TV mechanic-cum-salesman, Veerendra was returning from Ajmeri Gate after repairing a TV. He saw two matador vans, spreading rumours, via a loudspeaker that the Muslims of Ramganj had abducted twenty Hindu girls. When he reached Tonk Phatak he saw a big crowd where persons with lathis were telling that they had recovered three dead bodies of Hindus from Ramganj. Veerendra tried to sneak through the crowd to have a glimpse of those dead bodies but he was rebuked. He then proceeded towards Barkat Nagar where he heard that the 20 Hindu girls abducted by the Muslims were murdered in Ramganj. In retaliation the RSS kidnapped three Muslim girls but kept them safe without touching them. Veerendra also reported that some of the passengers in the matadors and jeeps, which were moving freely, appeared to be 'fake' policemen.

The SHO of Shastri Nagar, Nath Singh was on duty round the clock on 24th October. He reported that rumours were rampant with devastating effects. When he was returning from Chandpur, about half a kilometre from the police station, after dispersing a rioting mob, he was told that a rocket launcher was confiscated from Bhatta Basti by some persons. Nath Singh immediately went to Bhatta Basti to verify the allegation and found that the confiscated item was a children's 'hawai' cracker.

Arson and Police Firing

In brief, by 10.30 am on 24th October, 1990, the city was dotted with smoke and the moving mobs were fed with wild rumours. The situation was explosive throughout the city.

A social worker reported that police opened fire on an irate mob in front of Ramganj police station at 10.35 am. As a result, one person was killed. The thana-in-charge himself filed an FIR in that case. It was perhaps the first casualty on 24th October. Two persons were killed at 10.45 am., one in Tripoli Bazaar and another, known to be a 'meena' (Hindu Scheduled Tribe), at Hanuman Ka Rasta. Some persons reported that the 'meena' was killed when the DIG Gill opened fire.

Receiving that information Bhanwar Lal Sharma (minister), visited the spot, picked up the dead body and reported the matter to the Director General of Police. According to a senior police officer, five persons were killed in police firing on 24th October. In every case, he said, the mob was violent, indulging in looting and arson.

At Galtaji ka Rasta a mob of about 300 was organized in front of the local VHP Office by Pranvendra Kumar, an ABVP activist and the President of the Rajasthan University Students Union at about 10.00 am. In order to ensure that all shops were closed this mob proceeded from shop to shop. At 11.30 am it reached the shop of a *Lohar* (blacksmith), who was still working in his shop. The mob attacked his shop but the police was able to disperse them. At about 1 pm about 200 youth, known to be activists of the RSS, regrouped. And this time the mob was reportedly led by Kali Charan, the MLA from that constituency and Girdhari Lal Bhargav, an MP from Jaipur. The mob attacked many houses, shops and a mosque. They set on fire General Gramophone, a shop owned by Abdul Aziz Chameliwala (a well-known Muslim shop in the area which was attacked in the last riot too) attacked, looted and set it on fire. Thereafter the mob was on the rampage.

Riots in Paharganj

A TV mechanic in Paharganj, Abdul Wahab reported that in Koliyon Ki Basti, an RSS activist Koli, Nolay set his house on fire, despite many persons restraining him. He allegedly did it for filing a claim with the government; in the last riot too he had done the same thing. We visited Nolay's house, which was in fact destroyed in fire, but we could not trace him. In any case, the residents had reported the matter to the RAC Headquarters on 24th October.

A youth residing in Koliyon Ki Basti, active in Bajrang

Dal, receiving regular training in Brahmpuri *Akhara*, reported that most of the *kolis* had left the locality by 23rd October and the rest left after the riot but none wanted to return. The locality indeed looked like a ghost *basti*. The youth reported that the local Muslims set houses on fire. But he did not know, who set Nolay's house on fire. He showed us a house where two persons were killed. An old man was still around in a room near that house. He reported that the radio news of seven persons having been killed on 24th October was wrong. But he confirmed the death of two Hindus in the adjoining fire. It was also reported to us that a Muslim mob attacked the police picket near Phuta Khurra and a policeman was killed in firing.

Clearly there were cases of arson and killing in Koliyon Ki Basti and the Muslims were aggressive. But what seems to have happened later was even more shocking. Only an indepth judicial enquiry can reveal the real story. The available evidence, however, suggests the described scenario.

Receiving the reports of disturbances the RAC evidently surrounded Koliyon Ki Basti. They took up positions on a few multistorey buildings, especially a four storey house under construction, which overlooks the local mosque and from where RAC jawans could watch the movements of people down below. They also fanned out in the locality and tortured the Muslim residents on suspicion. The residents reported that a couple of jeeps with passengers disguised (in khaki dress) as policemen were moving freely in the locality. The residents also reported that the RAC fired indiscriminately. We saw many bullet holes on walls facing the house under construction.

Seven persons were reportedly killed in indiscriminate firing. The identity of these persons is not yet to be ascertained. Rajesh Sharma of *Rajasthan Patrika* reported on 26th October that three dead bodies were stacked in a gypsy and set on fire. But he did not enquire the identity of the dead nor the circumstances under which another maruti car was burnt at the same place. K.K. Purohit of *Navbharat Times* carried the Patrika report on 26th October but also mentioned that among seven Kolis burnt in Patali Gali, three belonged to one community and four to another community.

Our investigation revealed that seven persons were killed in indiscriminate firing by the RAC. They stacked these dead bodies in a gypsy and a Maruti car in a garage, set them on fire, and protected them from public rage until the dead bodies were burnt and all evidence eliminated. Apprehending that they were watched, the RAC blamed the police. When the police investigated the matter, the Muslim residents accused two Hindu brothers running a corner grocery shop. At closer investigation it was revealed that the two brothers were not in the city on that day. The matter being serious, because the police was implicated, senior police officers investigated and concluded that it was the handiwork of the RAC. This conclusion was confirmed by a senior police officer.

The killings in Koliyon Ki Basti was an important radio news on the evening of 24th October. And in the background of a surcharged atmosphere—smoke, irate mobs, firing, and wild rumours all over the city—the radio news was sufficient to ignite the retaliatory mob fury in several localities.

Terrified by the developments, the *basti's* residents, mostly Muslims huddled together inside their houses, some went up on their rooftops to watch the scene around. Golam Dagan Mosque is an interesting vantage point. From its roof one can watch the house of Haji Sarfooddin, a 65 years old Congress (I) worker and beyond that too, up to Rishi Galav Nagar. Many persons were on the rooftops of the mosque as well as the Haji's house. Some of them were seen using binoculars as well as telephones to inform others, including the police control room, about the arson and violence happening down below. The residents reported that they were receiving as well as supplying information to their friends through telephone. They had received the information regarding the fire in Chameliwala by 4 pm. They also noted on 24th October green and red lights flashing from a temple in the hill above Rishi Galav Nagar, allegedly signifying the movement of the police, especially of the senior police officers. In any case, whatever was being watched was also being communicated through phone to the police control room, to an ex-MLA, and other friends.

It seems that on 24th October the Muslim residents in Paharganj watched the RAC jawans on a shooting spree in their locality as well as the rioting mob in Rishi Galav Nagar. They regularly informed the police as well as their friends and sympathizers in other localities. The conventional administrative (intelligence) agencies were also doling out information to the administration. This information system perhaps unnerved the RAC. And the news of seven persons being killed was made public. But these persons were considered as Kolis because their identity was not announced.

Incensed by the public information system or suspecting a 'planning' for retaliation, the RAC targeted their terror on 25th October at the mosque and the Haji's house, the two vantage points from where the information regarding the RAC firing flowed to the administration and an ex-Congress MLA. Majeed (32) and Arab (62 years old sweeper), who were inside the mosque on 25th October reported that RAC jawans fired many shots at the persons offering prayer but fortunately no one was killed. We saw many bullet holes on the mosque's walls; two of them were distinctly marked, presumably by an official investigating agency, one on the front pillar at a height of about 5 feet and another on the inner wall of the mosque.

Haji Sarfooddin's residence was attacked at 2 pm. More than a dozen RAC jawans forcibly entered by breaking open the main door. Not finding any person on the ground floor they went up and beat up Ruksana, the wife of Riazuddin and daughter-in-law of Sarfooddin. She shouted for help and shrieked as RAC jawans tried to overpower her, pushing three children—Farzana, Shabana, and Maran—out of the room to the verandah. RAC pickets watching the scene from the roofs of other buildings, opened fire. The bullet holes inside the room indicate that the shots were fired from at least two directions. One RAC jawan was killed. Not able to make out, who shot their colleagues, the RAC raiders lost their nerves and retreated. Meanwhile Ruksana had escaped to the adjoining room and bolted the door from inside. Mortified by the incident seven of them, including Ruksana's old mother-in-law, Sarfooddin, and four children remained confined to that room for three hours. They opened the door when Ruksana's husband, Riazuddin reached the house along with the Search team.

Izhari Yazdani, a doctor in the locality reported that the firing continued until 3.30 pm. It stopped only after the mobile picket reached the locality. At that time (3.30 pm) RAC jawans were all over the roofs. The doctor was told of an RAC jawan having been shot down in the locality and that a house-to-house search would be conducted. Agreeing to the proposal, Yazdani suggested that along with the police party a prominent resident of the locality should accompany the search party. Ilyas Riaj Beg, Jagannath Verma, and couple of other citizens then accompanied the search party at 5 pm. The search party did not find any arms and did not arrest any person.

Rapes and Murders in Rishi Galav Nagar

The worst affected colony was Rishi Galav Nagar.

There, too, the mob had formed by 10.30 am. The mob intercepted two cyclists on the Delhi Road and asked them to say, *'Jai Sia Ram'*. Both of them responded. Nevertheless, the tone of one of them did not appeal to the person leading the mob. This was enough to infuriate him as well as the mob, who then attacked the cyclists. One was hacked to death. The dead cyclist was later identified as a truck driver, Seeraj from Bihar. The matter was reported to the police. Although the police was not able to arrest the culprit yet a police picket was posted in the locality.

The mob entered the locality in the night after 10 pm, noting that the policemen on duty were fast asleep or disappeared from the scene. The lady from the dispensary reported that she heard women shrieking at 11 pm. Babboo's wife jumped from the second floor to resist the attack on her and fractured her legs. A Hindu neighbour, later admitted her to a hospital. The Muslim woman told that she had good neighbourly relations.

On the night of 24th October, the mob killed 18 Muslim persons. A senior police officer reported that he saw a three-wheeler ablaze at 11.30 pm on the side of the road bordering on Rishi Galav Nagar. He was told that seven Muslim women were raped, their throats were slit, and were thrown into a ditch. He reprimanded the policemen on duty.

Many persons from a nearby locality, from where the mob was suspected to have attacked, were arrested that night. Most of the persons arrested were the RSS activists. When the local MLA came to know about those arrests, a protest was organised. On the afternoon of 25th October Ujala Arora, a BJP MLA along with her supporters approached Phool Singh Yadav, DIG Police and enquired about those arrests. The latter informed her that the police arrested some persons who were actively involved in crimes. Ujala Arora then enquired about two persons who were arrested. The DIG told her that he did not know whether the persons she was referring to were arrested or not. When Ujala Arora expressed her desire to meet the arrested persons the DIG told her politely that it was unfair for a respectable person like her to meet criminals in police custody; they would in any case be produced before the magistrate as soon as possible.

Not satisfied with the DIG's response, Ujala Arora broached the matter with some higher authority. And on the afternoon of 26th October the Director General of Police reorganised the police administration to handle the rioting situation by transferring the DIG, Yadav to his earlier position in the Police Academy.

Terror in Shastri Nagar

In Shastri Nagar Vyas Colony (Nargarh Kila), an unauthorized settlement was attacked by a mob from the east on 24th October. A senior citizen and an old resident of the locality, Shambhu Singh reported that a mob of about 200 youth, mostly outsiders came from the eastern side and ransacked all Muslim houses. Mortified by this rage, the Muslims did not return to their houses even after 40 days. Many, like Razia, have sold out their property and decided to live in Muslim majority localities.

The SHO of Shastri Nagar, Nath Singh reported that 'history sheeters' were not active that day, they generally remain behind the scene in such riots. The public men were in the forefront all over the place. He also reported that police force is too inadequate to handle such rioting situation when the entire city was disturbed. Whenever the situation gets out of control RAC is pressed in service. But unlike the police, RAC jawans are not familiar with local people and therefore their approach is generally brutal. In Jaipur the relations between the RAC and the police are not ideal. There was a sharp difference of opinion regarding the arrest of a criminal, Man Singh.

Sohan Lal a BJP leader and Girdhari Lal, Sarkaryawah of the RSS in Shastri Nagar reported that the riot in their locality was created by antisocial elements and that they had no idea, who created disturbances in other localities. They also admitted that their political position in fact strengthened after the riot.

In Kumharon ka Mohalla, Chand Bibi reported that the mob attacked her house at 11 am on 24th October. At that time she was taking bath. Hearing some derogatory remarks and observing the mob surging towards her house, half-dressed Chand Bibi escaped with her son to the adjoining *mohalla* where many Muslims had already gathered.

It is interesting to note that the house of Chand Bibi is a sort of landmark, with the Hindus dominating on one side and the Muslims on the other side, while a mosque is also located there. It is just outside an RSS run school, Adarsh Vidya Mandir and Chand Bibi has received threats from several officers to vacate the house.

The mob destroyed many Muslim houses and shops in the locality up to Chand Bibi's house. But they encountered resistance beyond her house, because the Muslims were in large numbers and also offered resistance. The RAC trampled that resistance on 25th October. They fired on unarmed people assembled on a *chabutra*. In the firing, Chand Bibi's son Abdul Amin was injured. On his visit to Jaipur, following the riot, Rajiv Gandhi incidently talked to this boy recovering in the city hospital. The RAC also fired at persons assembled in the mosque where a few bullet holes could be identified. Karuna Chand Sharma, who migrated from east UP 11 years ago and was working and living in that locality ever since, reported that he never saw such a large-scale destruction of property and such an 'indifferent attitude' by the administration towards the rioters.

Ghastly Murder in Barkat Nagar

The mob fury prevailed in the entire city. In almost all localities, the Muslim houses and shops were attacked. Even isolated houses or shops were not spared. The criminal mind was working at its worst in Barkat Nagar, a pre-dominatly Hindu colony, where well-educated University teachers and professionals live. A teenage school girl, who had an inkling of a plan by the RSS youth of the locality, to kill Babban Begum, the only Muslim woman in her neighbourhood, informed the latter to escape by the evening of 23rd. But the lady was too confident of the love, affection and decency of her neighbours to leave the locality. The mob attacked her, poured kerosene on her, and setting her ablaze, bolted the door from outside and moved on. No neighbour responded to her screams. Babban Begum somehow managed to save herself. But the mob returned after 35 minutes. The animal passions had seized them. Noting that she survived, they opened the door, poured kerosene, and again set her ablaze and vicariously watched until she died. This report was confirmed by a senior police officer.

War for Places of Worship

The mob fury was primarily motivated to terrorize the Muslims so that they leave their old habitat. A reordering of population is expected to consolidate the electoral votes of the BJP. But the mob was also motivated to grab land for temples wherever possible. We noted several cases of communal conflict for establishing Hindu temples—in Shastri Nagar, Brahmpuri and Neelgaron Ka Rasta.

A comic incident in Brahmpuri epitomizes such a symbolic communal war without confrontation. A group of RSS youth took a stone, inscribed 'Om' on it with red colour, placed it on the site of a Pir, and called it '*Pir Pachhad Mahadev*' (Mahadev defeating Pir) temple. Next morning the local Muslim youth noted it. They quietly removed that stone at night and called their action as '*Mahadev Pachhad Pir*'. This obviously infuriated the RSS youth, who again placed another stone inscribed with 'Om' and called it '*Pir Pachhad Mahadev Dobara*'. But this time they did something more. They went in a delegation to their leader and told him that temples were being destroyed in their locality. The MLA was obviously incensed at this heinous crime, when so many Hindus were willingly offering their lives for Ram Mandir. He moved the administration and got five RAC jawans posted there with an instruction, not to allow anybody to enter that premises.

Thus, the traditional resting place of the Pir is declared disputed by the state. Nevertheless the state is apparently neutral, because it is letting both the Pir and the Mahadev coexist, without letting any mortal approach the two deities anymore. The BJP Government in Jaipur is indeed practising a wonderful secularism.

We noted another incident, in Brahmpuri, which is more pathetic. A Muslim stone merchant has a stock of cement in a small shop and Kota stones on an open plot of more than 500 square yards at a prime location on the main road in front of prosperous shops. We noted the stock of stones worth lakhs of rupees still there in the open. The mob defied the curfew, painted 'Om' with red colour on a stone lying there, placed it in the centre, and called it a 'Curfew Mahadev' temple. Like the Pir Pachhad Mahadev temple, the Curfew Mahadev temple is also being guarded by the RAC jawans with the same instruction: do not allow anyone to enter the premises. What can the owner do ? He cannot sell his stock, he cannot leave the site lest RAC remove all or part of the stones at night, and he cannot file a claim as it is a disputed case. This is a case of fascist theocracy immobilizing business.

In Neelgaron ki Basti, a Waqf property is converted

into a Hindu temple. We saw a vacant plot with 7 feet boundary walls along with a mosque. The Muslim residents reported that the place was used for their children's education. On the front wall a fresh signboard is now fixed; it reads 'Satya Narain Lakshmi Mandir'. There, too, the RAC permits Hindus as well as Muslims to offer prayers, even though nobody has done so after 25th October. But they do not permit anyone to disturb the place by placing furniture or constructing a building. At the moment there is a heap of rubble inside the boundary walls, where RAC jawans freely perform their morning duties.

Tables 1 and 2 provide the details regarding the loss of property and lives in different localities.

Table 1: Persons Killed in Riots in Jaipur, June 1990

(number)

In police firing	5	
In RAC firing	8	(7 civilians + 1 RAC)
By Muslims	5	(4 Hindus + 1 policeman)
By RSS-BJP mobs	34	
Total	52	
Localities		
Policeman	1	
RAC jawan	1	
Galtagate ke pas	1	
Mohalla Visayatiyan	1	
Amgarh Ki Basti	3	
Salawatan	2	
Paharganj	3	
Barkat Nagar	2	
Jhhalana Dungri	1	
Lanka Puri	1	
Loharon Ka Khurra	5	

	Men	*Women*
Unidentified	4	—
Hindus	5	—
Muslims	30	13
Total	39	13

Continued on next page

Vidyadhar Nagar	4
Hindon	1
Karoliwala	1
Kolyon Ki Basti	7
Rishi Galav Nagar	25
Total	52

Source : Based on Relief Agency reports.

Table 2: Loss of Property in Riots in Jaipur, June 1990

Area	*Number*	*Amount (Rs. Lakhs)*
Ramganj		
Rishi Galav Nagar	31	10.38
Bandri ka Nasik	13	7.81
Moti Singh Bhumya Ka Rasta	6	3.07
Topkhana Hazuri	7	7.60
Suraj Pole	13	8.08
Manak Chowk (Ramganj Bazar)	3	8.13
Ghosyon Ka Rasta	5	6.80
Ramganj chhetra	17	17.28
Rauji Ka Khurra	3	3.25
Heeda Ki Mori	46	19.51
Kotwali		
Maniharon Ka Rasta	9	7.55
Nahargarh Road	25	24.19
Nahargarh Kila	8	6.45
Mohalla Neelgaran	25	6.96
Mohalla Purani Basti	3	1.25
Jaylal Munshi Ka Rasta	64	36.79
Khaijaron Ka Rasta	14	17.24
Chora Rasta	7	7.84

Continued on next page

Area	Number	Amount (Rs. Lakhs)
Mishra Raja Ka Rasta	14	17.24
Gangauri Bazar	19	14.09
Govindji Ka Rasta Kishanpole	44	48.28
Nahari Ka Naka	4	4.06
Kalyanji Ka Rasta	11	4.90
Unyaron Ka Rasta	17	18.65
Baba Harish Chander Marg	6	2.78
Sodala	8	4.15
Narsingh Colony	4	5.00
Bagru Walon Ka Rasta	20	22.42
Nala Neelgaran (purani)	7	2.40
Jat Ke Kuan Ka Rasta	9	6.95
Brahmpuri		
Gujarghat & JP Colony	22	6.61
Govind Nagar (W)	6	7.52
Ganesh Colony	9	14.86
Shivaji Chowk	5	8.00
Faqiron Ki Doongri	8	1.49
Brahmpuri Road	11	6.85
Santosh Nagar Colony	18	7.28
Rajiv Nagar	18	22.35
Manak Chowk		
Haldyon Ka Rasta	10	12.23
Pacherji Ka Rasta	3	9.30
Johari Bazar	2	1.67
Kanwar Nagar	5	4.68
Hawa Mahal	2	0.54
Vidya Dhar	2	1.30
Mani Rai ji Ki Kothi	6	5.25
Chandi Ki Taksal	4	1.91

Continued on next page

Area	Number	Amount (Rs. Lakhs)
Shastri Nagar		
Bhatta Basti	5	0.81
Parvat Colony	2	0.66
Nahari Ka Naka	3	2.01
Shivaji Nagar	11	3.28
Telipara	17	2.81
Vyas Colony	14	3.79
Pashupati Nath	12	4.09
Ashok Nagar		
Ganesh Puri	5	1.06
Gandhi Nagar		
Jhalana Dungri	2	0.26
Gandhi Nagar	4	0.77
Jhotwara	4	0.30

Source : Relief Agencies.

Summing up

It was an organised anarchy of a comprehensive order in a BJP ruled state that had no history of communal tension until 1988. On 24th October the BJP-RSS led 23 riot squads were on rampage in 56 localities. The mob fury prevailed everywhere; violence and mayhem was celebrated; and the rioters ruled the city for two days, despite the police, Homeguards, RAC and military deployed in large number under five DIGs—Phool Singh Yadav for the walled city, P.N. Raina for rural Jaipur, B.N. Hansuka for Ramganj, P.K. Tiwari for Kotwali and Arun Duggal for Manek Chowk. In the riots 52 persons, mostly Muslims (43) were killed, more than 144 injured, 229 houses and 163 shops were looted and burnt, 8 mosques and 2 *dargahs* were destroyed, many places of worship and open plots were rendered disputed, and property worth more than Rs 5 crores was looted or burnt.

What Congress (I) did (to the Sikhs) in Delhi, following the assassination of their leader, Indira Gandhi in 1984, the BJP accomplished (against Muslims) in Jaipur, following the arrest of their leader, Lal Kishan Advani in 1990. In both cases, the riots were planned and orchestrated by the ruling party to take revenge or subjugate the targeted community, the administrative compliance was glaring—no culprit was booked—and the political opposition to the communal attacks was ineffective even in making the offending parties defensive.

The riot left the city marred with fear and hatred. It is for the rational and social conscience keepers to decide how to respond to such organised violence. Speculators have their own way of dealing with the uncertainties created by the riots; they staked Rs 1.5 crores up to 30th November on the possibility of riots on 6th December, the second *kar seva* at Ayodhya. But for Alla Baksh who lost everything and for Babboo's wife whose legs are fractured, life goes on with complicated and painful struggle.

5

Communal Riots in Beawar: PUCL Investigative Report

Mahesh Bora, Nikhil Dey, Aruna Roy,
Chunni Singh and Vijay Lakshmi Joshi

Brief Account

23/10/90: VHP and BJP give a call for Beawar Bandh. In an effort to close Jai Mandir Cinema Hall, a skirmish erupted between students and its employees. The RSS and BJP gave this skirmish a communal turn. A report was lodged against only Saif Mohammad, who was not even present there, and no complaint was made against Hindu employees.

The BJP-VHP organized a public meeting at 7 o'clock in the evening. The speeches and slogans at the meeting incited communalism in an effort to turn the whole atmosphere into a communal atmosphere.

24/10/90: During a visit by Trilokani and Virendra Sindhi to the Muslim Mohallas at 8 o'clock in the morning, pressure was exercised to close the shops despite the fact that shops were a part of residential houses. Threat was issued to come in large numbers if the shops were not closed and to settle the matter then resulting in the atmosphere begining to deteriorate.

At 10 o'clock at night The Mohammad Ali School was set ablaze. Later on a Hindu crowd burnt Muslim shops and reduced them into ashes. In Muslim *mohallas* Hindu owned shops were damaged by Muslims but the the wreckage was minimal. Peace loving Hindus and Muslims put an effort to stop arson and looting.

Hindu crowds encircled Muslim *mohallas* from all around. Police tried to disperse Muslim mobs inside the *mohallas* and Hindu mobs outside. This action made the Hindus militant and the situation got almost out of control. The police thus resorted to lathi-charge, teargas and firing. Later, curfew was clamped and the situation controlled. VHP and BJP were wholly responsible for these communal riots and for this purpose they used students and it was felt that any religious procession or celebration should be banned if it was communal in nature.

On 23rd October, the VHP, BJP and Bajrang Dal gave a call for Beawar Bandh from 2 pm onwards in protest against the arrest of L.K. Advani. This was being announced in the whole town through loudspeakers mounted on autorickshaws. The city shops started closing. The shopkeepers who did not close were threatened and forced to close. These were the days when students were carrying on anti-Mandal reservation campaign. Due to this the students had gathered in large numbers. Ugam Raj Mehta, Hari Kishan Trilokani, Devi Shankar Bhatia and Rajendra Kumar Aggarwal, prominent leaders of VHP-BJP, were able to bring these students into their fold and tried to bring the whole trade and commerce to a standstill. In this process the crowd reached the Jai Mandir Cinema around 3 pm and asked the proprietor to close the cinema. The employees of the cinema house appealed to the crowd to wait a few minutes when the show would be over and promised not to begin the new show but the mob insisted on the immediate closure. Babel was leading the student mob and he was injured when the cinema employees and the students clashed. The students started dispersing from there but in the process they broke a hand *thela* parked near the cinema. This *thela* belonged to Saif Mohammad who was an employee of the cinema. After this the student leaders, Ugam Raj and Babel went to the police-station and filed an FIR against Saif Mohammad accusing him of physical assault on students. The BJP, Congress and Muslim leaders confirmed this fact. The various statements regarding this incidence are almost identical, timely and important, except with a difference as to the role and participation of Saif Mohammad in this whole clash. The BJP and RSS hold that Saif Mohammad was very much present at the time of the clash between cinema employees and the students, while others deny the fact. Babel named Saif Mohammad on the persuasion of Ugam Raj Mehta because he wanted to give the whole clash a communal colour.

If one looks at the whole series of events it is very clear that Saif Mohammad was nowhere to be seen during the clash. All the cinema employees except Saif Mohammad were Hindus. Ugam Chand and other VHP leaders were with the students. Hence Saif Mohammad's *thela* was burnt and an FIR was filed against him. The offence comes under IPC 323 and hence no FIR could be registered. RSS and VHP leaders used this mob of students and turned this clash into a communal riot. But nothing more could be done and the students dispersed quickly.

BJP and VHP organised a public meeting at 7 pm in which almost all the speakers gave communal speeches and turned the Jai Mandir Cinema clash into a communal incident though it was not so.

The BJP and VHP gave a call for Bharat Bandh on

24th December, 1990. There was also an announcement for Beawar bandh on this date. Supporters of the bandh came out in the streets announcing the bandh and forcing the shopkeepers to close the shops. Most of the shops in the main bazars were closed but some shops were open in the streets and *mohallas*, which were closed forcibly. There was no tension. The situation started deteriorating when Hari Kishan Trilokani, Virendar, Manjit Singh, Zoiti Shankar Bhutra and some others went to Jama Masjid near Basai Mohalla around 9 am and insisted on closing of shops. The shops in Qasai Mohalla are part of the houses. The inhabitants said that they would not sell anything that day but they could not close the door of the shops as these were the entry to the house through the shop. This led to tension. The supporters of the bandh wanted the door closed and the inhabitants wanted the door to be kept open. According to the BJP sources, Trilokani and Virendra were beaten by the Muslims, but the inhabitants say that Trilokani and others threatened them to bring a crowd of 1000 people to get the door closed. According to the subsequent talk with the local administration officials and with others, the fact came to light that Trilokani and others had tried to close the doors forcibly and had threatened to bring in a big mob. This provoked and infuriated the Muslim youth, who told them that they would meet the challenge. It led to the deterioration of the situation in the city. Trilokani and others proceeded from there to Loharon ki Chaupar and started spreading rumours of being beaten in the Qasai Mohalla.

The process of spreading communal tension in the city in a preplanned and organized manner started from here. Rumours of students being arrested by the police were spread. On 24th October, 1990 anti-reservation students along with BJP and VHP went to the police station during the bandh and demanded the release of the arrested students. The police officers tried to pacify the students and said that no arrests had taken place and for their satisfaction they were taken inside the police station on the orders of ASP Shri Reddy to show that there were no students under custody. Students started returning after getting assured. In the meantime, under the leadership of VHP and BJP leaders, a large number of Hindus started collecting at Loharon ki Chaupar and other entrances to the Muslim *mohallas.* SDM and ASP were present there with some force and tried to prevent the Hindu crowd from entering the Muslim *mohallas.* The angry mob was bent on entering these *mohallas.* People of the Muslim *mohallas* started gathering in their *mohallas.* The situation could have become explosive any moment. The administration and the police were continuously trying to prevent this confrontation by appealing to the Hindu mob to disperse. At that moment they received a message that Mohammad Ali School was set ablaze. The ASP and SDM took some force to the school and found that the furniture in two rooms had been set ablaze. The fire was extinguished but this news spread like wildfire in the whole city and as this news reached Muslim *mohallas,* the mob became furious. The Muslim mobs started demanding that they be allowed to go out of the *mohallas* in order to safeguard their property and shops outside the *mohallas.* The police did not allow them to go out in order to avoid confrontation between Hindu and Muslim mobs. But while the SDM and ASP had gone to the school, the Hindu mob had burnt Muslim shops in Halwayon Ki Gali resulting in a loss of property worth lakhs of rupees. When the Muslims heard of it the Muslim youth started damaging Hindu property and burning Hindu shops, but moderate Muslims totally opposed this action. Consequently, only four Hindu shops were gutted and a few more nominally damaged while the Muslim shops were gutted in large numbers. On talking to the Hindu shop owners whose shops were put to fire, it was confirmed that their loss was not much. They also admitted that these shops were guarded by their Muslim neighbours. But the situation became volatile. The SDM and ASP on hearing the news of shops being set ablaze ran back to the Loharon Ki Chaupar and tried their utmost to persuade members of both communities to disperse, but to no avail. After these incidents of arson, the Hindu mob armed with lathis and iron rods encircled the Muslim *mohallas* and started throwing stones at the police and the Muslims. During this some angry Muslim youths took out some weapons like kitchen knives from their houses. On appeal from SDM and ASP, the Muslim mob receded back some distance but the Hindu mob which was ten times stronger did not budge. The situation was such that they could break the police cordon any time. The police had to resort to lathi-charge and teargas firing. They failed to control the situation as there were only 30 to 40 policemen.

The police sources say that messages were sent to Ajmer for extra force but the force did not come for quite some time. The majority of the Hindu mob consisted of students led by Babel, Trilokani and Ugam Chand Mehta, etc., and were not ready to budge from there at any cost. The police had to resort to firing in which five persons were wounded with no deaths. Only after this could the situation be controlled and subsequently Curfew was clamped. The BJP sources also admitted that more Muslim shops were burnt but the damage was not extensive because the goods had been removed by the owners beforehand as if they preempting in advance that these shops would be set ablaze. But the claims later on and burnt goods testify the fact that these shops were full and most of the goods were destroyed in the fire. We had a talk with the inhabitants of Harijan *mohalla*, which is adjacent to the Muslim *mohallas*. This talk was very important as these people put the whole situation very objectively before us. Tandas Bharati, the chief of the Balmiki Yuva Morcha and some others told us very openly that the BJP had approached them to help them to attack the Muslim *mohallas*, but they categorically refused. On the other hand they foiled the attempt of the BJP to penetrate these *mohallas*. Some Muslim youth also came to the Harijan Mohalla in an attempt to set ablaze some shops belonging to the Sindhi community. They also put a stop to this effort. As a consequence, there was no incidence of arson in Harijan Mohalla. In the whole situation the role of the Harijans was appreciable as they did not take side with any community.

Causes of the Riots: History

Beawar does not have a history of communal riots but one also cannot say that there has not been any communal riot. With the partition of India in 1947, Beawar did see the spread of poison of communalism. Consequently, there were riots in 1947 and 1949 resulting in a considerable loss of property. Eyewitnesses of those incidents do state that thc RSS had its hands in these riots. Progressive and secular forces had tried to maintain communal harmony but their number was negligible. After 1947-1949 peace did come to Beawar and for some years to come there was no communal tension. In 1986 a Naga baba was murdered in Sojat city in Rajasthan. A number of Naga babas were brought to Beawar. In this murder case, a Muslim youth was also accused. The RSS under the leadership of Ugam Raj had made arrangements for the stay of these babas and had spread rumours against the Muslims. This fact was brought to our notice not only by the Muslim community but by many Hindus as well. The prominent among them being Vishnu Batar—a Congressman. Hence atmosphere of Beawar became communal after the arrival of Naga babas. In 1986 Mehndi procession just before Moharram started from Jama Masjid and went towards the main bazar, Teja baba was holding a *jagran* there. The communal Hindus asked for the change of the route of the procession. This was done. At the time of *tazia* procession, it was not allowed to pass by Mahadev

Ki Chhatri, resulting in a very tense situation between the two communities. After discussion and mutual understanding, the *tazias* were taken back to the Jama Masjid. Some minor clashes did take place but due to police vigilance these incidents were few and were controlled. A day after Moharram, a large number of Muslim shops were set ablaze. The administration and the police did nothing. After 1947 the deflagration of communalism was evident in Beawar in 1986. Since then no other incident had taken place but the city remained under communal tension.

Local Tension

After 1986, communal tension was prevalent but before the present riot no local causes were evident. After talking to the inhabitants of Beawar, one comes to realize the fact that there does not exist any major local cause of tension between the two communities.

National Circumstances

This fact supports the idea that the Mandir-Masjid dispute had effect in Beawar too. But there has been no open confrontation between the two communities over this issue. The fact has come to light after talking to different views on the problem of Mandir-Masjid, but they do not consider this to be a worthy cause of involving themselves in communal riots. The majority of the people want a peaceful solution to the problem.

Communal Element

The main cause of the present riot is incitement of the public in a pre-planned manner by the communal element. As far as local tension and national situation is concerned, some solution can be found out by opening an all-embracing dialogue but till the communal elements are identified and isolated from the public, communal tension and consequent riots cannot be stopped. Communal elements spreading communal fire can really be identified in the present riots.

Face of Communalism

In a cultured and civilized society respect for all religions and communities is a must but if people from one religion start shout inflammatory slogans against the people of other religions, communal tension is bound to arise.

From the evening of the 23rd, large groups of Hindus had started shouting inflammatory slogans, two of these are : *Babar ki auladon ko, jute maro salon ko. Jo mangega Pakistan, Woh Jaega Qabristan.* These slogans were shouted in the Muslim majority areas. In the morning of 24th these slogans were shouted more vociferously and by larger groups. The communal tension on 24th was mainly intensified by these slogans, which bed to the riots. This fact was testified not only by eyewitnesses but by the administration and the police. On 23rd and 24th the police and the administration tried to dissuade the Hindus from shouting these slogans as these lead to the worsening of the communal situation, but the Hindus turned a deaf ear to it.

Incident at the Cinema Hall

The dispute between the proprietor of Jain Mandir Cinema and the students was intentionally turned into a communal incident. One of the cinema employees was Muslim—and the rumour was spread that he had beaten up a Hindu boy. The FIR lodged with the police in which only this Muslim employee was named goes a long way to prove that a definite effort was made to turn a small incident into a communal riot.

Rumours and Incitements

During our survey tour the fact came to light that an appeal was issued to the Hindus of the city through loudspeakers to collect at Loharon Ki Chaupar. BJP leaders went especially to Harijan Mohalla to appeal to unite with them to fight against the Muslims. It clearly shows that riots were preplanned and provoked knowingly.

The Use of Students in Riots

The most painful fact is that students have been used in a condemnable manner in these riots as they were involved in the anti-Mandal agitation. It is true that arson, looting, stone pelting, and slogan mongering were indulged in by the students but the BJP and VHP leaders chiefly Ugam Raj Mehta were mainly inciting them. Ugam Raj himself was seen shouting communal and inflammatory slogans on 23rd at the cinema hall. He also went along with the students to the police station to lodge an FIR and demand the arrest of the Muslim employee of the cinema hall. The police and the administration arrested students on the basis of photographs taken during the riots. The administration showed us these photographs. In these photographs the students were seen openly brandishing *lathis* and rods in their hands while setting the shops ablaze and taking out a procession in a very belligerent mood. Immediately after the riot, the inciting leaders went underground in order to escape arrest.

Causes of the Present Situation

The fact which hurts most came to light during our survey that some Hindu as well as Muslim families left their residences and went to live in places where their communities were dominant. This leads to a sense of insecurity among both the communities and leads to greater tension. It is imperative to check this aspect.

Change of Religion

Mehrat community lives in a sizeable number in rural areas surrounding the Beawar city. Mehrat religion is a mixture of traits from both Hindu and Muslim religions. The leaders of both the religions keep pressurizing this community and hence conversion goes on taking place. This conversion leads to communalism and is an added factor in communal tension. If Mehrat community is left to itself and if religious leaders do not exert pressure, communal tension can be minimized.

Religious Procession

Religious procession taken out by both the communities are a cause of communal tension. Chalking out of the route of a procession always causes tension. In 1986 this was mainly responsible for communal riots, and was so in every other communal riot. Thus the administration should pay special attention to religious processions and take some strict steps so that communal tension is reduced and harmony prevails.

Lack of Secular Forces

The vocal, active and courageous and organized secular forces are absent in Beawar. Some persons from both the communites were trying to stop the incidents of arson during the riots but these people were only a handful, and such examples are also few. It is true that a very small part of the population takes part in riots. It is also true that the majority of the population is a mute witness to the riots taking place and the consequent destruction. Hence it is imperative that majority of the people should come out and be vocal to quell the riots. Otherwise, a handful of persons with rested interests communal tendencies will be able to divide the society in the name of religion. The prime need of the society today is communal balance. This can only be possible with vocal, organized, active and secular section of the society.

Role of the Political Parties

It is expected of the political parties that they would assume an active role of secular forces but the situation in Beawar city exposed the fact that they were a total failure in this respect. As far as the BJP is concerned they have polluted the atmosphere by putting their communal activist forces under the banner of VHP and

RSS. The Congress (I) has categorically blamed the BJP for the present riot. But it played no role in stopping the riot. Congress (I) confined itself to taking out a *sadhbhavana* rally and asking the administration to rectify the situation. The CPI only published a poster though they accept that they played a significant role in stopping the riots in 1947/1949. Now they were satisfied with the poster. As far as Muslim communal forces are concerned, some people did name the Jamat-i-Islami and Students' Islamic Organization but could not name any leader or activist of these organisations who participated in the riots. We could not talk to the office bearers of these organizations. We did see some posters by the SIO but the address on them was of Delhi and not of Beawar, but the fact that the BJP and its allies are continuously spreading Hindu fundamentalism came out to light very clearly. In one section of Muslims, especially among the youth, Muslim fundamentalism is also spreading. If unchecked this can lead to dangerous consequences. No political party has a programme to fight this fundamentalism. All are engaged in safeguarding their vote banks. This may lead to farreaching consequences.

Role of the Administration

The role of the administration in the riots and during curfew in Beawar is debatable. The administration was very active during the riots and hence it is imperative that its role should be examined. Dr. B. Shekhar was the SDM and Shri Ravi Reddy was the ASP during that period. They were known for their honesty and earnestness among all sections of society. Leaders of both the communities, before the riots, accepted that these two officers were non-partisan. The talks held with the BJP and its allied organizations, as well as Muslim leaders and journalists make it very clear that no one had a complaint or grudge against these two officers. All agreed that they performed their duty without being pressurized by anyone. They also tried to sort out and solve the legitimate problems of the public but during the riots due to the role of the administration, the Hindu fundamentalists turned against them and the Muslims had a special fear of them. During talks with the people and the administration, it came out not before the incidents of 23rd and 24th that the administration had very cordial relations with all the political and religious leaders. The administration was also aware that no untoward incidents should take place. Whenever religious meetings or processions and celebrations took place the administration always arranged for video recording, and taking of photographs, etc., so that they could restrain inciting slogans and speeches. This had a good effect as people were afraid that consequent to the video recording if any law and order problem arose, action would be taken against them. As regards the 23rd and 24th incidents, the police promptly reached the Jain Mandir cinema hall and prevented the situation from becoming explosive. When students under the leadership of Ugam Raj reached the police station, Reddy was present there. He made it very clear that their dispute was with the management and not with a particular community. It is not out of place to say here that the proprietor of the cinema hall and employees are Hindus. Hence this incident could not be viewed from a communal angle, nor should rumours be spread to start communal riots. With a view to the call of Bharat Bandh on the 24th, the peace committee of Beawar called a meeting on 23rd night in which all the political parties including the BJP promised that they would not indulge in any incident and would keep themselves under control. This was told to us by the members of the peace committee and the administration.

On 24th, when confrontation took place at Qasai Mohalla between the two communities the police reached there with the SDM and the ASP. They were able to control the situation and reduce tension. On hearing the news of Mohammad Ali School being set ablaze, both the officers moved from that place to the school. When they reached the school they heard that arson and looting had started in the city. They immediately proceeded to Loharon Ki Chaupar. On reaching there they found that the Muslim majority areas were surrounded by angry Hindu mobs. Some shops had already been set ablaze. Both the officers intervened and did not allow the Hindus to penetrate the Muslim areas, nor did they allow the Muslim mobs to come out. Both the communities support this fact. Despite the continued efforts of the administration and their advice, the Hindu mob was not ready to lift the encirclement of Muslim areas. On the other hand they would go into the Muslim majority area from time to time and Muslims also started gathering in great numbers. The administration issued warning to both the communities to disperse failing which force would be resorted to. The Muslim community did listen to this advice but the Hindu mob with lathis and rods were not ready to budge. They were shouting inflammatory slogans. A light lathi charge was resorted to. It had no effect. Then teargas was used. The quality of teargas was of very low grade according to the administration and it failed to disperse the crowd. The fury of the mob reached dangerous proportions by this time and the police force being very small, the administration held that if the mob did not disperse, loss of life and property was bound to occur on a large-scale. They gave a warning of opening fire. When this had no effect, an order to fire in the air was given. On this the Muslim mob did disperse and went inside their houses but the Hindu mob stayed on and continued their effort to penetrate the Muslim *mohallas*. In this situation six rounds of firing took place, as a result of which five persons were injured. Whether firing and curfew were needed is a debatable point. The BJP and its allied organizations contend that the firing and the curfew were wrong, that the administration had unnecessarily resorted to firing on Hindus and caused inconvenience to the people. The BJP leaders say that the administration started firing when people were already dispersing. They also say that the Muslims would get into their houses when they saw the police and come out and indulge in stone throwing at the Hindus when the police was not there. They say that the firing on Hindu mobs showed partisan attitude of the administration. Some people from the Muslim community say that a large Muslim mob had gathered in the *mohalla* but they were outnumbered by the Hindus. Some angry and incited Muslim youth threw stones at the Hindus and were inciting others to come out and protect their shops in the Hindu *mohallas* which had been burnt down or were being set ablaze. They wanted to confront the Hindus. But they could not succeed as the police did not allow them to come out of the *mohallas*. Many of the people went back to their houses—while shots were fired in the air till the whole mob dispersed. Some eyewitnesses and non-partisan people including journalists who were present there accept the fact that Hindus outnumbered the Muslims and that they were in an aggressive mood. Despite firing in the air the Hindu mob did not disperse. In these conditions it became imperative for the police to resort to firing. Otherwise the situation would have deteriorated. The statement by the administration, eyewitness accounts, and the prevailing conditions and the statements of the BJP leaders lead this team to the conclusion that in order to safeguard life and property, resort to firing by the police was absolutely essential.

Regarding curfew, the Hindu fundamentalists say that curfew should not have been imposed. After talking to local administration, Ajmer Collector, Muslim leaders and neutral individuals the conclusion was reached that without curfew it would have become impossible to control the situation. After firing and declaration of the imposition of curfew, it took the administration three hours to enforce the curfew effectively. According to the Muslims the curfew was essential for security.

Everybody including the administration and the police admit that certain excesses did take place during the curfew. Most of the complaints were regarding excesses on the violation of the curfew and indiscriminate arrests at that time. As far as cases registered under the IPC are concerned the ratio of both the communities is almost equal, but in Beawar, Muslim population comprises only 8 per cent of the population. Hence more Muslims were arrested than Hindus. The explanation given by the administration was that it was easier to identify the Muslims and because the Hindu mob was very large, identification was not so easy. Hence the administration had to depend upon the photographs taken during the riots and the local police also knew some individuals and this led to the arrest. Both the communities were very critical about the arrests —Hindus being more so as they say that on the scrutiny of the list of the people arrested it was found that most of them were students and also persons who were politically and economically influential. Most of the students were sons of influential people. Hence there was a lot of resentment among the Hindus. The agitation against the Mandal quotas going on at that time was turned into a communal confrontation.

People also complained about the promulgation of TADA besides the arrests. All political parties, religious leaders and the common public think that there was no justification for TADA. The administration also could not give us a satisfactory answer to this. According to our viewpoint the situation did not call for imposition of TADA. After having a talk with the administration, our impression is that effects of the provisions of TADA were not very clear to the administration and it was promulgated without much thought. Our team agrees that there was no necessity for TADA and in future the administration should not commit such mistakes as

TADA is special law and should be used only in special circumstances.

Many demonstrations were organized in protest against the role of the administration, arrests, and promulgation of TADA after the riots in Beawar. The BJP and allied organization wanted the transfer of the SDM and the ASP as according to them they sided with the Muslims. We had a talk with many people regarding this. The BJP, VHP and RSS demanded the removal of these two officials, while the Muslim leaders and other political parties like Congress (I) and Janata Dal and Harijan leaders opposed this demand. On the other hand those parties and individuals who were against transfers said that the administration tackled the situation in a correct manner, otherwise there would have been a great loss of life and property. Many Muslims said that they felt safe because of the two officials, otherwise the Hindu militants would have destroyed their property to a larger extent. The neutral persons say that spreading of communal riots and resultant bloodshed was avoided because of the prompt action by these officers. Therefore such officers who are devoted to their duty and have presence of mind to tackle the ticklish problem should not be transferred, otherwise it would result in frustration to all.

Peace Committees

The administration formed peace committees to maintain communal harmony. These peace committees comprised of representatives of various political parties and religious organizations and others. The main aim of the administration was to bring people of divergent views to a common platform so that they could work for peace together. In fact these were the very people who indulged in rioting. In reality these committees were reduced to forums for false assurances and levying accusations and counter-accusations. Most of the arrested people belong to these peace committees. The administration should not organize such committees and should bring together secular and democratic forces to fight communal elements. Communal forces should also be exposed in public. It should organize programmes which strengthen the hands of secular and democratic forces and encourage communal harmony. The present peace committees in Beawar feel proud of spreading communalism as extreme communal elements were present in these.

During our talks we came to know that peace committees were organized in each *mohalla*. In reality only secular and democratic forces should have been organized to form these committees. Only then could they help the administration to maintain communal peace. Otherwise the communal forces will keep on forcing the society into a communal conflagration. Even during the riots such peace committees will have a vital role to play. Otherwise all efforts after the riots become meaningless. To quell the riots should be the main task and after the riots, promotion of communal harmony should be their aim.

Check on Religious Processions and Other Meetings

The administration should promptly stop religious and political processions and meetings which are organized to propagate communal frenzy as the slow poison of communalism spreads through these. With ignition of a small spark, the situation becomes explosive and rioting starts.

The administration in Beawar sometimes used video camaras, tape recorders and photographs to identify communal elements but the use of such devices was negligible. The government should make available special funds and provide adequate facilities to the administration so that these can be used in a useful manner to combat communal forces.

6

Communal Riots in Jodhpur City

Vijay Mehta

The city of Jodhpur, for the first time in its existence of nearly 560 years was caught in the franzy of communal riots on and from 24, October 1990.

Communal atmosphere generated by the Rath Yatra, better known as Rakt (Blood) Yatra was further accelerated with a call of 'Bandh' given by BJP, VHP, Bajrang, Dal, etc, to protest against the arrest of L.K. Advani. Chief Minister of Rajasthan issued a call to make the Bandh a grand success, Thus the government. and the ruling BJP and its front organizations joined hands to register its protest against the arrest of the BJP supremo.

Communal hysteria was let loose on the eve of the Bandh. Slogans like. "हम सब राम के लाल सब राम के, हिन्दुस्तान में रहना होगा हिन्दू बन के रहना होगा नहीं तो पाकिस्तान या कब्रिस्तान जाना होगा।"

(All of us who live in Hindustan are children of

Ram. If we have to live in India one can live as children of Ram otherwise they will have to go to Pakistan or Kabristan.) ran into the air. Not a single slogan could be heard against the arrest of Advani or for his release. As a matter of fact the call of Bandh was given for generating communal passions with an aim to take political mileage as also to demoralize the minority community and secular forces.

Right from the morning of the Bandh one could see BJP leaders including MLAs terrorising a section of people by using physical force and provocative communal slogans. By 11.30 am the Bandh took a communal turn though it was entirely a one-sided affair. Right under the nose of the police, just adjacent to the police post on the main square of the city, stone throwing on Muslim locality began. There was none to stop them. Within a few minutes curfew was imposed. The District Magistrate with a microphone in his hand came on the scene affirming the imposition of curfew. The bandh supporters gheraoed the car of the District Magistrate and raised communal slogans. The District Magistrate had to Virtually run away leaving the main square of the city under the control of rioters.

It was not a one-way traffic. People seeming Muslim by their appearance began to be stopped and be mercilessly beaten. Then started the looting and burning of the shops belonging to the minority community. These shops were identified by the BJP leaders. Instructions were given not to burn particular shops but only to loot them because their landlords were Hindu. The looting commenced hardly 10 yards away from the police post. The police force with many officers present on the scene remained passive spectators. There was none to stop the looters. For hours together this orgy continued. Lootings soon spread to other parts of the city. More than one hundred houses, factories, and shops were looted, burnt and destroyed. The stones of city wall weighing more than 100 kgs and more were pulled down with tools on the houses of other community situated by the side of city wall. This continued for two days during the operation of curfew.

Political parties were refused curfew passes while BJP leaders, many of them named as accused in the FIR's were favoured with curfew passes. Thus the administration left the city in the hands of BJP and the criminals spread all kinds of terror. After much effort a few passes were managed by leaders of CPI, MCPI and TUs. Without loss of time they seriously plunged into the task of organizing the relief work and mobilizing the secular forces.

At the initiative of the CPI joint and separate meetings of CPI, MCPI, CPM, Janata Dal, Congress and Progressive nonparty elements were organised. Relief work was organized by many of these parties separately. Padyatras were undertaken by the leaders of the secular political parties in the affected areas. This helped in restoring confidence among the people. All this was done during the days of curfew. After lifting of the curfew in spite of the restrictions of Section 144, marches for communal harmony were also organized. The administration even refused to give permission to take out these processions.

People by and large were found to be anti-communal. In all *mohallas* consisting of Hindus and Muslims, residents exhibited exemplary good neighbourly relations. They helped each other in procuring ration/water, milk, etc. Essential commodities and articles of daily use were made available to each other by the residents by passing them through their housetops.

In some areas where there was a lone shop or house of one community inhabitated by another community people who guarded these properties and there was not even an iota of damage to such properties, though it would have been the easiest thing to take 'revenge'. It was again established norms that masses in general believe in communal harmony.

Of the role of the administration, the less said, the better. The administration not only shielded and protected the miscreants but took anti-Muslim postures. A reign of terror was let loose in Muslim *mohallas*. Hundreds of arrests were arbitrarily made. Many of them were booked under the TADA.

The CPI and others took up the matter of paying compensation to the administration. Progressive lawyers under the banner of Indian Association of Lawyers were in the forefront of this struggle. They took up the matter inside and outside the court and were able to obtain marginal concessions.

The Lessons

Masses are secular and anti-communal but lack courage to take initiative to fight back the communal elements. Mobilization of secular forces and their united action is the necessity of the day. Not a single party, however big it may be, can generate confidence and mobilize the secular forces but united action by secular forces can generate a qualitative change in the situation. Unitedly the masses can be put in action, Secular forces cannot depend upon the administration. It is the united action of the secular forces which alone on the one hand can compel the administration to take remedial measures and on the other hand defeat the communal game.

7

The Dreamland of BJP: Madhya Pradesh Riots

N.B. Ruhi

The recent wave of communal frenzy which swept several parts of the country has also left an indelible scar on Madhya Pradesh, thc state which is a well known citadel of communalism and feudalism and hence also famous for its socio-economic backwardness and orthodoxy. However, today its characteristic is that it has the chance of being ruled by the BJP which has obtained two-thirds majority in the State Legislature. That is why the Patwa Government was least affected by the political turmoil that had overtaken various states after the fall of V.P. Singh Government at the Centre, as a sequel to the withdrawal of support to it by the BJP. Thus, MP Government is well settled and is in a position to materialize its dreams on the soil of MP.

In socio-economic life there is prominence of new BJP culture overloaded with orthodoxy, religiosity and *laissez-faire*. People belonging to a certain community and having communal approach are feeling exalted and are unhesitatingly vocal about their views, while the people belonging to the other community seem not only distressed but at some places their reaction is also matching the exaltation of their counterparts. This reaction was demonstrated in Indore during communal violence. At Jabalpur, the rational leaders of the minority community intervened and could stop the youth of their community from reacting against violence of other community while the minority reacted violently at Indore.

It is obvious that the recent communal violence in MP was a reaction of Rath Yatra by Advani, Ayodhya *kar seva* and its aftermath. The disgraceful provocative propaganda that was let loose during the Rath Yatra and *kar seva* could have turned even worse but for the peace-loving people, the centuries old traditions of harmony and goodwill, humanitarianism and rationalism prevailed.

Predetermined Explosion

October 30, 1990 was the day earmarked to start *kar seva* at Ayodhya to construct Ram temple after pulling down the Babri mosque. Evening editions of several MP newspapers were lying in wait for the occasion and published extremely provocative matter like loaded machine guns which boiled the blood of the youths in both the religious groups. Consequently the volcanoes erupted in Indore, Jabalpur, Mhow, Dewas, etc.

After the eruption of violence, as a matter of routine, many voluntary fact-finding committees and delegations rushed to riot hit cities. They have placed some facts on record. The present report is based on that.

Indore

The city of Indore was extremely tense on the day, i.e. Oct. 30, 1990. People were restlessly waiting for the news from Ayodhya. As soon as the news of *kar seva* broke out rallies started from different parts of Indore.

People were jubiliant and raising slogans to give vent to their emotions. They were also raising some indecent and provocative slogans. Members of other communities naturally felt offended. According to a report, the mob in a rally went berserk and took an aggressive and violent posture. The shops and houses belonging to the other community were attacked and set ablaze. The hutment-dwellers were worst hit after which it was the turn was that of the minority community. Their reaction was equally violent. According to some observers this community was fully prepared that year for any eventuality. During the riots that took place in 1989 the community had lost 16 out of the total of 23 killed in riots. Last year they had suffered bigger losses due to the violence committed by the police along with the rioters of the other community. It is said that, in general, the whole city was waiting for the event but this community was ostensibly in a pensive mood. They had sent their families to other places. In view of their previous experience and peculiar feature of the present State Government they were more in distress and hence prepared for their security.

The local press played havoc by carrying reports of demolition of Babri mosque, presence of military in Ayodhya and killings of hundreds of people there. While the Hindus expressed mixed feelings of pleasure and anguish, the Muslims were terrorized. The riots erupted like a volcano resulting in large-scale violence, arson and loot. The most regretful is that all this happened during curfew hours. 13 persons were dead and 26 injured, more than a thousand were arrested. Community-wise ratio of deaths was 6:7. in an instance the right hand of a young girl was amputated. She was the sole bread earner in her family and earned her bread by sewing. Her aged parents and younger brother and sisters were dependent on her. There may be many more such ghastly stories which did not come to light.

Jabalpur: Appeals for Peace

Alarmed by tense atmosphere in the city the anti-communal elements came into motion. Progressive Writers Association, Front for Communal Harmony, CPI, CPI, JD and BSP, etc, appealed to the people to be peaceful and not to be led by provocative and communal propaganda. 20,000 copies of handbills for appeal for peace were distributed. Police administration, District Collector and other officers were also apprised of the situation. They were alert .and there prevailed good cooperation between the peace-loving people and local administration. However, one sided aggression could not be averted. There was a rumour (which later proved false) about the damage to a temple. Anti-social elements belonging to that community went on rampage from 10 am on 2nd November, 1990 to 12 noon the next day, allegedly under the protection of lower ranks of local police officers. There was arson and loot on a large-scale. Shops and houses were looted, and set on fire and a reign of terror was let loose. One innocent person was killed isolated in the crowd. Four to five mosques were blown up by time bombs. Dozens of mosques including *Idgah* were badly damaged. The tombs and shrines worshipped by both the communities were also not spared. Shops of vegetables vendors were totally ruined. The families who were isolated in the localities of the other community fled away. The rioters noted their houses and worship places and set them on fire. Previously such families were guarded by the rational members of other community.

It was also alleged that some influential political leaders obtained about 1200-1300 curfew passes and distributed them among the anti-social elements and they used them for violent acts even during curfew. According to an estimate, property worth Rs 40-50 lakhs was destroyed. It was also alleged that the members belonging to Khateek, Kanjar and Oriya castes who were economically quite well-off and politically influential (usually they are able to send their elected representatives in the state legislature) together with some of commercial classes who are members of Bajrang Dal and RSS were involved in the violence. It was also alleged that the son and nephew of a local MLA were caught redhanded. Despite various types of pressures, the collector and the SP refused to release them.

National Intervention

In a population of about 15 lakhs 70-80 thousand belong to the minority community, who are weavers, manual labourers, tonga drivers, careers (cleaners of cotton). They were worst hit by the crisis in handloom industry. People working in this profession have now turned into mechanics, *thela* and rickshaw pullers and vegetable vendors. There seems no conflict in the economic interests of the two communities.

When there was already a one-sided offensive, about 1000-2000 youths of the other community gathered at a place and were ready to pay back in the same coin. It is told that aged and rational people of the same community which included workers, leaders and members of CPI persuaded them to be peaceful and thus the communal aggression could not be turned into a communal riot and changed the whole situation radically. It became easier for the police to detect the culprits and arrest them. The rumour that any temple was damaged could be refuted. Similarly, the Hindu comrades did not allow the rioters to enter into Muslim localities though they had to tolerate their abuses and challenges.

Victims of violence opined that BJP and Congress (I) both were responsible for the incidents because both wanted to capture political power at the Centre.

Role of Top Police Officials

Within a day or two the top police officials of both

the places, Indore as well as Jabalpur were determined to check violence and refused to accept any political pressure. Next day the police was called from other cities and the situation was controlled with their help though incidents of arson still continued but they were soon overcome.

There was general consensus that due to neutrality and promptness of top police officials the riots could be checked within a short time. Not only that, they were neutral and also alert and took stern action against the rioters.

Sense of Insecurity

Jabalpur has already witnessed terrible riots in 1956 when a statue of Ganesh was damaged and in 1961 when one unlawful relationship between two persons belonging to different communities became public the memory of which is still hair-raising. Those who have witnessed all the three riots (1956, 1961 and 1990) were of the opinion that due to BJP at the helm of affairs in the state members of minority community felt more insecure and terrorized. People who had never deserted their houses in the past were now compelled to run away. The administration did not take any initiative this time to form traditional peace committees even when the city was very tense.

Death of a Cow

Apart from the rumour about the temple there is one more illustration to suffice enough that the violence was preplanned. One day prior to the eruption of violence a cow died in an accident at Fountain Chawk in Jabalpur. Some people covered it with red cloth immediately and burnt some incense sticks. Around 100-150 boys also gathered on the spot. However, the anti-communal forces and civic authorities took prompt action and the cow's carcass was disposed of before it could create any problem.

There are various examples throughout the length and breadth of India where holy places of two different communities are built in the same complex side by side. There may be many more examples in Jabalpur too but we could come across only one where a tomb and a temple are existing side by side. Their entrance is one. This worship place is situated in a Hindu locality who look after it. When the rioters came there to damage it, the Hindus protested but they didn't listen to them and damaged it. However, when our delegation visited there, Hindus were getting it repaired. In our presence one Hindu worshipper came there and offered prayer on both the places.

There were stray incidents in Mhow, Dewas, Satna and Bina too. Raisen and Raipur had already sufferred the shocks. There was violence in Mhow. One mosque was damaged in Satna but the local Hindus came forward to get it repaired.

We were also told that the common masses were not involved in these incidents. Only a handful of rioters went on a rampage. People were accusing newspapers bitterly for their partisan role. One victim suggested that such newspapers should be banned.

However, it will be incorrect to conclude that the story is finished here. The conspiracy is much deeper to render the minority ineffective and if possible to neutralize them in the Indian politics. The slogan of Hindu Rashtra is to deprive the Muslims of their political rights and equality, and its push them back economically. The BJP government is not only utilizing its party and police cadre to suppress and crush the minorities but there is a very systematic attempt to crush and suppress the entire weaker section of society—minority as well as the downtrodden. There is overhauling of entire state machinery for that purpose. Some police officials who were transferred from Indore for their dubious role during communal rights of 1989 were again posted there by the new government despite the opposition of the director general of police. Moreover, two of them were promoted. A district collector who had refused to demolish a mosque was transferred overnight and an ordinary government employee who is a worker of VHP had threatened him publicly for not demolishing the mosque. However, this government employee who was dismissed by the previous government for his open political activities was reinstated by the present government. Not only was the civil administration made the political subservient to the BJP rule but about fifty thousand state government employees were transferred by one stroke of pen immediately after the BJP came into power. The action was politically motivated. Anarchy prevailed at every stage of administration from block, tehsil and district to state level.

There was intensive anti-encroachment drive in the name of beautification of cities and towns throughout the state. Thousands of people were dislodged from their shelters and business installations. They were rendered roofless and jobless during the rainy seasons. There was lot of discrimination and favouritism in dislodging as well as in reallotments. People are still running from pillar to post for the relief. Most of them belong to the minority and downtrodden sections. In this regard the following observations made by a journalist are mentionable. "The Turkman gate devastations in Delhi during the Emergency look like a picnic compared to what happened in Bhopal under the benign rule of BJP". Recently when the cold wave was sweeping the state the poorest of the poor were thrown under open sky. Heartrending reports of the miseries of infants, women, old and sick thrown to the mercy of chilly winds were coming in. All of them may not belong to one community but atrocities committed against one section of society act as a deterrent to other weaker sections. Here is one more illustration. During the birth centenary of Dr Ambedkar, his followers were compelled to fight a tough battle with the state police and administration over the disfiguring of Ambedkar's statue by some miscreants right under the nose of the state government in Bhopal. The agitators were demanding that the culprits should be arrested and duly punished and that the statue should be restored. The miscreants who were allegedly BJP workers were roaming about openly and Ambedkarites were subjected to police atrocities. According to a newspaper report, "it was virtually a seige of Ambedkar Nagar on 13-1-1991 when policemen in huge numbers mercilessly beat up men, women and children with a fury that is astounding." Observers opined that the action of the police can by no stretch of imagination be described as civilized or restrained. It was a brutal assault on the Ambedkarites with a vengeance. Women were dragged by the hair, children were thrashed, lathi blows were hurled on old women and men who were mercilessly beaten up. Later, a group of 50 injured women stormed into a local newspaper office to narrate their tale of police atrocities. The event is a deterrance to all those who may think of agitating against the BJP workers. A journalist working in a local press at Raipur who dared to publish a news item against BJP was warned of severe consequences and threatened to be burnt alive. Such is the dreamland of BJP.

BJP Culture in Administration

On the day of Diwali, the chief minister officially greeted the officers and citizens by posting them greeting cards which carried the picture of Lord Rama on its title with the wordings in the bottom "Jai Shri Ram". Religious rituals have become more common and are exhibited with pomp and show. The Bharat Bhawan is a centre of cultural activities and having obtained international repute is now completely at the mercy of BJP to promote their own type of culture after doing away with its autonomy.

Last but not least is the theory of *laissez-faire* being practised in the state. The chief minister has publicly declared that public enterprises will be privatized. MP Electricity Board, MP State Road and Transport Corporation and State Milk Dairy are undergoing the process. These things may look as not directly the concern of minorities but it is certain that they are directly hit by the discriminatory policies pursued by the State Government with a communal approach deeply afflicting the nerves of the administration.

8

Communal Divide in Indore

L.S. Herdenia

The roots of communal divide have deepened in Indore. Apart from some sensible and rational minded persons, Indore has become polarized into communal camps. Despite the fact that there have been communal occurrences in the past, mutual hostility had never been witnessed on such a large scale.

In October, 1989, on the occasion of the Milad-un-Nabi procession, communal violence occurred. In 1990, communal riots started on 30th October. Right from early morning there prevailed an atmosphere of communal tension. The people of Indore waited with anxiety for the moment when the *kar seva* was to begin in Ayodhya. As soon as the news of beginning of *kar seva* reached Indore, it was engulfed in a strange tension. According to a high official, Indore was witnessing an unprecedented flood of emotional upsurge. The city was decorated all over. Saffron flags were flying atop all buildings. The roads were all along covered with yellow dust, called *Ram Raj*. The same day the President of

India arrived in Indore and after a few minutes' stay at the airport, proceeded to Ujjain. He was accompanied by the Governor, Kunwar Mahmood Ali and the chief minister, Sundarlal Patwa. All the high officials of Indore had gone to the airport.

As soon as the news of *kar seva* at Ayodhya reached Indore, processions started coming out in various parts of the city. During these processions the participants were shouting slogans not only expressing pleasure and happiness but also provocative insulting to the Muslim minority. Soon these processions assumed aggressiveness and attacked the houses and shops of the minority community. During this rioting and arson, the shops, houses and hutments of the latter were burnt. The communal violence spread like wildfire throughout the city on that day. With the passing of the first round to this orgy, the city was put under curfew. After this, the other community took turns. A retaliatory attack was launched. In 1990 as against 1989, the community was in full preparation to fight back. In 1989, 22 people lost their lives; out of these 16 belonged to the minority community. Apart from the atrocities by the police, the majority community had inflicted heavy losses on them. Even though the whole city was waiting for some happenings on the 30th October, the people of the minority community were afraid of the worst. Hence most of them had sent their womenfolk and children from Hindu majorty areas to safer places. Keeping in view the experience of 1989 riots and the political character of the government, these people were then extraordinarily worried. They, therefore, had made preparations for protection to self.

Some local newspapers had brought out special issues on the occasion of the commencement of *kar sava* in Ayodhya. In these issues the news was given in a specially inciting language. For example, one newspaper wrote: "Babri Masjid has been destroyed in Ayodhya; Army had been called; hundreds of persons were shot dead, etc. etc. This created a sense of pleasure and anger among Hindus and the minority community became terror striken. These writings created more tension in the city. Because of this, violence and communal incidents erupted one after the other on a large-scale. What is ironic is that it occurred during curfew hours. 13 persons were killed out of which 10 died on the spot and three in the hospital, 223 were injured and 1182 were arrested. Among the dead, seven belonged to one community and six to the other community.

Both the communities suffered on this account and the proportion of casualties varied in different localities. The occurence in Vyasphalan *mohalla* has become an object of fierce debate. Here as a result of firing by a policeman, one person died and five were injured. This incident became controversial because the policeman belonged to one community and the victims to the other community. It has been alleged that the policeman knowingly fired at the victims because they belonged to another community. The person who died on the spot was Kamal. He was 30 years old and a married man. Of the injured three persons belonged to one family. Similarly, a child on the fourth floor of a building was injured. A newspaper published a false report that 5 persons were killed by policeman belonging to a particular community which could be no greater evidence of irresponsible reporting. It is very painful to observe that the police is also being divided communally. The policeman is being blamed because he belongs to the minority community. One must take this event as the honest performance of duty by the policeman. It must be remembered that at that time, that area was under curfew and the police had orders to shoot at sight those who violated the curfew.

Many of the persons injured during communal violence were admitted to the hospital where both Hindu and Muslim victims were being treated together, even though communal violence had gripped the entire city. Observance of these persons proved the fact that only poor people were the victims of the riots. Many others lost their livelihood during the riots. From among the injured in the hospital a woman's right hand had to be amputated. She said. "I and my family have been deprived of our livelihood. I was looking after my aged parents and younger brother and sisters with earning from stitching clothes. Now I won't be able to do so."

Another event was being discussed vociferously in Indore city. An attempt was made to attack the police colony at a time when womenfolk and children were alone in the colony and the menfolk had gone out. But due to the alertness of the police, not much damage was done. But this occurrence worsened the atmosphere in the city. It was felt that this event be thoroughly investigated and its causes pinpointed.

Like in 1989, the people of Indore were very angry with their elected representatives. They said that they were repeatedly deceived by them. Nobody came to sympathize. They were particularly angry with the BJP MP Sumitra Mahajan. She and other BJP elected legislatures had gone to Ayodhya to participate in the *kar seva*. They were told that with the prevailing tense condition in the city they should not have gone there leaving Indore; they had elected them not for *kar seva* but for service to the people.

May be Babri mosque was not destroyed in Ayodhya alone, for in Indore some antisocial elements destroyed a mosque.

In spite of all this, it can be said that more destruction could have taken place in Indore but owing of the alertness and vigilance of Ayukt Vijay Singh, I.G. Police Surjit Singh, the District Magistrate and other police officers the situation could be brought under control.

9

Communal Virus Spreads in Agra

Vinny Jain

The very name of Agra conjures up visions of the majestic Taj Mahal, of medieval royalty grace and splendour, of the times when Agra was the capital of the mighty Mughal empire. As a consequence, the city attracted a large number of people of the majority as well as minority communities seeking patronage and favours at the Mughal court. These communities have since lived and worked together in peace and harmony thus making the city considerably renowned for its secular traditions. Muslims forming nearly twenty per cent of the city's total population have felt and safe secure. The city had never seen a communal riot, not even in the trying times of the Partition till communal violence raised its hideous face in December, 1990.

The period between July and December, 1990, saw a series of calamities engulf the city. The first blow of the Jat versus Jatav caste riots at Pansari village on the outskirts of Agra in July, 1990, was followed by six months of high tension between the Hindus and the Muslims, culminating in virulent communal rioting by the end of the year. As city after city succumbed to the communal malaise in Uttar Pradesh in the wake of the Ayodhya dispute, Agra fought hard to save its sanity, but to no avail. Considerable loss of life and property resulted and the official death count was placed at 21, the number of injured at 47, and moveable and immoveable property disputes at 361.[1] Unofficial figures for all the above categories are much higher. According to Mr Ajay Singh, Janata Dal MP from Agra, the bulk of the 22 persons killed were Muslims, at least eight of whom were eliminated by the Provincial Armed constabulary.[2] Local residents put the number of dead around 50. To one who has spent a lifetime in the city, it fears today a changed countenance grotesque and unrecognizable, peace has fled, perhaps never to fully return again. What follows is an attempt to trace the trajectory of events leading up to the riots, based on a close scrutiny and analysis of reports in the local press, as well as countless interviews with local residents, politicians and religious figures.

The Genesis

The bitterness generated due to the Jat versus Jatav clash in July at Panwari, over something as inconsequential as the route to be taken by a Jatav marriage procession, had barely died down when tensions of a different nature surfaced in October. As the BJP-VHP lead campaign in Ayodhya mounted so did tension in the city. Agra had been made prominent by the fact that the administration stopped a large number of '*Ram bhakts*' and '*Kar sevaks*' from Rajasthan, Gujarat and Madhya Pradesh here and held them at improvised jails set up in local sports grounds. Their presence further inspired the local BJP and VHP units already active in the campaign. The BJP had in the 1989 elections, won for the first time all the three urban Vidhan Sabha seats and held the Municipal Council seats as well. A local *kar seva* committee was set up, chaired by Bhagwan Shanker Rauat, a BJP nominee for the Lok Sabha. Hardwar Dubey, Krishan Gopal and Satya Prakash Vilal, sitting BJP MLA as well as VHP leaders like Kesho Mehta, led numerous processions in violation of administrative orders, demanding that the Babri masjid be handed over to the Hindus, clashing several times with the security forces seeking to enforce curfew orders, and courted arrest in turns.[3] As tensions mounted, a preventive curfew was strictly imposed which was relaxed only on the 7th of November when the situation began to return to normal. A direct clash between the two communities was avoided, while the two communities now stood face to face, distrustful of each other.

Tension began to rise again with the arrival of Uma Bharti, the vociferous BJP parliamentarian, to the district on the 30th of the November. She addressed more than two dozen public meetings, which attracted a vast number of people. Her characteristic mix of BJP rhetoric with religious and mythological references clearly left a profound impression on the local audience.[4] She had, by then to some extent, become the symbol of the aggressive Hindu stand and was completely alienated from the Muslims. Numerous interviewees of the Muslim community told this writer that they regarded her mere presence as a provocation. This was further corroborated by the fact that Uma Bharti's next stop at neighbouring Ganjdundwara, resulted in a communal riot there on the 4th of December after her cavalcade had been attacked by angry Muslims.[5]

The '*Asthi Kalash*' containing the ashes of the *kar sevaks* killed in Ayodhya during October and November, returned to Agra on the 7th of December. The administration, already apprehensive of a riot carefully chalked out a route for the procession, avoiding 'communally sensitive' areas, requested the press to maintain a restraint in reporting extensively on communal issues and assigned a contingent of the police to travel with these processions[6] while passing through the Muslim dominant areas such as Tajganj, Mantols, Dholikhar, Lohamandi, Shahganj, Vajirpura, etc. Accompanied by slogan shouting crowds chanting : "*Bachha Bachha Ram Ka, Janambhoomi ke kam ka*", or "*Kasam Ram Ki Khate Hain, Mandir Wahin Banaeyege*"etc.,..., they were likely to provoke and inflame the Muslim populace, prepared to fight to preserve their religious identity, symbolised by the Babri Masjid.

The next week from the 7th to the 14th of December was fraught with high drama and tension. Attempts by the administration to prevent the 'Ram Bhakts' from entering Vazirpura on the 9th were met with stiff resistance, a sit-in was undertaken for over two hours on the road and an insistence on the part of local BJP-VHP leadership to press forward in the face of which the administration ultimately caved in. This was a pattern which was repeated at New Agra, at Motikunj, etc.,[7] over the next few days. Tempers and tensions continued to rise and the conflict seemed to draw closer and closer.

An official communique dated the 10th of December warned the BJP and the VHP that if they insist on taking the *Asthi Kalash* through communally sensitive areas and desist from inflammatory speech making, otherwise the processions would be banned altogether.[8] This threat was however never converted into action.

The Riot

Large scale violence broke out simultaneously at Loha Mandi and Tajganj on the 14th of December at about 11.30 am The *Asthi Kalash*, amidst palpable tension toured Lohamandi that day. The administration after the usual doubts, allowed the procession to go up to Anta Bagh in this Muslim dominant area. While it was returning, the procession was attacked by Muslims from rooftops with stones and acid bombs. The *Ram Bhakt* retaliated and a pitched battle ensued which soon spread to Punic Bagh, Telipadha, Raja-ki-mandi, Gali rangrejan, Alamganj and Motikunj.[9]

At Nanda Bazar in Tajganj, 20-year-old Mohamad Masud Alam was attacked by knife wielding youth of the other community. The entire area had already been tense for the past few days, after the explosion of a bomb in which three children of the minority community had been injured. The police had accused the Muslims for the incident. The unifying incident fueled the simmering resentment and large-scale Hindu-Muslim rioting spread to the surrounding areas. Six police station areas (of the total nine in Agra) were put under curfew, These were Tajganj, Shahganj, Lohamandi, Mantola, Nai-ki-mandi and Kolamali.[10] Indefinite curfew was extended to M.M. Gate and Chatta Bazar Police stations for the next two days.

The PAC, the CRPF as well as the army were deployed in large numbers, the latter staging flag marches throughout the city. One CRPF jawan stated that if the force had been delayed in arriving for even ten more minutes at Tajganj, the entire area would have been put to fire and the Muslim population slaughtered by violent mobs of Hindu men.

The next four days saw repeated attacks planned and mounted with concerted effort by members of both communities on selected targets. Countless horrific accounts of stabbing, looting, arson and people dying of bomb explosions and police firing, as well as men and women fleeing their homes in peril of their lives are recounted by the local populace. Many shops belonging to members of the minority community were ransacked and put on fire. There were numerous shops looted but left intact with the contents burning outside on the road. Inquiries generally revealed that the owners of the shops were usually Hindu while the tenant were Muslim.

It is difficult if not impossible to capture the sheer

terror one experienced during the riot. It was a nightmarish experience which seemed a little unreal when it ceases to exist. The army returned to its barracks on the 22nd of December and a semblance of normality began to return.

In Retrospect

Communal riots in several northern states in the wake of the Ayodhya agitation have brought into sharp focus the imperative need to sustain the secular character of the Indian society and polity. They have also forced upon us the debate as to the very definition and meaning of the concept of secularism and its application in the Indian context, the rights, status and position of the minorities *vis-à-vis* the majority community, as well as several other related concerns. All these and many more issues confront the citizens of Agra as well as those of other riot affected areas. These are broad, far-reaching problems which the nation must pay attention to. What was the role of the administration, the security forces and the politicians ? Was the riot engineered ? Has the riot altered public perceptions with regard to national issues and concerns. These are some of the issues that are discussed below.

During the riot, several reports in the local press, revealed a mysterious unidentified maruti van followed by three ambassador cars which went around the city at night. Local residents talk of hand-grenades being thrown, shots fired in the air and inflammatory audio and video cassettes being distributed by the occupants of these vehicles[11] Security forces apprehended a maruti van on the 19th of December and arrested four young men with explosives and video cassettes, going around the city in the dead of the night. Was the riot deliberately incited ? A large number of inflammatory audio and visual cassettes, banned by the authorities were freely available in the city. Many illegal firearm manufacturing units were also raided during the riot. Did the administration have no information about their existence before violence broke out? These are questions which nobody is willing to answer, at least not in an objective manner.

Perceptions also differ as to the role of the police, the PAC and the CRPF. SSP Karamvir Singh was transferred on the 17th of December in the midst of the riot amidst allegations that he had deliberately created conditions leading to the riot in Tajganj in order to reap a huge amount of monetary profit on the local betting (*satta*) bazaar. Dr Mohammad Amin, from the academic faculty of St Johns College as well as the heir apparent to the '*kadri*' Muslim religious sect, is of the opinion that the Muslim community breathed a sigh of relief after this transfer. The Hindu community on the other hand saw this as unjust and sent in protest appeals for the reinstatement of Karamvir Singh. Dr Amin holds the PAC to be clearly partisan. The Hindu-Muslim riot, he believes, converted to a PAC versus the Muslims' affair. Muslim residents interviewed at Mantola and Kholikhar relate incidents of the PAC men entering their homes with the express purpose of harming them. Leaders of the VHP and the BJP dispute this claim. Rajendra Gupta, Chairman of the UP State unit of the BJP visited Agra on the 20th of December and praised the role of the police and the PAC during the riot. He claimed that a large number of local residents had also done so.[12]

Most of the PAC men were observed to be intensely religious, organizing on the occasion of Ramnavmi, a continuous recitation of the *Ramayana* on loudspeakers and celebrating the event with great enthusiasm and fervour. Religious belief is no doubt a personal prerogative. Such enthusiastic faith however is likely to cloud one's judgement, especially in conditions of duress and stress. The riot was better handled by the CRPF and the army according to all accounts.

It was apparent that the administration was ill

prepared to meet such a crisis. Distribution of essential commodities to curfew bound areas was woefully inadequate. Amal K. Verma, District Magistrate received his transfer orders on the 26th of December. Significantly, this came two days after the visit of Mulayam Singh Yadav to Agra. The chief minister had to face heavy criticism and abuse at the hands of the local residents, protesting against his Ayodhya policy. His cavalcade was even attacked and he was prevented from entering riot affected areas.[13]

Local politicians too did not earn much glory. Agra's representative to the Lok Sabha, Ajay Singh of the Janata Dal, did not come to Agra for the first three days, and when he did come, he did precious little to ease the situation or help the people. Sitting BJP MLAs were actively involved with the *Asthi kalash* processions. Hardwar Dubey, MLA from Agra cantonment in an interview categorically stated that Mulayam Singh's policy of appeasing the minorities was responsible for the riot, the genesis of the riot in Agra (as elsewhere) lay in disproportionate importance and undue favours being granted to the Muslim community. Angry Hindu reaction to this was inevitable.

Rajendra Gupta (Chairman of the UP unit of the BJP) while visiting Agra on the 20th of December said that the riot in Agra was preplanned by the minority community. He blamed the chief minister, Mulayam Singh Yadav for the riot. Mr Gupta named Haji Islam Kureshi, Ahmed Hesan and Mobarak Kureshi as responsible for the riot and demanded their arrest.[14] Mobarak Hasan was a Congress (I) Councillor and was held by the police under the National Security Act on charges of inciting the riot. This charge was severely contested by the Muslim community. The Janta Dal (S) has nominated Haji Islam Kureshi as its official candidate for the parliamentary seat in the coming polls. Prof. Ram Gopal Chaudhari former head of the Hindi Department of the Agra College said : "The riot is bound to affect voting patterns in the ensuing elections and most of the political parties are seeking to establish equations that would yield beneficial results in this background. *En-bloc* Muslim votes (which are about a lakh out of nine lakh total voters) in favour of any one political party would greatly improve its chances *vis-à-vis* the BJP, and all political parties are wooing the Muslims." Dr Mohamad Amin, as well as several others reveal that the Muslim voters in meetings held at Mantola and Kholikar had decided that their main concern would be to keep the BJP out of power. The riot in Agra, he believes, occurred because the BJP-VHP combine deliberately enraged the masses on religious issues. The Muslims must protect their distinct identity within the Indian nation. (Subsequent elections showed that the BJP benefitted from the riots).

The considerable loss of property, as well as loss of business to the main industries of tourism and leather works is also bound to influence the Vaish votes in Agra. The riot has had a negative affect on BJP popularity in some circles although it has also hardened the committed BJP supporter. Religious issues are now inextricably linked with political ones.

A majority of the deceased in the riot belonged to the Muslim community, which also suffered a heavier loss of property. Many Muslims vow that this would not happen again. They would be better prepared the next time. Already many talk of young men coming from Aligarh to train the local youth in the manufacture and use of firearms. They would be prepared to go to any length to safeguard their religious, social and cultural identity; which would be symbolically sacrificed if the Babri Masjid was surrendered.

Such intractable attitudes, displayed by both the Hindus and the Muslims at the local level are bound to complicate the issue. The fallout of the riot has been a hardening of hearts, a loss of trust and goodwill that has vitiated the atmosphere in the city. Both sides blame each other for the riot and for ensuing problems. One can only hope that efforts to solve the Ayodhya dispute by peaceful means would bear fruit and that peace would be given another chance. Agra, as indeed the nation, can ill afford another conflict which would prove fatal for basic human goodness and values.

References

1. *Amar Ujala*, Hindi Daily, edited by Ajay Agrawal, published at Amar Ujala Press Agra, 3 Jan, 1991.
2. Times of India, Delhi, December 2, 1990
3. *Amar Ujala*, op. cit. Jan 3, 1991.
4. *Amar Ujala*, op. cit, Dec. 2 and 3, 1990.
5. *Amar Ujala*, op. cit, Dec. 4, 1990.
6. *Amar Ujala*, op. cit, Dec. 8,1990.
7. *Amar Ujala*, op. cit, Dec. 10, 1990.
8. *Amar Ujala*, op. cit, Dec. 11, 1990.
9. *Amar Ujala*, op. cit, Dec. 12, 1990.
10. *Amar Ujala*, op. cit, Dec. 15, 1990.
11. *Ibid.*
12. *Amar Ujala*, op. cit, Dec. 17, 1990.
13. *Amar Ujala*, op. cit, Dec. 29, 1990.
14. *Amar Ujala*, op. cit, Dec. 25 and 26, 1990.
15. *Amar Ujala*, op. cit, Dec. 29, 1990.

10

Communal Riots in Meerut

Devendra Singh

Violence, communal tension and riots have been a destiny of this city. The people have grown accustomed to the communal disease. During the period of 44 years of Independence, Meerut saw 25 riots with a cumulative loss of 2500 human lives and about 3000 persons wounded. About 18,000 persons were arrested in this connection and nearly 500 crores worth of property destroyed.

In every riot many a persons were declared missing without any trace and they never returned homes. It will be no exaggeration to state that the history of this city after independence is marred by bloody violence. The psyche of the city has suffered enormously enundating it with hatred, ill-will and mistrust on several occasions.

According to the UP Govt. report, Table 1 reflects the number of incidents of the communal riots suffered by the state from 1946 to 1970. (Meerut being a major shareholder).

TABLE 1

COMMUNAL RIOTS IN UP DURING THE PERIOD 1946-70

Year	*No. of Incidents*	*Year*	*No. of Incidents*	*Year*	*No. of Incidents*
1946	374	1947	464	1948	467
1949	35	1950	458	1951	7
1952	23	1953	8	1954	14
1955	11	1956	30	1957	8
1958	16	1959	14	1960	14
1961	84	1962	12	1963	3
1964	5	1965	7	1966	50
1967	10	1968	62	1969	22
1970	3				

After 1970, the city again witnessed communal riots during 1973 and 1982. In 1982 riot spread due to dispute over a religious centre of worship claimed by two communities. In this riot, a Hindu priest was killed. Whatever be the reasons otherwise all the communal riots in this city after 1982 have centred around the dispute of Ayodhya Temple versus Babri Mosque issue. During 1986, Vishva Hindu Parishad celebrated the event through the Ram-Janki Rath Yatra in the entire length and breadth of the nation. The event was telecast on the national T.V. network. Some persons opine that the outbreak of violence in the Kashmir villages was the direct consequence of telecast. Similarly Congress governments in UP and Delhi appeased fundamentalists first by passing Muslim Women's Bill and later on by unlocking the temple-mosque at Ayodhya. Thus, the government itself encouraged and strengthened the fundamenalists from both the communities.

Later on the Babri Masjid Action Committee was

formed to bring this issue in focus at the national scene. Syed Shahabuddin and Imam Bukhari gave a call to Muslims to boycott Republic Day ceremony. This created adverse reaction in the minds of the people and sensing the mood of the nation the appeal was withdrawn leaving a deep scar on the Muslim psyche. Later on a rally was organised by Muslims leaders at Boat Club (New Delhi) on 30th of March, 1987 on the issue of Babri Masjid. Apart from inflammatory speeches, a banner was imposed in front of the stage inscribing, "*Na Ghabrao Musalmano Khuda Ki Shan Baqi hai, Abhi Islam Jinda Hai Abhi Quran Baqi hai, Ve Kafir Kya Samajthe Hain, Jo apne Dil Main Hanste Hain, Abhi To Karbala Ka Akhiri Maidan Baki Hai.*" In loud voice, the anti-Hindu slogans from the stage surcharged the atmosphere. Slogans from the stage "*Babar Aur Mahmood Gaznavi Bharat Ki Taqdir Banenge*" rent the air. A large number of Muslims from Meerut participated in the Boat Club rally and after their return they tried to exploit and excite the Muslim passions. Subsequently the city walls were found painted with these slogans. Thus, such activities further aggravated reactions in the minds of people and enhanced militancy among the communities.

Hindus were by no means less aggressive. They gathered round the call for Hinduism. If the Muslims could unite on the cause of Babri Masjid and form Babri Masjid Action Committee, the Hindus felt glorified in the name of Rama their God incarnate and the disputed place being his birth place. Subsequently they gave a "slogan" *Saugandh Ham Khate Hain, Mandir Vahin Banayenge* (We swear in the name of God that we will construct temple at the same place) further, *Yadi Bharat Mein Rehna Hoga, Bande Matram Kehna Hoga.* Gradually the militancy in Hindus increased after exciting speeches of VHP leaders and the advent of audio cassettes arousing religious sentiments and calling the Hindus to unite for protecting their religious heritage. The Hindu daily *Prabhat* published news on 22nd September, 1990 that the audio cassette *Bhaye Prakat Kirpala* (God the Benevolent appeared) was very much popular in Meerut. In the same issue it was reported that a Video Rath was to be started on similar lines which would propagate the Hindu passions in the villages of Meerut District. Thus, with the increasing militancy new slogans *Tel Lagao Dabar Ka Nam Mita Do Babar Ka*", "*Hindu Ka Hai Hindustan, Katuo Jao Pakistan*" and "*Bachha Bachha Ram Ka Musalman Ha Ram Ka*" formed place in the tongues and on walls. Thus, inflammatory slogans and speeches forced both Hindus and Muslims to stand face to face with the consquences of rioting.

The following are the reasons which created communal tension and riots since 1970 in the city of Meerut:

1973—The local Gudri Bazaar was the focal point after a Hindu cyclist met with an accident with a Muslim-thelawala.

1982—The dispute between a temple and *Mazar* in the shahabgasha locality began with the incidence of killings of Hindu Priest;

1983—The Muslim dominated Firozabad suffered a bomb-blast injuring Muslim children;

1986—Opening of the locks of Ayodhya temple-mosque disputed structure;

1987—On the occasion of Shab-e-Raat there was a display of fireworks and in this incidence a confectionary shop was gutted in fire and the Hindu owner was killed.

The communal riots of 1987 were the most fearsome and deadly in the history of Meerut since India's independence. The city was completely bisected in two divisions—Hindus and Muslims. There was evacuation of Muslims and Hindus to safer places in the vicinity of their majority. Both the communities had shattered faith in each other. The somewhat remaining confidence was destroyed by the Rath Yatra.

On 6th August, 1990, the Mandal Commission Report was made public for implementation. The BJP felt that the implementation of commission report may erode their political base. Before announcing the commission report, the then Prime Minister Mr V.P. Singh did not take into confidence the BJP which was supporting him in Parliament. To weaken the commission's force, Lal Krishan Advani, the BJP president announced the Rathyatra from Somnath to Ayodhya to stir and stimulate the political environment in India. The journey commenced on 25th September, 1990 covering a distance of ten thousand kilometres to be completed on 30th October at Ayodhya and *Kar sevaks* had to assemble there for doing *kar seva* to build temple. Advani knew full well that his determination would force the Central government to stop the Rath Yatra. He also knew that VHP and Bajrang Dal had gathered enough force during past 9-10 months on the above issue and they would rally round in case his journey is stopped and he is arrested.

The VHP infused the spirit of militancy among the Hindus in the Meerut city on the issue of building temple in Ayodhya. August 16th 1990 was observed in the city as a *Chetavani Divas* (warning day); that on a fixed date temple construction will begin. A little later, brick collection campaign was started which was called *Shila-Pujan* (consecration) ceremony. These bricks were to be used in the construction of the temple. Thus, this initial stage for preparing ground for temple construction was stamped with religious sanction. *Jan Sankalp Divas* or Determination Day was observed during the night of 17th August, 1990 prior to the commencement of the Rath Yatra by beating bells and blowing conches. This was done for creating a spirit for temple building. In a nearby town at Phalwada, the above ceremony was also observed next day. On third September, 1990 Vishnu Khanna Deputy Chief of Shiv Sena announced at Meerut that" *Kar sevaks* will proceed to Ayodhya on 29th October and a memorandum would be given to Mulayam Singh Yadav, chief minister of UP to remind him of their determination of building the temple. In spite of strict police vigilance Ram-Jyoti was carried in a procession on 18th September. On 21st September the Hindus went on *Prabhat Pheris* to repeat their determination. The women and children were the main participants in the *Prabhat Pheris* and the men folk abstained fearing their arrest. The ladies team was castigated as Durga Vahini. From 23rd September, communal tension began to increase when *Ram Shobha Yatra* participants *gheraoed* CO City D.C. Misra and SDM Surendra Kumar Dwivedi by chanting slogans. On 22nd Sept, the district administration ordered a police and PAC flag march. The entire UP city turned into an explosive situation by this strategy of VHP.

On the other hand the UP chief minister Mulayam Singh Yadav to prove himself a 'strongman' adopted a policy of confrontation which boomeranged, adding fuel to the fire. As a result of this policy, communal tension spread wherever Mulayam Singh Yadav organised Sadbhavana (Goodwill) rallies even prior to the arrest of Advani. For instance there was tension in Bareilly but soon after Yadav's Sadbhavana Rally there were high passions among the fundamentalists. On 15th September, VHP, Bajrang Dal and Shiv Sena youths called for a *Bandh* in Bareilly. Muslims had not observed Bandh and their shops were open and within no time these were looted, ransacked and burnt down. Mulayam Singh Yadav's Sadbhavana rallies could not bring harmony but remained instrumental in fanning communal disharmony and subsequently turning into communal riots.

The Old Delhi suffered communal riots on 14th October due to Rath Yatra and exciting slogans. The arrest of Advani in Bihar on 22nd October led to the withdrawal of support of the BJP to the V.P. Singh Govt., and BJP's call for Bharat Bandh on 29th October, engulfed the entire nation in violence. The entire area around Delhi-Shamli, Muzaffarnagar, Aligarh, Bijnor, and Modinagar was engulfed by communal violence. The city of Meerut remained an isolated island of peace, surrounded on all sides by curfew and riot affected cities. However, the environment was tense. An ominous element of (Satta) betting for the violence to take place or not played havoc with the lives of citizens of Meerut. However, it was a ray of good luck that Advani's Rath Yatra did not pass through Meerut yet VHP, BJP and Bajrang Dal made an effort to carry Ram Jyoti in a procession. The Ram Jyoti processions were stopped in Mawana and Aminagar Sarai, the sattelite towns of Meerut city as the city of Meerut was fully tense and highly explosive. According to the census of 1981, the population of the city of Meerut stood at around one million, consisting of 53 per cent of Hindus, 45 per cent Muslims and 2 per cent others. The city contains nearly 550 temples of different Hindu sects and about 150 mosques. According to intelligence reports, there were 5000 Bajrang Dal members, 150 Shiv Sena and 800 RSS workers at the time of Rath Yatra. It is difficult to workout the members of VHP during the Heyday of Hinduism. However, 8000 *kar sevaks* proceeded to Bareilly on way to Ayodhya from there to do *kar seva*. However, the *kar sevaks* returned from Bareilly to Meerut on being refused help to move forward. However, some of the *kar sevaks* reached Ayodhya. After their return, they inflamed the Hindus by telling fabricated stories of atrocities committed on Hindus by the UP Government headed by Mulayam Singh Yadav.

The wounded and injured persons from Bijnor were admitted in the Medical College at Meerut on 30th October. These persons had suffered at the hands of police in Bijnor jail struggle. Two constables were also injured. Nearly 747 persons were sent to Meerut jail, who were arrested in various demonstrations where the local newspapers called them *Kar sevaks* and not demonstrators . On 31st October they stood in revolt in the jail, broke open the doors after manhandling the jail staff and proceeded therefrom in procession towards Budhana Gate shouting slogans.

"*Lathi Goli Khayenge Mandir Vahin Banayenge* (we will bear lathi blows and gunshots but temple will be built there) and *Ye Andar Ki Bat Hai Pulis Hamare Saath Hai* (it is secret that police is with us).

In raising the communal ogre of violence, local and other newspapers have played no mean role. These newspapers provided sufficient space in their columns giving only sensational news to the riot-hungry communalists. Their sensational reporting increased their sale four-fold, casting aside the norms of reporting. They indulged in glorifying the Rath Yatra, and its victory. In their reporting thousand people became a lakh strong. In the name of press freedom, *Dainik Jagran* reported that the corpses coming from Bijnor to Meerut were buried instead of being assigned to flames as per Hindu rites. *Swatantra Bharat* of 30th October and 2nd November, and *Swatantra Chetna* reported sensational excessive stories. *Jagran* reported that peace hidden under the shadow of Sri Ram brigade will chop off hands and legs of Sri Mulayam Singh Yadav. 'Devotees' under intensive firing: 10 killed, thousands wounded and corpses all around Ayodhya" "the city of Ram has became a river of blood, etc". The Press Council of India has condemned the sensational reporting expecially of four Hindi newspapers of UP, viz. *Dainik Jagran, Swatantra Bharat*, and *Swatantra Chetna*. The council said that all norms of fair reporting were thrown to the winds. One *Hindi News* published from Meerut—'*Mayrashtra*', '*Hindu*', and *Prabhat* and others, turned every news into rumour and every rumour became news for them. The Urdu papers published from Delhi did not lag far behind in their false reporting. '*Mashk-e-Avaj*' and '*Nai-Duniya*' poisoned the minds of their readers. Even government sponsored TV and All India

Radio did not lag far behind in their news bulletins. Meerut was declared curfew bound by them on 31st October whereas the truth was that city was still peaceful. The next day Hapur, Ghaziabad and Dibai (Bulandshahr) also caught fire of communal violence and subsequently curfew was imposed there.

The calm and quiet city was at last engulfed by the outbreak of communal riots on 2nd November, 1990. It was inflamed with the stabbing of a scooter rider. But it was not an isolated event. Similar 20-22 such incidents occurred during the same time at different spots. On November 3, curfew was imposed in five police-stations of Delhi Gate, Kotwali, Lisari Gate, Brahampuri, and Nauchandi, for indefinite period. As a precautionary measure, the military flag marched through the sensitive areas of the city. Thus, riots and curfew were forced on this unwilling city—untouched by Rath-Yatra of Shri Lal Krishan Advani. The curfew continued from 2-11-90 to 24-11-90 with little let-up and further incidents of arson, looting, stabbing and killing necessitated further imposition of curfew till the advent of New Year. Thus, the city remained disturbed for nearly two months, jeopardizing business, transport, schools, colleges, medical services and official transactions for months together. According to official reports 31 persons died, 69 were wounded and 669 persons were arrested during this period for causing unrest.

Therefore, within less than five years of unlocking the long disputed religious place at Ayodhya BJP, VHP and its allies made their continuous efforts in extracting more political capital by raising Mandir-Masjid issue. Rath Yatra of Advani compelled V.P. Singh to leave the lead he had over Government and created circumstances for the downfall of his government. Subsequently an interim government of Chandrashekhar with support of Congress (I), was installed. BJP did not stop its campaign and continued its excitment propaganda. The BJP visualized the inevitability of mid-term polls and gained more political strength out of it. Ultimately after fall of Chandrashekhar government mid-term polls were declared to be held in 3rd week of May, 1991.

May 20, 1991 was scheduled to be the poll day for Meerut, both for Parliament and Assembly. The main contestants for Parliament were—BJP (Thakur Amar Pal Singh), Congress-I (Shri Manjoor Ahmad) and Janata Dal (Shri Harish Pal). During 1989 polls the parliamentary seat was snatched by Janata Dal candidate, Harish Pal from twice representing Congress (I) candidate Mohsina Kidwai. Meerut constituency consists of five assembly seats including two assembly constituences of Meerut city and Cantt. Earlier this parliamentary seat was won by undivided Janata Dal candidate, Harish Pal, having electoral alliance with BJP Similarly BJP held possession over city and Cantt., by Laxmi Kant Bajpai and Shashi Mittal respectively. But now the situation was altogether changed. The earlier joint alliance between BJP and Janata Dal against Congress (I) was broken. The Janata Dal also split into Samajwadi Janta Dal and Janata Dal. Considering Muslim votes for parliamentary constituency Manzoor Ahmed was a rival for Janta Dal candidate Harish Pal. Similarly Dharma Diwakar, Congress-I candidate from Meerut city was a rival for Janata Dal candidate Ayub Ansari. BJP was expecting and depending on Hindu votes. It adopted a strategy to cast their Hindu votes in the early hours of the poll day rapidly and simultaneously to slow down the Muslim vote and casting by raising frequent objections on the identity of voters. This practice was adopted both by Hindu and Muslims in their areas of respective influence. The Congress (I) candidate Manzoor Ahmed when objected over these tactics, was attacked and sustained injuries. Anyhow he escaped from there. Meanwhile in another locality of Budhana Gate two innocent Muslim scooter riders were stabbed and within no time the nearby cinema hall Nigar was attacked by antisocial elements, killing about a dozen persons. The report of looting ballot papers and poll grabbing dismayed the district administration and in such circumstances one sided polls continued for hours in the areas of influence of candidates or parties. Under the circumstances helpless administration ordered to stop polling and imposed curfew in the city. As there was no sufficient police force with the district authorities, they could not control the situation immediately. District Magistrate, ex-officio returning officer of the election, ordered to cancel the polling of city and Cantt constituencies. Curfew remained imposed in the city and continued till 12th of June. This unwanted violence took 32 lives, 78 persons were injured and 1055 perrson were arrested for looting, arson and breaking curfew laws. Later on, the election of whole Meerut constituency (including assembly) was countermanded by the Election Commissioner of India.

The shocking statistics of communal hysteria, resultant of Ram Janam Bhumi Babri Masjid, from 1986 to 1991, reveals that it has played with the lives of more than 500 persons, in Meerut alone. The statistics from the compensation record of the UP Co-operative Bank Ltd, Meerut is given in Table 2 as follows :

TABLE 2

COMPENSATION RECORD OF UP CO-OPERATIVE BANK DURING 1986-92

Period	*Total Amount*	*No. of Recipients of 20,000 Rs.*
1. June 1986 to June 1987	20,50,000	14
2. July 1987 to June 1988	50,61,800	133
3. July 1988 to June 1989	9,82,000	41
4. July 1989 to June 1990	14,06,600	46
5. July 1990 to June 1991	84,12,833	39
6. July 1991 to Feb. 1992	11,41,667	220
	1,90,54,900	493

According to the Table, an estimated 493 persons have so far been paid a sum of Rs. 20,000 each for death. This assessment of bank record does not mention the cause of payment whether for the loss of life or property leaving it incomplete. Still more than 50 lakh rupees are lying undisbursed for distribution as compensation to the victims of riots.

During and after every riot, house to house searches were conducted in all sensitive areas of the city. Even the licence holders of weapons were asked to surrender their weapons. In large number seizures of firearms including telescopic rifles, pistols, single and double barrel guns, rifles and plenty of country made firearms and ammunition used in riots, were seized. Highly inflammable chemical powder was also seized from the mischief mongers which was used to ignite fire without any spark. However, largely the incidents of killing and injuring, were done by iron rods, knives and sticks.

It is evident from the gruesome picture of this city that the violence and riots have frequently devastated so many people. Many were left orphaned, destitute and with ruined dwellings. The business and other establishments were either burnt or looted. The daily wagers were left to starve and outside labourers were either killed or escaped. UP Government tried to pick and choose the victims and award compensation. The government machinery in discharging their function never showed clemency or clarity. Poor and weak could not get anything. Hindu shopkeepers tried to create artificial scarcity of consumer goods during curfew and sold them on high prices. Thus, the daily earners were sandwiched between the twin monsters of high price and no income.

Muslim organisation Jamat-e-Islami, came forward to help the devastated and destitute Muslims with missionary zeal. It distributed eatables, clothes and money for repairing the mosques, dwellings and shops. They distributed sewing machines to widows and provided financial help to rickshawpullers. According to the balance-sheet of Jamat-e-Islami, it incurred expenditure amounting to Rs 9,53,878 in Meerut city to rehabilitate the persons affected by communal riots. Hindu victims were also helped by RSS in many cases.

For the first time an inquiry commission was set-up in 1967 to probe into the riots spread over Meerut, Muradabad, Varanasi, Bareilly, Bulandshahr and Kanpur. The commission was headed by Raghuvar Dayal. Col. B.H. Zaidi and M.N. Philips were its other members. The commission was to enquire into the incidents of communal riots, which occurred during 1957 to 1967. The commission along with its other recommendations suggested death sentence to the rioters responsible for looting and arson. After 1971, communal riots for Aligarh became very common. In the same year, Aligarh with other towns of Firozabad, Varanasi and Muradabad, etc., caught fire of riots. UP Government appointed a judicial inquiry under Justice D.S. Mathur to enquire into the riots in Aligarh. Justice Mathur in his report suggested that Aligarh Muslim University should work in a democratic framework. To ensure the democratic norms he suggested that its students should be brought into the mainstream of the nation. Accordingly, he suggested amendment in AMU's structure. The third inquiry for riots of 1978, broke out from Sambhal, Muradabad and expanded to other towns of UP. It was announced by the then Janata Party Govt. of UP, which was withdrawn in 1980 by Viswanath Pratap Singh the then chief minister.

Since then numerous curefews due to communal riots were imposed in UP and particularly in Meerut but no serious investigation was ever made. After a lot of hue and cry, in 1987 riots of Meerut the UP Government announced two inquiries: (i) judicial inquiry of the incidents in Maliana area for the alleged atrocities committed by the PAC on Muslims, and (ii) Gyan Prakash Inquiry Committee for the rest of the riots in Meerut.

Thus the riots were also divided in separate heads. The reports and findings of all such committees and commissions were thrown into oblivion without any use for them. These reports are still secret and even the serious scholars have no access to them. It is ridiculous that even after incurring so much expenditure of public money on the commissions they are still beyond their reach. Further, their recommendations have never been implemented to prevent and cure this chronic disease for which they were constituted. Thus the commission and omissions proved nothing more than a mirage or an eyewash.

The role of the Provincial Armed Constabulary (PAC) in riots, has also attracted the attention of the people. In 1978 at Aligarh, 1980 at Muradabad and later in Meerut and other UP towns it got notoriety for siding with Hindus and killing Muslims wherever it was deployed. Muslims repeatedly opposed the deployment of PAC in riot affected areas. Much earlier in 1971 this issue was also raised before Mathur Commission but he did not agree with the proposal of separate security forces for the Hindus and Muslims. But in the later years its role aggravated the situation during riots and became very much controversial. The allegation of brutal kilings in 1987 in Maliana and Hashimpura of minority people, and other inhuman atrocities on their innocent children old and disabled, levelled against PAC, are still pending before the above two inquiries. Worst of all, even the leaders of the ruling and opposition parties played communal role, even the secular branded persons were seen siding with their respective communities. They helped in siding either the brute actions of the police and PAC or coaxed them to do so. The supply of essential commodities to the curfew bound areas in the city was also done on the communal basis both by Hindus and Muslims.

History will record that on such moments of manmade misery, no Gandhi undertook a fast unto death, no

Nehru ran into mob, no Jai Prakash jumped into fire. No liberal, no democrat, no humanist, no leftist, ever made it a question of conscience or even of political priority. Brutalized and power hungry politicians, rootless leadership, neo-rich careerists, exploited the sentiments of the innocent persons to extract political capital. In the interest of the national integration of India, the re-affirmation of the basic values of our freedom struggle and our Constitution, are badly needed. Good sense should prevail in Meerut for people to understand the price of this hatred and illwill.

11

Communal Riots in West Bengal

Panchanan Saha

Communal riots took place in different parts of our vast country in the wake of Rath Yatra by L.K. Advani. Even the left-oriented West Bengal was not spared. The communal virus started to sap the very lifeblood of Bengali intellectual tradition. The idea of Hindutva has been deeply penetrating even among a considerable section of intelligentsia. It seems that the Hindu communal organizations have started to hijack secularism in West Bengal. Though the situation has not turned into an alarming proportion, yet the idea of *Hindutva* has surpassed the influence of the Hindu communal organisations in the state.

On the other hand, Muslim communalism has not remained far behind. The influence of Muslim fundamentalists has been increasing at an alarming pace during the last few years. Some observers allege that huge amount of petrodollars have been flowing from the Middle-East into the coffers of Muslim fundamentalists. Communalism of all sorts—Hindu as well as Muslim is complementary to each other as one breeds the other.

One has to go deeper to understand the basic causes of communal flareup in the state recently. Since the past few years, the Hindu communalists have been carrying on mischievious propaganda which was not properly counteracted by the secular parties and organisations. One of the arguments of the Hindu communalists pointed out the danger of rapid growth of Muslim population in comparison to Hindus. It is argued not without historical evidences that before the eighteenth century, the Hindus far exceeded the number of Muslims in Bengal. Even in the overwhelmingly Muslim populated district of Dhaka, the revenue survey of 1868 observed that the population consisted of more or less equal number of Hindus and Muslims. Thus, rapid increase of Muslim population made Bengal Muslim majority province within a few decades and the price had to be paid in 1947 when the country was divided on the basis of religion. The Hindu communalists point out that the rapid increase of Muslim population in West Bengal, particularly in the border districts—Malda, Murshidabad, South and North 24 Parganas, Nadia, and West Dinajpur are due to two factors: (a) Muslim personal law allows a male to marry more than one wife and religious taboos prohibit birth control; (b) regular inflow of poor Muslims from Bangladesh who easily mingle with the local Muslim population in the border districts. If it continues, they argue, one day West Bengal will turn to be a Muslim majority province and it will not be astonishing to find another movement growing to make a Muslim majority independent state seceding from India. Besides, the rise of Muslim fundamentalism across the border, has been cleverly utilized by them to create a sense of panic among the Hindus in the state. This attitude is clear from a letter published in *The Statesman* (4th December, 1990): "It is absurd to reject the overwhelming evidence in support of the provocative and intolerant attitude of Muslims towards other religions. As long as the concept of 'jihad' is not renounced as a holy edict, it is impossible for this community to live in peace with others". The writer further states: "It is not uncommon to see Indian Muslims cheering sports teams from Islamic countries, and not their home side... Certainly Hindus have been too tolerant and for too long."

The idea, that the Muslims of India have not accepted India as their motherland from the core of their heart and that they still harbour extraterritorial loyalty, is very much current among a very good section of Hindus in the state. The idea of 'secularism' initiated by Jawaharlal Nehru is also under fire. It is argued that most of the political parties in India pursue a policy of appeasement towards the Muslims in order to get their votes in the general elections.

The secular parties in West Bengal either did not give due importance to this propaganda or considered the influence of secular parties among the masses too much. The complacency of the secular parties has tarnished the image of West Bengal when they failed to arrest the communal riots in the wake of Rath Yatra of L.K. Advani. The Rath Yatra organised on the question of Ram Janam Bhoomi-Babri Masjid controversy spoiled the whole atmosphere. It is strange to see that how communal passions led ordinary people to forget for the time being even the pressing problems of the day like unemployment, inflation, rising prices, lawlessness, etc.

Rath Yatra and Bharat Bandh

L.K. Advani's Ram Rath passed through Jhalda, a small town on the border of Bihar. His subsequent arrest and the call for Bharat Bandh received little response in the state. Except for Nadia, and to some extent Malda, Murshidabad and Burdwan the *Bandh* call elicited marginal response. But the *Bandh* has shown how BJP and other Hindu communal organisations have already made a dent in certain pockets of West Bengal. The *Bandh* supporters made unsuccessful attempts to obstruct road and rail traffic. Nearly 1,100 activists of the BJP and other allied groups were rounded up in different districts. At Katwa, in Burdwan district, which has returned CPI(M) nominees to the State Assembly and the Lok Sabha, about 2000 supporters of BJP had blocked the railway tracks disrupting of railway services for several hours. The police fired six rounds, killing one *Bandh* supporter and injuring another after bursting teargas shells failed to disperse a mob that attacked a place of religious worship and hurled bombs at the SDO's office. The mob burnt an ambulance and tried to storm the municipal office. It was infuriated as, according to sources, a bomb had been hurled at their procession. Even the BJP supporters went to the local CPI (M) MLA, Anjan Chatterjee's house with the dead body and 'heckled' the MLA's mother in his absence. *The Statesman* reports on 25 October, 1990 that Mr Jyoti Basu admitted that the BJP had pockets of influence at both Kalna and Katwa "though the MLAs belong to our party in both places". The government of West Bengal had awakened from slumber and became very much concerned when reports of deaths and clashes from Pilkhana in Howrah and Jhalda in Purulia reached Calcutta.

Pilkhana Riot

Pilkhana is a mixed pocket of Hindus and Muslims in Howrah city—the other side of the Ganges from Calcutta. On Wednesday the 24 October, 1990, trouble started there over a trivial issue following an altercation between two groups of Hindus and Muslims in the evening. Senior police and administrative officials convened a peace meeting with the representatives of both the communities. The meeting was over at 9.30 pm. At about 11.30 pm. there was fresh dispute over trivial issues and the heated arguments snowballed into widespread violence. Both the warring groups used bombs and firearms freely at each other. Strangely enough the violence continued till 2 am in the morning without any effective intervention by the state police. Even when the police force came in full force, it had a hard time chasing away the warring groups who often emerged from the numerous lanes and bylanes of the dingy Pilkhana area to hurl bombs and fire from the sophisticated weapons. Rumours were spreading in the whole locality since the clash between the two communities in Domjur which is not very far from Pilkhana. The rumour was that a demonstration of Hindus led by the VHP and the BJP was attacked by local Muslims in which some of the women demonstrators were seriously wounded and some were missing since then. Wild rumours like this always play an important role in instigating people into violence. Nobody cares to verify such rumours with a cool mind and rationally. It is observed that in all communal clashes, the anti-socials and criminals emerge as the real "saviours" of each community. The Chief Secretary of West Bengal said that the dispute at Pilkhana was between two groups of inebriated criminals.

Callousness of Administration

It is alleged by local people as well as some political elements that the government machinery remained callous and almost inactive even after the spread of rumours on Domjur incident on October 23, 1990. Despite the tension mounting in the area and appeals for more police pickets, only three constables were sent to man the area. They also fled to save their skin as soon as the violence erupted. *The Statesman* reported on 26th October, 1990 : "Reinforcements were sent an hour later consisting Eastern Frontier Rifles and State Armed Police personnel." The local people allege that they were deployed almost two hours after the trouble had actually begun.

On the evening of 25th October, there was fresh trouble. Bombs were hurled by two warring groups against each other. The EFR personnel took stern measures. They used teargas shells to disperse the crowd and had to resort to firing. Section 144 was clamped in the area.

In Pilkhana riot three men had been killed and twelve injured in violence and police firing.

Jhalda Riot

The Jhalda riot was also caused primarily by incessant rumours. The small town is situated in the district of Purulia. Incidentally Purulia was a part of Bihar not long ago. It was given to West Bengal on the recommendations of the State Reorganization Commission on the basis of language. The town is situated on either side of a highway leading to Ranchi.

The riot was triggered off when a motorcyclist belonging to a minority community knocked down a man killing him on the spot on 25th October morning. The victim happened to belong to the Hindu community. Rumourmongers described this accident as a planned communal killing. Jhalda town was already surcharged with communal passion after the Rath Yatra. It seems to be a fall out of the confidence within one community bolstered by the passage of the *Ram Rath* through Jhalda five days before.

Jhalda town is preceded by four villages populated by about 6,000 people belonging to minority community. The town itself, with a population of 15,000 people, has about 400 people of the minority community. According to newspaper reports the local police officials and residents of the town alleged that some of the villages harbour hardened criminals and their frequent depredations have been suffered by the townsfolk.

The following account of the direct cause of the riot was reported in *The Statesman* : "On Thursday morning, a village youth was dragged out of a bus, and was paraded with a rope tied to his ankle. Subsequent assaults resulted in his death in hospital. Rumours about the assault spread and nearly 400 people from Hussain Bihi, Bandaghat, Katdihi and Dangal stormed about on the outskirts of Jhalda town, damaging shops and hurling bombs. The only jeep of the police station was engaged, forcing the officer-in-charge of Jhalda *thana*, Subhajyoti Choudhury, to run about one kilometre to the spot with a number of constables. Bent on preventing the mob from entering Jhalda town and confronting the townspeople, the police fired seven rounds. A wireless message was sent to the Superintendent of Police, Purulia, 40 km away, for reinforcements and fire brigade personnel.

While the police held the villagers at bay, news of the advancing mob reached the town. A much larger mob assembled in the town and went on the rampage and the few policemen left behind in the police station were unable to prevent the violence. Police sources said a section of the people of the town burnt, looted and killed. The targets were innocent and hapless men of the same community. Nine men were hacked to death with sharp weapons. By the time the District Magistrate and the Superintendent of Police of Purulia arrived, it was all over. The marauding crowd had disappeared, and the police was left to pick up the bodies."

The hour-long act of violence left a trail of destruction in which 20 houses and 44 shops were damaged. "It began all of a sudden. We had no inkling of what was coming", said Mumtaz Alam Khan. "All we had heard were wild rumours since morning."

Inside the Jhalda police station precincts, groups of men and women took shelter to escape the rampaging mobs armed with choppers, iron rods and sticks. Well-meaning members of the other community, stupefied by the sudden violence, failed to prevent the frenzied mob.

Appeal for Sanity

After the sudden shock and bewilderment, the saner elements took initiative to stop carnage. Appeals by some municipal commissioners and town elders to stop the orgy fell on deaf ears. Some persons of the majority community boldly gave shelter to many families of the minority community. "We took to protecting and sheltering as many as we could," said Manakosh Mukherjee. Many were escorted to the police station. "We have lived here for a long time in total amity and cannot believe that this could happen," Mukherjee added. (*The Statesman*, 28 October, 1990).

Responsibility of the Administration

The district as well as state administration cannot avoid responsibility of Jhalda riots. The administration had not taken timely precaution to avoid communal flare up and seemed to have suffered from complacency. It is true that when *Ram Rath* passed through Jhalda, only a few people welcomed it lining the roads. But Jhalda observed a complete welcomed bandh on October 24, when BJP called a "Bharat Bandh". In Jhalda Bandh was called by BJP, the VHP, the Bajrang Dal and the RSS jointly. A meeting was called by the organisers on Bandh day. It is reported that two Muslims were beaten up at the venue of the meeting. Despite a report to the local police, no action was taken by it to prevent the violence.

Security personnel did not discharge their duties impartially. "Security forces, which are supposed to be secular, did not act in a manner which could have prevented the attack on the minority community in the town", wrote *The Statesman* of 30 October, 1990.

The police, district administration as well as secular political parties should be held responsible squarely for Jhalda riot. Since Jhalda was the only place in West Bengal through which the BJP president, L.K. Advani's Rath Yatra passed, the State Government ought to have arranged for adequate police pickets and should have strengthened the Jhalda *thana*, at least on a temporary basis.

The district administration's role has also been questioned. "No one thought it was necessary to keep an eye on the area which has a mixed population," a businessman said.

The secular political party leaders like CPI(M), the Forward Bloc and the Congress(I) were nowhere in evidence on October 20 when the Ram Rath went through Jhalda. They were unable to read the signals. They seemed to have been ignorant of the meetings that took place in the Muslim villages before the Ram Rath passed. They were also equally ignorant about the meetings that took place among some VHP and BJP activists after Rath Yatra.

The Statesman gives an instance of callousness of administration. "The tension which built up after three cycles were snatched and a recurrence of the incident too seemed to have passed unnoticed in a town which is quite small. The rumblings within the majority community following the snatchings was ignored by both police and the politicians. Preventive arrests and intervention by the political parties even as a youth was being beaten up with a rope tied to his ankle, would have prevented the subsequent outbreak of violence." (*The Statesman*, 30 October)

The *Emarat-e-Shariah* of eastern India and the Muslim Action Committee of Bihar in a memorandum submitted to chief minister Jyoti Basu strongly and unequivocally charged that the police personnel posted at Jhalda connived with the culprits to attack the Muslims. The memorandum also blamed the police administration for its callousness when the tension was mounting since October 20 itself at the time of Rath Yatra.

It is also alleged that the mob, armed with lethal weapons, moved freely in different areas and burnt houses and shops of the Muslims which were located very close to the police station. It is even charged that some policemen were among the frenzied mob. A party of West Bengal Socialist Unity Centre of India has also levelled the same charges against the police. A spokesman of that party said in Calcutta on November 3, 1990 that a "BJP-police nexus" had been active in Jhalda during the recent violent incidents there. The district leaders of the CPI(M) and the Congress (I) had done nothing to stop the violence.

Conclusion

It appears that the secular parties of West Bengal have been suffering from complacency. The recent communal flareups caught them unawares. The Rath Yatra could have been stopped at the border of West Bengal. It seems that political exigencies have prevented from taking such a decision.

It appears from the statistics presented by Nandgopal Bhattacharya, the state CPI secretary in a booklet, that the growth of communal organizations in West Bengal has taken place at an alarming rate in the recent years. Out of twenty thousand RSS branches all over India in 1988, the number of functioning branches in West Bengal was only one thousand. But by 1990, the number of RSS branches increased two and half fold, i.e. to 2,500 with 22,270 full-time workers and 34,278 members (*swayamsevaks*) and 47,251 supporters. The state RSS had collected Rs14,68,120 as *gurudakshina* from its members in 1988-89. The annual budget of the RSS in the year 1988-89 was only 20 million rupees which doubled in 1989-90. Besides organising Ram Jyoti processions throughout the state, a big Hindu conference was also organized in Calcutta on 21 October with great fanfare. It is estimated that more than twelve lakh rupees were spent for it. A few thousand *kar sevaks* were also sent by them from West Bengal to Ayodhya. The major secular political parties in the state like the CPI(M) and the Congress (I) seem to be unperturbed at this increasing danger of communalism.

It has been found that wild rumours create communal passions resulting into communal flare up. The government and secular parties have failed to counteract such rumours in Domjur, Pilkhana or in Jhalda.

It is interesting to note that whereas the hardened criminals are involved in communal riots (like Pilkhana) bombs, guns, and even sophisticated weapons were used freely. But in Jhalda riot, where the frenzied mob was involved, traditional weapons like choppers, knives, iron rods, sticks were used more than bombs.

The state police has generally failed to discharge its duties impartially. The nexus between the police and the rioteers was also evident.

12

Communal Virus Introduced in Karnataka

U.S. Venkataraman

Karnataka is known for peace and tranquility and tradition of communal amity was in the grip of violence and terror unleashed by communal and political forces. Thc main cause was the threat to building of Sri Ram Temple by demolishing the Babri Masjid in Ayodhya. South India in general and Karnataka in particular were peaceful. But, the BJP and its frontal organizations, RSS and VHP fanned communal passions. The worst communal riots took place between the first week of September and the end of December, 1990 and sporadic incidents continue till now. The number of persons killed is placed at about 60 (on a very conservative estimate) and the loss of property is estimated at about rupees three crores. Davanagere, Ramanagaram, Kolar, Channapatna and Tumkur were most affected. These riots took place in both urban and rural areas.

During these riots, the state administration was literally paralized since the chief minister Veerendra

Patil himself actually suffered a paralytic attack and was in the sick bed. He was removed from chief ministership by the Congress high command for his inability to check the riots. The law and order enforcement machinery acted differently at different places depending upon the angularities of the enforcement officials. As reported in *The Times of India* dated 7 December, 1990, Renukarya complained to the chief minister that the deputy commissioner of Tumkur was inciting communalism. There are also instances of police officials acting impartially and preventing riots by timely prophylactic measures. Subash Bharani, the DIG of Dharwar Range was honoured in a public meeting organised by the autorickshaw drivers and the CPI, for his impartiality and prompt action.

After S. Bangarappa took over the chief ministership from Veerendra Patil, he took some political initiative to form a state level committee for bringing communal harmony. He also threatened to use TADA (Terrorist and Disruptive Activities Act). However, while constituting the committee, he had left out the left parties which are consistently secular in their outlook and approach. It was only after CPI urged for inclusion of left parties, that they were also included. *The Hindu* dated 29 October, 1990 reports a speech made by S. Bangarappa at Davanagere, one of the worst affected places :

The chief minister wondered whether it was his misfortune or distinction of sorts that the first task that he addressed himself to after assuming office was the situation arising out of the unprecedented communal flareup in the state.

Though he reiterated that the police department had been given the full powers to quell the disturbances, he had given clear instructions to his staff not to hesitate to wake him even during night hours, when the law and order problems occurred so that the extent of loss to life and property could be minimized. He said "I am keeping a round-the-clock vigil on communal disturbances."

It can be stated without any reservation that the main cause had been the "Rama Janmabhoomi-Babri Masjid issue." *The Hindu* dated 14-11-1990 made the following observations: "Rama Janmabhoomi-Babri Masjid issue which witnessed turbulent scenes in the North, has had its echoes felt in the four districts of Hassan, Madikeri, Mandya and Mysore, resulting in the deaths of ten persons and damaging property estimated nearly 1.5 crores of rupees."

The continued rampage of events that shook these districts for over three weeks, was the backlash of Ayodhya issue where passions sored high eventually leading to some miscreants taking advantage of the situation to settle old scores.

As is well known, it was Vishwa Hindu Parishad which took up the Ayodhya issue and it was ably supported by RSS and BJP An organization called Citizens for Democracy investigated the riots that took place at Davanagere.

The Hindu dated 28-10-1990 reported : "The citizens for democracy has attributed the communal riots in Davanagere, to the intense competition between the Muslims and the Hindus in celebrating Id-Milad and Organizing Ram Jyoti Yatra.

In an interim report, the organization (CFD) blamed a local organization, the Hindu Yuva Sakti for the events leading to the riots, even while demanding an enquiry by a sitting judge of the High Court.

CFD alleges that the Hindu Yuva Sakti enjoyed the blessings of BJP and the VHP.

Yuva Sakti members raised provocative slogans leading to ill-will and tension.

CFD has alleged that Yuva Sakti systematically spread hatred against the Muslims and displayed excessive zeal in removing buntings and the flags."

Similarly, Janata Dal has also held BJP and its front organizations responsible for the riots.

The Hindu dated 23-11-1990 reported : "Janata Dal Members lashed out against the BJP and VHP on the Rama Janma Bhoomi issue, during the discussions on the recent communal riots in parts of the state, in the legislative council. "Mr. B.R. Patil (Janata Dal) said that the BJP had now revealed its true colours and had identified itself fully with the RSS and VHP which in the past it was refusing to admit its links with RSS The BJP took up the Rama Janmabhoomi issue as it had no concern for the poor and the backward classes. It was the ordinary people who went to Ayodhya to offer *kar seva* and were called and not the leaders who raked up the Ram Janmabhoomi issue."

"Another Janata Dal member Mr V.R. Sudershan, went to the extent of saying that VHP was cheating the people in the name of Lord Rama. Quoting the chief priest of a temple of Ayodhya, he said that VHP had raised money in the name of Lord Rama."

The chief minister, Bangarappa said on May 12, 1991 that the corps of detectives (COD) had found *prima facie* evidence that the BJP was responsible for the riots in Karnataka in 1990.

Though the cause is definitely not known, the Muslims, either on their own or in retaliation, have also indulged in violence. *The Hindu* dated 1-11-1990 reported: "In another incident reported from Coorg last night, a group of Muslims attacked the house of Sudhakar Yadav and ransacked and damaged it, when the victims including the three brothers of Sudhakar Yadav were on their way to the police station to lodge a complaint, the same group waylaid and damaged the jeep. The people in the jeep, travelling with fire arms opened fire in which one person died on the spot."

In an atmosphere surcharged with tension and mutual mistrust, even a burst of a cracker ignited riots.

The Hindu dated 7-11-1990 reported : "At Chamarajnagar, police said, a cracker burst in front of a shop owned by a Hindu triggered the clashes, while Hindus believed that the Muslims had attempted arson, The Muslims believed that Hindus were assembling only to attack them. Both the groups armed with lethal weapons including lathis and cycle chains clashed in which three persons sustained serious injuries."

Religious passions were so highly aroused that unrelated innocuous incidents lead to riotous situations. Looking at these instances we see that :

> A bailiff with an eviction order from a court had come to serve to order on a shopkeeper whose shop was close by to a mosque. To chase away the bailiff, the shopkeeper's men started hurling stones. A few of these stones fell on the mosque. Men in the mosque had reasons to believe that their place of worship was being attacked. However, local people and the police, explained the facts and convinced the men at the mosque, that there was no communal attack.

In Gulbarga, an accidental fire in a footwear shop (due to electrical short circuit) was sought to be attributed to communal violence. But the rumours were dispelled.

On the first of February 1991, there was a sudden eruption of communal violence in Sullia town in South Kanara District, which took everybody by surprise. It was for the first time that Sullia witnessed an orgy of communal violence. There were 160 houses and shops that were either damaged or destroyed belonging to one community, which bear testimony to the communal frenzy let loose on the town. The town now wears a deserted look. While the government has estimated the loss and damage to property at Rs 80 lakhs, other estimates exceed Rs 1 crore.

The *Deccan Herald* (February 15, 1991) reported : "The Sullia trouble is said to have started on the night of January 31, when a tempo following the Pejawar Swamiji's car was stoned. The windowpanes of the tempo were broken but nobody was injured in the attack.

The next day, a few organizations staged a march in the town to protest against the alleged attack on the Swamiji. The day also happened to be the one on which the Babri Masjid Action Committee had called an all-India *bandh.* When the march reached a place of worship, some people raised provocative slogans. This provoked counter-slogans from people in the place of worship. The confrontation snowballed into a major conflict by evening and shops and houses all over the town were set ablaze. The small police force in the town did little to control the violence. Stoning and torching of isolated houses in villages around the town continued for about a week."

It was for the first time in its history that Sullia went through such an agonising experience. The suffering of the riot victims is poignant. Sheikh Mohammed Hussain, an 80-year-old man who retired as *Dafedar* from the Sullia *taluk* office several years ago, now lives, with his wife, daughter and grandchildren, including a 20-day-old baby, in a cow shed.

Fatimabi, a widow living in Court Road, was making preparations for her daughter's wedding when the violence broke out. The rioters robbed her of 160 gm of gold and Rs. 15,000 in cash. Ironically, all that she has got by way of compensation from the government is ten kg of rice and half kg of dal.

The communal flare-up did not stop people from helping one another, however. When rioters tried to set fire to a house belonging to a woman, people belonging to the other community stopped them by saying. "If you want to set fire, set fire to our house first". There are other such instances of people of both communities providing shelter to each other.

The apparent cause of the trouble—the attack on the tempo of the Swamiji's follower—is itself shrouded in mystery. The Swamiji and his followers had no engagement in Sullia and the local people could not have known that they were passing through the town on the night of January 31 to reach Mysore. Then who stoned the tempo? The question cannot be answered but they tend to support the view that the violence was preplanned.

The visits of the chief minister, the home minister and other government leaders to the town have had only symbolic significance. The government compensation programme has hardly satisfied the riot victims.

Left to themselves, the people in a neighbourhood maintain communal harmony and they will ignore provocative actions of outside mischief makers. In Savana Durga, in Magadi *taluka*, Bangalore district, some outsiders, deliberately to provoke the Muslim community, demolished a small *Dargah* adjacent to Sri Laxminarasimha Temple. The Muslim community which has friendly relations with Hindus was aware that it was the mischief of outside elements and hence did not retaliate. Local Hindus joined the Muslims in requesting the government to rebuild the *Dargah*, which was readily agreed to by the government.

There are changing patterns and disturbing trends in the eruption of violence. Arson, looting and stabbing are the common features. Burning of auto and cycle rickshaws and huts and attacks on poorer toiling men, and burning and looting of shops, occurred in almost all areas affected by communal riots. But heightened activity of destruction was seen at Srinivasapur, where mango trees in an orchard and a cinema theatre, were set on fire.

Attacks on places of worship and damaging them this time is the worst kind of vandalism hitherto not witnessed.

The Hindu of 3-11-90 reported : "Three persons were killed and 13 places of worship were partially damaged yesterday and early today in different parts of Karnataka."

So far, we have seen the present situation and it is necessary to look at the past and think of the future. The future depends upon the lessons we learnt from the past and how we mould the future.

Despite the existence of many religions, by and large, Karnataka has the tradition of religious tolerance and respect for each other's religion. Religious synthesis has been the cardinal principle followed by successive rulers of the State.

- Satavahana Kings were followers of Vedic religion, while their queens were Buddhists.
- Vishnuvardhana became a Sri Vaishnava, his senior queen Shantala was a Jaina and her father was a Smartha Brahmin.
- Vijayanagara Emperor Devaraya II got a mosque built for Muslims at Vijayanagara and he used to show reverence for *Quran* as testified by Ferishta.
- Speaking on the religious policy of Vijayanagara Kings, Barbosa says :

  "The King allows such freedom that every man can come and go and live according to his own creed without suffering any annoyance and without enquiry whether he is a Christian, Jew, Moor or a heathen."

"Though religiously devout the Bahamani Kings were not oppressive or intolerant towards their Hindu subjects. Both Jainism and Hinduism flourished as numerous temples of the period bear witness."[1]

"Even, in regard to religion, the idea that Hinduism was always held in contempt by the early Muslim rulers would not bear examination. In fact, we have ample evidence that even under the most bigoted kings like

Allauddin Khilji and Firoz Tugalak, the Hindu religious leaders received honours and recognition. From Jain sources, we know that Allauddin held religious discourses with Acharya Mahasen who had to be brought from the Karnataka country for the purpose."[2]

In Bhagwan S. Gidwani's *Sword of Tipu Sultan*, we find several references to Tipu Sultan giving munificient grants to several Hindu temples and his religious tolerance.

Tipu's declaration on religious tolerance is interesting. "Religious tolerance is the fundamental tenet of Islam."[3]

"The *Quran* holds that there can be no compulsion in religion. The right discretion henceforth is distinct from error."

"The *Quran* calls upon you not to revile the idols of an other religion for it says revile not those unto whom they pray beside Allah lest they may wrongfully revile allah through ignorance."

"Vie with each other in good works."

The Sufi sect "believed in the integration of the principles of Islam and Hinduism and was popular in Karnataka. The tomb of Bande Nawaz Desu Darwaz at Gulbarga is venerated by all.

In modern times too, a Veerashaiva going on pilgrimage to Tirupathi or an orthodox Brahmin attending an *Urs* to fulfil an oath is common. The *Urs* at Baba Budan Giri, Yamanur, Gulbarga and other places are attended by the Hindus in huge numbers. Some of the Veerashaiva *mathas* like the one at Savalgi in Belgaum district is visited by Muslims too.

The Dharma Raya Karaga is a popular Jatra of Bangalore. In simple terms, Karaga is the procession of a flower-bedecked religiously ordained person carrying the crown of Dharmaraya propagating the message of Dharma. It is customary for the Karaga to visit Mastan Sahib Dargah.

These are the hoary traditions of communal amity in Karnataka. It is lamentable that these secular ideals are being swayed by communal indoctrination leading to division of people on religious basis. The secular forces must assert themselves in order to wean away the masses from the clutches of the communal forces. It is good augury that all secular forces are coming together irrespective of political affiliations to combat the evil of communalism. In the recent days, we have seen a number of mass contact programmes disseminating the message of unity and fraternity among the people of Karnataka.

Yet, the communal forces, which are disruptive by nature and disposition are intolerant of the efforts made for bringing communal amity and they disrupt such excellent efforts. According to a report in *the Hindu* of 9-12-1990: Mangalore: "When Mr Jayakumar, Secretary, Democratic Youth Federation of India accused the BJP and the VHP of encouraging communal tension in the country, slogan shouting, Sriram Bhajan singing youth tried to disrupt the meeting and indulged in stone-throwing. Police intervened and after isolating the groups resorted to mild lathi charge to disperse the crowd."

References

1. Panicker, K.M. *A Survey of Indian History*, p. 147.
2. *Ibid.*, p. 131.
3. *Ibid.*, p. 229.

13

Communal Riots in Hyderabad

A. Prabhakar Rao

The Union Home Ministry had long back identified Hyderabad as a city prone to communal riots. The purpose of identification of such areas prone to communal riots all over the country is to keep the respective state administrative machinery alert in advance to cope with the communal trouble likely to take place on certain of occasions. The possibility of clashes in Andhra Pradesh between the two communities Hindus and Muslims was there on the occasion of certain festivals of the two communities falling on the same day or with a week's gap. They are like Vinayaka Chavithy of Hindus and Phanka Jhulus of Muslims in Hyderabad, and Dussehera and Moharram all over the state. The police administration normally takes precaution to avert any untoward incident taking place on such festive occasions.

The reason behind identifying Hyderabad as city prone to communal clashes was the predominance of Muslim population in the old city, in additior. to being the headquarters of Hyderabad State ruled by Nizam before it was merged in the Indian Union consequent to the police action in September, 1948. A quick glance at the past will enable us to have a correct outlook on the forces behind such inhuman riots.

The freedom struggle in Hyderabad State was also part and parcel of anti-Nizam struggle. While the Andhra Maha Sabha and later the Communist Party mobilized the people including the peasantry not only against the Nizam but also against the landlords who stood by the Nizam for their own class interests, the Vandemataram movement and Arya Samaj mainly concentrated on mobilizing Hindus against the Muslim ruler. On the other side, by and large, most of the Muslims felt psychologically that they were safe only under Nizam's rule, though they too were among the millions exploited by the landed gentry and the *subedars, jagirdars*, etc., of the Nizam. There were no communal organizations as such in Hyderabad city at the time of the formation of Andhra Pradesh in November, 1956.

An organization called *Majlis-ettehadul-Muslimeen* (MIM) was operating earlier under the leadership of Kasim Razvi, who roused Muslims against the Hindus during the freedom movement. Kasim Razvi, who was put in Pune jail, was released in 1960 and asked to leave Hyderabad and go to Pakistan. When the former president of MIM, Abul Khair Siddique, an advocate, refused to revive the organization, Abdul Wahed Owasi, father of Salauddin Owasi, MIM member of the Lok Sabha rapidly revived MIM.

The Jana Sangh and the RSS were already there in existence, deriving mainly from Arya Samaj, though the founders of Arya Samaj like Swami Ramananda Theertha and others were not in favour of Hindu communal organizations. Several of Swamiji's followers like P.V. Narasimha Rao had joined the Congress Party much earlier. These two political formations based on religion did not, however, get much mass support from the people belonging to their respective religions, whose champions were supposed to be either the Jana Sangh or the BJP. It was the faction ridden Congress Party that gave political respectability to both Jana Sangh and MIM in 1907 assembly elections, when three members from each of the two communal parties were elected. In earlier 1962 elections one section of the Congress got a cabinet minister Mrs. Masooma Begum defeated at the hands of a MIM candidate in one of the old city constituencies. In 1967, BJP contested seven of the eleven constituencies in the twin cities and won three, defeating even the home minister Mir Ahmed Ali Khan. (Present member Mr Salahuddin Owaisi) thanks to Congress groupism. The polarization of votes on communal lines between the Jana Sangh and MIM in every booth in old city constituencies had taken place for the first time in 1967. This has continued to be a phenomenon even to this day in that part of the city.

This was a brief history of the rise of communal parties in Andhra Pradesh and frequent communal clashes went on in Hyderabad thereafter with MIM and Jana Sangh (now BJP) whipping up communal passions. Though communal clashes have taken place in Hyderabad earlier several times, the nature of riots that took place in October, November and December, 1990 were unique. They were well planned, better organised, adopted improvised techniques, and widespread when compared to all earlier communal riots right from the formation of the state of Andhra Pradesh. At times they even surpassed brutalities of the notorious Razakars during the Nizam period.

Though some sporadic violence had taken place during the prolonged Ratha Yatra of L.K. Advani here and there, it was in October, the killing spree was begun following the arrest of BJP chief, L.K. Advani in Bihar. The aggressive mood of the BJP men with saffron coloured caps was very much in evidence when they threw the burning effigy of V.P. Singh on a police officer posted on duty right at the State Secretariat.

From October 25 to 28 it was a free-for-all in the old city and in certain adjoining villages in Ranga Reddy district. Mostly stabbing was the method used in which a 40-year-old man, an assistant sub-inspector of CRP on duty and two boys aged between 10 and 15 were the victims of the frenzy let loose by leaders of both the communities. The 40-year-old man, a supervisor of an oil mill at Chandrayan Gutta,was found dead on the road with a deep knife injury in his throat. In these six days a score were killed in stabbing and double the number injured. These figures of dead and injured were based only on official releases.

Suspecting the stabbing-spree more widespread on October, 30 due to impending *kar seva* at Ayodhya, the State Government imposed a 36-hour curfew from 6 am on October, 29 as a precautionary measure. Never before in Hyderabad was the curfew imposed covering 43 police stations out of 60 in the state capital. It was almost the entire city, except the posh Banjara Hills and Jubilee Hills, which was under curfew for such a long time at one stretch. It was also for the first time that communal clashes and incidents of stabbings on a large-scale were reported outside the old city and the residents of this otherwise calm city too had the taste of the curfew.

The credit for igniting the communal fire must go to the BJP and its militant RSS under the shelter of Ratha Yatra, *kar seva* and Ram temple. But its counterpart, the MIM, too did equal damage to the heritage of Hyderabad city by retaliating and killing innocent men, women and children in certain pockets of the old city where the religious minority community is in numerical majority.

The city police commissioner Gurunatha Rao, a very efficient police officer, acted swiftly in rounding up the antisocial elements from both the communities inviting ire from the political highups in the ruling party, Congress (I). Army was called out to assist the civil administration and flag marches were undertaken on all major thoroughfares in the Old City on October 29 itself. However, some stray incidents did take place in which four persons including two boys around 15 years were stabbed to death.

Ironically, not a single legislator or a corporator belonging to BJP and MIM was arrested, though it was a known fact that they were directly behind this communal carnage for full six days. Another interesting aspect of the entire tragic drama was that the chief minister Dr M. Chenna Reddy did not find time to visit the old city to get first hand information on the goings on for himself, but also did not go to console the people and infuse confidence in the fear-stricken people and to assure them that the government would provide the much needed security. What did Dr. Reddy do on October 30 ? He had created a world record. Imagine what it was. Was it a "mounavratha" (to keep silence) ? No. Then what ? Dr. Reddy invented a unique method of getting first hand information on communal killings for the past one week in the city, a method as unique as that of the one adopted by the human blood suckers of both the communities in Hyderabad. 3,00,000 pamphlets were printed in Telugu and Urdu appealing to the people of the twin cities by Dr Reddy as Chief Minister of Andhra Pradesh to maintain communal harmony. Curfew was further extended till 6 am 1 November.

The chief minister Dr Reddy, ably aided by his two sons (one of whom had donated his kidney to Dr Reddy) and top civil and police officers, had a 40 minute aerial survey of the curfew-bound areas of the state capital. The 3,00,000 pamphlets in Telugu and Urdu containing his appeal for the maintenance of communal harmony were meant for airdropping. There must be at least one wise man in the helicopter who was supposed to have given him a sound advice against the airdropping of the pamphlets. Hence, that was shelved. A politician with over 40 years of active public life alone could invent such unique method of visiting the curfew areas not by road but by air. It is a world record, as to my two decade and odd journalistic experience. I have never come across any chief minster of any state in India or political head of any State on the globe, who took a helicopter for an aerial view of an area where roads, lanes and bylanes were motorable and not even a single drop of water (not blood) could be found anywhere in the area meant for aerial survey.

After the *kar seva* and the successful hoisting of saffron flag on top of Babri Masjid, with pictures of a damaged mosque published in the local dailies the 'victorious' BJP and RSS devotees of Ram were again on the rampage from 1st November, and caused minor or major damages to over 30 places of worship of the other community in villages around Hyderabad.

Now the killing and stabbing technique was changed. Scooters and motorcycles (two wheelers) were pressed into service. It was the 'holy duty' of the pillion rider to knife a person of the other community found on the way, while the driver took care to speed up the vehicle after the 'holy job' was done by the person riding pillion.

From October, 23 to November, 3 there was curfew which was lifted only twice for a couple of hours to enable the people to buy essentials. During this period over 20 people were killed and hundreds injured, in addition to damaging the places of worship not only in Hyderabad and its neighbouring Ranga Reddy district but also in certain select places in Telangana district.

The pattern of stabbings in these particular communal riots in Hyderabad city were totally different from the earlier ones. It was undoubtedly not a spontaneous reaction or outburst, as used to be on earlier occasions. The *modus operandi* was identical for both communities.

Normally in any such troubled situation, the anti-social elements indulge in looting of the valuables. But this time (October, November and December, 1990) it was not so. The pattern of stabbing arson, damage or destruction of religious places clearly indicated that it was the preplanned action of the gangs wanting to fan communal passions and thereby create unrest, probably keeping in view the elections for Lok Sabha due to the hung Parliament and expecting elections any time with the withdrawal of support to National Front Government headed by V.P. Singh by the dictating BJP after the arrest of Lal Kishan Advani even before he reached Ayodhya to participate in the "holy ceremony" of *kar seva* in which the then prime minister V.P. Singh had reported to have agreed to participate having allowed Advani to take out his Ratha Yatra from Somnath Temple.

In this two and a half month long communal flareup, the BJP leaders in their public speeches and slogans have concentrated their fury against Mr V.P. Singh on the ground that he had agreed to participate in the *kar seva* and allowed Advani to take out his Ratha Yatra from Somnath Temple. Other issues the BJP leaders raised during the course were that the Congress (I), communist parties, and others were pseudo-secularists and were pro-Muslim, and the BJP was the genuine secular party in this country providing equal rights and opportunities to people belonging to all religions.

Coming back to the communal riots, it was established beyond doubt that the persons engaged in the carnage were professional gangs of criminals, some of them being brought from other states. The type of multiple injuries mainly on the vital parts of the body, like stomach, lower part of back and the chest was described as clear indication that the persons engaged for the job were well trained professionals. The knives used were not ordinary knives. They were sharper and twisted at the end so as to inflict a very serious injury once it is pushed inside the body and while taking it out it would damage the intestines and other vital parts of the body. In certain cases the knives were driven up to to the hilt in the back resulting in instantaneous death.

By November 7, day curfew was lifted and much to the relief of the people local papers published news on page one with banner headlines: "City heading to normalcy"; "Incident-free day" and the like. But the Hindu population had already started leaving their houses in the Muslim dominated old city and started migrating bag and baggage to the new city crossing Naya Pool (new bridge). Relief camps were opened for the people fleeing from the old city in Gandhi Bhavan, headquarters of the Congress (I) party, mostly from the Hindu community leaving their properties and belongings behind. This had created a new dimension to the communal carnage in the normally peaceful city beyond Naya Pool. BJP again took the initiative to beat the Muslims in this part of the city wherever they were in small numbers.

From November 7 onwards the situation started slowly improving as the police commissioner G. Gurunatha Rao rounded up hundreds of known and suspected antisocial elements from both the communities irrespective of their political affiliations. During the second and third weeks of November, hardly three people were killed and twenty injured in the sporadic stabbing incidents. Day curfew was lifted in the entire city by then and night curfew was restricted between 9 pm and 5 am in certain sensitive parts of the old city.

The chief minister Chenna Reddy and his friends instead of appreciating the strenuous efforts of the Police commissioner, started bringing pressure on him to release some of the antisocial elements. The role played by M.M. Hashim, Congress (I) member of Rajya Sabha and a staunch follower of Dr Reddy is worth considering here. He went egging on the police commissioner to release some of his followers in the old city on the ground that they were not the followers of MIM but of Congress (I). The police commissioner was firm in his attitude towards those he had rounded up and told Hashim that he refused to differentiate between the anti-social elements based on their political affiliation. An antisocial element was so because he indulged in antisocial activities was the curt reply Hashim got from the police commissioner. Gurunatha Rao did not oblige even the son of chief minister, who was the office bearer of the state Congress (I). The result was that he was shifted and an obliging officer was posted as city police commissioner. This was in the third week of November. This act, naturally, had a demoralizing effect on the police.

To everybody's shock and surprise, on November, 24, two persons including a *muni* of a Jain temple in Secunderabad were axed to death and another was injured seriously. This happened at 4.30 am on that day. However, no untoward incident had taken place till the end of the month.

The legislators and corporators belonging to BJP and MIM were moving freely asking their respective followers to damage the places of worship of the other community. The second spell of communal killings had started in the first week of December. On December 5 Majid Khan, a right hand man of the MIM, member of the Lok Sabha Salahuddin Owaisi, was attacked with butcher's knife on some personal animosities by three caste Hindus. It had nothing to do with the communal clashes which had taken place earlier. But the fact that some Hindus attacked a Muslim and that too a right hand man of Owaisi was enough to provoke the Muslims to attack Hindus. While Majid Khan survived the attack, in the so-called retaliation by Owaisi's followers, next day a certain Ramesh was killed. While returning from the funeral of Ramesh, the mob had again started attacking the people belonging to other community indiscriminately. The communal avalanche that swept for full ten days was spine-chilling and heart rending, and defies description.

While 50 people were killed and about 120 injured in the month long first spell of stabbing starting on October 23, the second spell which commenced on December 5, witnessed 165 deaths and about 350 injured in just ten days. Thereafter it was sporadic and hardly any deaths were reported. Table I gives the details.Thereafter it was sporadic and hardly any deaths were reported.

TABLE 1

CASUALITES OF RIOTS IN HYDERABAD DURING DECEMBER 1990

Date	*Persons Killed*	*Persons Injured*
Dec, 6	1	16
Dec, 7	16	35
Dec, 8	40	52
Dec, 9	20	72
Dec, 10	13	60
Dec, 11	8	30
Dec, 12	10	24
Dec, 13	14	30
Dec, 14	5	15
Dec, 15	6	23

It is reported that a section of Congress (I) leaders, mostly from Hyderabad city, were also involved in this unabated violence resulting in the loss of over a hundred people. Though it is very difficult to substantiate the charge, their role in the killing spree in the second spell could be construed due to the fact that the violence had subsided with the chief minister Dr Chenna Reddy announcing his decision to resign on December, 15. But other factors too have played a major role in controlling the riots. Let us look at the events that have taken place in this second spell of communal riots.

When the situation was going out of control and chief minister Dr Reddy was not taking enough steps to put down the killings with a stern hand, the Congress (I) President Rajiv Gandhi being upset had despatched a 'high powered' team to study the situation and report back to him. The delegation consisted of former Speaker of Lok Sabha, Balram Jhakar, former Minister of State for Home Mr P. Chidambaram, Mrs Mohsina Kidwai, Mr M.J. Akbar and Mr Janardhan Pujari. They arrived on December, 10. This five-member team went round the lanes and bylanes of the old city and were shocked at the gruesome stories narrated by the people and found several lapses in dealing with the situation.

In fact, after the visit it was Mr Chidambaram, who gave firm instructions to the Chief Secretary, Director-General of Police and the Police Commissioner of the various steps they should take to put an end to the communal carnage. How unconcerned the chief minister was during the second round of clashes could be established by the fact that five MLAs and 21 corporators belonging to BJP and MIM were arrested by the police only after instructions to that effect were given by the former Union Minister of State for Home Mr Chidambaram. He also gave a stern warning to the police and literally directed them to bring the situation to normalcy quickly at any cost. Chidambaram asked the police commissioner to take certain measures after which he visited the affected areas in the morning and again went to the area in the evening to see for himself whether the "orders" he had given to the commissioner in the morning were carried out or not. He was satisfied as the police complied with his orders.

The violence and the gruesome killings in this second

spell were of totally different nature when compared to earlier occasions. This time groups of people of one community forced entry into the houses of other community and dragged people—men women and children—out and killed them. Petrol and kerosene was used for the purpose. In some cases acid was also used. 80 year old Ramakka's nose was cut and the visiting Congress (I) delegation had to make arrangements to send her to hospital with nose dangling. The women told the delegation that the culprits after attacking her butchered her two buffaloes and carried them away. When some local Congressmen were trying to tell something to the delegation during their visit, they were told curtly by Mr Chidambaram; "Please go away. We want to go on our own and assess the situation ourselves." PCC (I) President V. Hanumantha Rao had accompanied the delegation throughout.

The residents of Pardiwadi in the Shakkarnager area of old city behaved bravely and staunchly saved the lives of many. A mob entered the area around 7.30 pm, the power supply was switched off and telephone lines were out. Then the mob forced entry into some houses, pulled out the inmates and attacked them with swords and daggers. There they found that a woman who was stabbed was still alive hence they poured kerosene and set her on fire. An ex-serviceman somehow gathered some youth and virtually built a sort of fortress around a cluster of houses. One of the youth approached a local peace committee leader and informed him about the attack. But strangely, a person standing next to the peace committee leader stabbed the youth in the chest with a dagger and fled. This is how the so-called the peace committee leaders came to the rescue of the suffering people.

An 18-year-old girl said that her mother was virtually cut to pieces in front of her. Another boy said his father and aunt were killed in his presence. He said during the killing spree, he called back his brother who was going to a troubled spot. The miscreants nabbed his brother, found out to which community he belonged and killed him.

In this period, rows of houses were either burnt or ransacked, household articles, scooters, cycles were reduced to ashes. On December 12, a most shocking incident had taken place. An assistant commissioner of police asked a police constable to be on duty at a particular point. The constable refused. Then the ACP asked ordered the constable to follow him to that spot. The constable after walking few yards behind the ACP, loaded his gun and shot the ACP dead. They belonged to two different communities. Such a thing had never happened earlier. It showed the extent of hatred towards persons belonging to other community which had entered even in the police department, though on a small scale yet.

Even children as young as two and five years old were not spared in the heinous communal carnage, a new phenomenon never heard of in any of the communal clashes that took place in Hyderabad since 1956. Again for the first time women too were killed in large numbers.

The doctors in the Osmania and Gandhi General Hospitals found it difficult to cope with the injured bodies being brought in every minute. On certain occasions lorries had to be pressed into service to pick up the injured struggling in pools of blood in lanes and bylanes. The number of people killed and injured as reported in the print media was mostly based on either the one given at official briefings or collected by the mediapersons from the hospitals. It is feared that some more were taken to certain private hospitals by the near kith and kin who refused to reveal for the safety of the remaining. Similarly, certain causes of death were also not made public in their own interests and and the last rites conducted the burial or cremation ceremonies according to their religious faiths without informing the officials.

As stated earlier, the alleged involvement of "dissident" Congressmen had to be construed putting several things together. The five-member team of the Congress (I) that came from Delhi at the instance of Rajiv Gandhi held discussions with a cross section of the partymen and others. During the discussions, a section of Congress (I) legislators, who were followers of Dr Chenna Reddy, told the delegation that a couple of Congress (I) legislators of the twin cities were also behind the riots and added fuel to the fire to discredit the leadership of Dr Chenna Reddy. Even the chief minister Dr Reddy told newsmen on one occasion that some people from Vijayawada had come into to the city to intensify the communal violence. Dr Reddy had in mind, when he said so, V. Ratna Kumari, MLA from Vijayawada proper. She is the widow V. Mohan Ranga, a Congress (I) MLA from Vijayawada who was brutally murdered by the TDP men when he was on fast unto death demanding protection from the government when TDP was ruling the state. She won the seat with a huge margin in 1989 elections on sympathy wave. She later joined the dissidents camp organised by Dr Rajasekhar Reddy, a young and rebellious leader and MP from Cuddapah in Rayalaseema.

This correspondent had the occasion to meet her later and asked her why she was disturbing the calm of the people of the state capital. Her reply was: "My life itself is in danger after my husband's death. You can see the number of securitymen in my jeep and in the one that follows. That apart, we don't know the lanes and bylanes of the old city. What business we have got to poke our nose in Hyderabad riots." She had her own problems in Vijayawada in terms of not only her safety but also to look after the safety of her followers there. Her involvement, directly or indirectly, as suggestively made by the chief minister Dr Chenna Reddy, was totally beyond anybody's imagination taking into consideration her own condition in Vijayawada city.

Some of the followers of Dr Reddy questioned the authority of Mr Chidambaram in ordering the civil and police authorities while ignoring the presence of the chief minister who was incharge of law and order. When mediapersons asked him during the course of the day how was he competent to instruct the police, expectedly he said that it was a big lie to say that he had given instructions to the police. The purpose of their visit to Hyderabad was only to assist the chief minister and to have a first hand information on the goings on, so as to brief the AICC (I) President, as asked by him.

The Congress (I) internal politics was introduced in the communal riots only on December 10, when the party high command had despatched the five member team. The chief minister did not even guide the team during their visit to the affected areas. Rather he was sore at their arrival.

Having told his followers to make a complaint against the dissidents when they met the high powered delegation, Dr Reddy even stooped to such a low level as to direct the Inspector General of Police (Intelligence) to brief the high command delegation, when asked by them, in favour of the dissidents' hand in the communal carnage. But to his "misfortune" the I.G. (intelligence) did not oblige the chief minister and told the delegation, when he was called, that he had no information to implicate any Congress leader in the communal riots.

The five-member delegation, after day-long discussion with partymen, police officials and others, went to Tarnaka to talk to the chief minister before leaving for Delhi. Dr Reddy had developed such a contempt towards the delegation that he told them: "Why are you in such a hurry to go to Delhi ? Why can't you wait for a couple of days more and maintain the law and order in Hyderabad ?". But Chidambaram curtly told Dr Reddy that their job was not to maintain law and order in

Hyderabad, but to give their own assessment to the party president Rajiv Gandhi.

This was the scenario at the time of the exit of Dr Chenna Reddy, who became the chief minister of the state for the second time.

One would naturally wonder how could Dr. N. Janardhan Reddy, who was sworn-in as chief minister on December 17, bring the situation under control within a week's time. There is every possibility for any intelligent person to jump to the conclusion that the dissident congressmen must be behind the riots at a later stage and withdrew from the field once. Dr Reddy was replaced. Though a certain element of truth in that assumption could not be ruled out, it would be farfetched to come to such a wild conclusion. The moment the new chief minister Janardhan Reddy took the oath of office and secrecy, he told the police point blank that there would be no political interference from his side in controlling the communal carnage. He had virtually given a free hand to the Director General of Police, R. Prabhakar Rao, who was also known for his integrity and efficiency, in dealing with the twin-problems faced by the state—the communal clashes in Hyderabad and the Naxalite menace in Telengana. Police did get the required support and encouragement from the political leadership of the state and put down effectively the unprecedented communal riots that were witnessed in the state capital for over two full months. The curfew was totally lifted in the entire city and it was lifted from Ranga Reddy district only on February 13, 1991, though day curfew was lifted in most parts of the city from December 16, onwards in a phased manner.

Former Prime Minister, Mr V.P. Singh, General Secretary of CPI (M) E.M.S. Namboodiripad, and the saffron clad National Front chairman N.T. Rama Rao tried their best to fish in troubled waters (or blood) by demanding the state Congress to get fresh mandate, as they lost control over the situation. The timely intervention of Rajiv Gandhi saved the state from total destruction.

The loss of valuable lives of men, women, youth and children and the destruction of property could have been saved to a large extent, had the political leadership of the state administration taken a firm stand to round up the BJP and MIM leaders in addition to known antisocial elements at the earliast stage, say in the first week of November, 1990, if not in the last week of October. Even though the wounds of the two-month-long communal carnage were healed, the scars would remain forever and the bitterness would continue between the two communities for a long time to come. Let us hope the happenings of October, November and December, 1990 would not recur in the 400-years-old city. This tragedy happened at the time when the 400th year was being celebrated by the people here.

14

Communal Riots in Delhi

Dinesh Chandra Varshney

15th October 1990 was the day when the BJP-Advani's Ram Rath Yatra passed through Delhi going through the walled city area. The Rath had the Lotus which is the election symbol of BJP on it. Approximately ten thousand people of which most of them of Bajrang Dal, VHP, and RSS cadre accompanying the Yatra. Bajrang Dal was in the forefront of the Yatra. Most of the above-mentioned participant organizations cadre had various type of weapons in their hands which included *tridents*, swords, knives, long *lathies*, *bhala* and some of them even were carrying two-barrelled gun. The Bajrang Dal cadre were having the maximum weapons. They were brandishing these weapons. Not only that, the slogans shouted in the rally were of very communal and provocative nature, and were meant more to create the panic, communal hatred and develop fear in the minds of the minority community than to serve the cause of the Bhagwan Ram who from every source of literature and history was tolerant as the god of welfare. Nowhere in any dream or in any practice and theory would have

Ram according to epics ever thought of or approved the following slogans:

Saugandh Ram Ki Khate hain, Mandir Wahhi Banayenge, Baccha Baccha Ram Ka-Janam Bhoomi Ke Kam Ka, Ram Lala Ham Ayenge-Mandir Wahi Banayenge, Musalman Ke Do Sthan Pakistan Ya Kabristan, Hindu Baccha Ram Ka-Musalman Baccha Haram Ka, Babar Ki Aulado Ko-Mar Bhageo Salon Ko, Hindu Jab Jab Jagega-Katua Sala Bhagega, Tel Lagao Dabar ka-Nam Mitao Babar Ka, Bharat Me Rehna Hoga-Bande Matram Kehna Hoga, Saugandh Ram Ki Khate hain-Masjid Hum Girayenge-Mandir Wahin Banayenge, Hindustan Me Rehna Hoga-Toh Hindu Hit Ko Kehna Hoga, Joh Hindu Hit Ki Baat Karega-Wahi Desh Pe Raj Karega, Hindu Sikh Bhai Bhai-Yeh Musalman Kom Kahan Se Ayee.

These slogans clearly indicate that this Rath Yatra for the construction of the Ram temple at disputed site was not for serving the cause of Ram nor to propagate his teachings. Basically BJP could understand very well that the Mandal Commission was going to erode its base and the seats in Parliament will be lost if something were not immediately done. The so-called Ram Janam Bhoomi problem was the best opportunity for them and they realised it in a very calculated manner that this type of Rath Yatra can defend its bases. That is why we find that these slogans are very much communal, vulgar and abusive against the one particular community to just create the Hindu vote bank as well as in long run to continue to develop its roots on the basis of communal politics; and increased its strong hold in politics.

Because of this communal nature of the Rath Yatra, it has created serious communal tension as well as riots in Delhi. When this rally was passing through the walled city, i.e. Chandni Chowk, its very first incident of violence was by a group of 30-40 participants of rally who attacked the Nayab Imam, Deputy Imam of the

Fatehpuri Masjid. First he was attacked by stones and then blows and finally he was attacked by *tridents*. Thanks to a chance which could save him because by chance the *trident* injury was not very deep. Around 7.45 to 8.00 pm he was coming out of the mosque after the *Namaz*. He was attacked at this time without any provocation. After inquiring about the rally or the Rath Yatra at various places in Delhi, many facts have come to light. As soon as the news of the attack on Nayab Imam spread to other areas of Delhi, riots broke out in Lal Kuan and Jama Masjid Chowk. Thanks to the efforts of seniors and senior leadership of the minority community could these riots be controlled immediately. Next day a complete *Bandh* was observed in the walled city, Okhla, Seemapuri, and also at Agra, Muradabad, etc. But one very serious fact has come to light that is that the Rath was empty from Town Hall to Khari Bawoli. Advani was not in it. He had travelled by a car from Town Hall to Khari Bawoli by the side of the Old Delhi Railway station. Why did he do is open to conjecture.

Had the organisers planned in advance the beating and stabbing of Nayab Imam at Fatehpuri Mosque. If yes, then was it approved by the leadership of the Rath Yatra. Definitely many more questions come into mind why the Rath travelled vacant only for this short distance.

Here the role of the police is also very dubious because the police as such did not act promptly to arrest the stabbers even after repeated indication by the Nayab Imam about the persons who had stabbed him. Why was the police not able to arrest the culprits even after the two reminders by the Nayab Imam to the DCP to cover the sensitive area. In no way can police claim to control the expected riots in the area after the stabbing of the Imam.

After talking to the persons belonging to the minority community in Ballimaran, Jama Masjid, Lal Kuan and some other areas of the walled city it became clear that most people did not object at all to the construction of Ram temple. They said that everyone of them had great respect for God Ram. Even their children do go and see Ramlila and Dussehra festivities. Hindus and Muslims greet each other on *Id* but it is the vested interests of some people in this city as well as in the country who flare up communal hatred so they can continue their vote politics. Both the Hindus and Muslims staying in these areas said that the slogans shouted in the Rath Yatra rally were filthy, abusive, communal and indecent and these types of slogans cannot be approved of by any senior person who cherishes national integration and communal amity in our country. No sincere person of the country or the world can approve these type of cheap slogans that too in a Rath Yatra which is supposed to serve the cause of Ram, the Ram who was a tolerant wellwisher of each and every citizen of his land.

cement, the politics was Mandalised. What happened in Patna is due to a section of Koeri population led by ex-legislator Ramdeo Matto of BJP along with RSS and VHP men who took greater interest in communal euphoria. But this time the backward caste people specially the Yadavs were apathetic and against it. Yadavs from Jalla area and Diara acted against communalism only because of reservation politics. These people also thought that if the communal orgy continued, the Laloo Yadav government would be overthrown. The role of the Bihar government and a few people in administration did play a positive role in fighting communalism. It must also be borne in mind that this time the anti-reservationists were all along sympathetic to communal people. The son of an ex-MLA Braj Kishore was beaten by Muslims so he wanted this feud to be turned into Hindu-Muslim riots but could not succeed in his plan.

Ranchi

Former Yadav leader Rajendra Roy had been with BJP but this time came forward for the defence of Muslims. Gulsan Azmani, BJP MLA left no stone unturned for this communal tension. He himself came forward but was pushed back by Muslims and Yadavs. Here CRP arrested only Muslims not the Hindus but the Ranchi SP and the DM were strict. It is noteworthy that Kande, Hatia and Khijari constituencies belonged to BJP. They all cooked several stories for the communal flare-up. In Hind Pirhi they succeeded in creating create some incidents but ultimately failed in their ugly design. Even Ramtahal Choudhary, the defeated BJP MLA, stood against BJP MLA Azmani. The reason of this action is obvious. BJP were divided sharply on reservation issue and ultimately this party was split. BJP MLA under the leadership of Samresh Singh and Inder Singh Namdhari formed a new party—Sampurna Kranti Dal (SKD). All this phenomena was the result of the Mandalisation of Bihar politics.

In Sitamarhi a riot like situation developed. Anti-reservationist forces acted for communal tension and planned to kill a few minority persons but due to Mandalised politics it could not succeed. Yadavs fully sided with minority community and riots stopped.

In Bhojpur, Piro is a small town. In this town there are altogether 50 shops of Muslim community. Nearby this town there is a village dominated by Bhumihars. During idol immersion procession tension developed between Bhumihars and Muslims. Bhumihars were driven back. Later Bhumihars wanted to mobilize all Hindus against Muslims but they could not succeed because not a single backward community people came forward. Yadavs told that they had no interest in their personal affairs. Thus we see here the riots could not take place due to the same reason.

In Amnour and Marhoura (Saran), Kurmis, *baniyas* and Muslims were united against, Bhumihars and Lumpen elements of Rajputs. In Bhagalpur there was constant feud between Marwaris and others, once Marwari *hatao* movement had started. Seeing this Marwaris communalized the Hindu masses for their own interest. They succeeded in increasing riots in towns and villages. Thousands of people were butchered and heavy loss of property were reported. Backward castes people were mainly utilized by Marwaris. But this time they failed because the backward people were for the implementation of Mandal Commission Report in toto.

Through all these examples it is obvious that this time Mandal Rath was very much successful in checking the Ram Rath of Advani saving the Bihar people from communal catastrophe.

Now it is a time for a constant vigil for communal peace and harmony. Anti-communal rallies, seminars, symposiums, etc, should be regularized to halt the communal carnage. But secularism in India has to make a distinction between religion and culture. Our culture is one while living in multistructural, multireligious, multilingual country. Religion is personal but culture is collective. The lives and literatures of saints and prophets are common cultural heritage of all Indians. Sufism makes us feel the composite cultural treasure of our land. Religion and state should be separated. The debate about religion and politics is not set today in proper perspective. The values of all religions are valid for individual. After the dawn of participatory democracy the relevant values have been incorporated in the Constitution and the civil and criminal codes. It is mutual respect for each other's religion that will bring about resolution of the contradiction of the communal conflict to some extent and undercut the base of the communal people. Violence will breed violence and hatred will breed more hatred. So let us put a stop to this in our mutual interests and in the interest of communal harmony and for national integration.

Then why VHP, BJP and RSS people are doing all these acts is the moot query ? Clearly political move for gaining votes in the coming election to the Lok Sabha and to help move forward towards the establishment of Hindu *rashtra*.

In January 86 an order from a court was manipulated for unlocking the disputed place and for unrestricted entry of Hindus for pooja and darshan. Lock was broken open within 40 minutes of the order. T.V. personnel had arrived in Ayodhya even before the formal order was passed for shooting and televising the unlocking. As planned the "Hindu victory" was telecast all over India that very evening. This was a clear-cut tampering of religious sentiments of Hindus which emboldened the communal forces. Later on *shila poojan* was allowed at disputed plot of land and this time Advani's *rath* was glorified by the T.V., the AIR, magazines and other mass media.

So in order to make secular India much more powerful, it is the responsibility of all patriotic people to delink religion from state and education from religion. For this we have to inculcate the scientific temper at least among the new generation.

16

Communal Danger Spreads to Assam

Phani Bohra

The Hindu-Muslim communal tension heightened by the Babri Masjid-Ram Janma Bhoomi controversy has travelled to every nook and corner of the Indian sub-continent. Even the land of blue hills and green valleys of the north eastern region of India which was known to be free from religious and communal tension was not spared. During the Ram Rath Yatra of the BJP leader, L.K. Advani to occupy the Babri Masjid and to start the construction of Ram Mandir, tension was running high throughout the country particularly in October, 1990. At the height of that rising tide of the communal tension, the sleepy district and the town (of the same name) of Hailakandi was suddenly set ablaze by communal fratricidal riots. Killing each other, burning of houses, looting of shops and other properties became the order of the day in Hailakandi, in Assam from 24th October, 1990. The communal carnage went on unabated.

Beginning with the puja rituals to purify bricks (*Ram Shila*) for *shilanyas* of Ayodhya, organized by the RSS, VHP and BJP, Hindu-Muslim tension began to rise wherever the two communities lived in considerable number. Had there been a campaign for building a Ram temple without reference to any demolition of the very old mosque Babri Masjid there would have been no cause of tension and in Assam the Hindus of all the religious sects and many Muslims would have joined the campaign for a Ram Mandir with enthusiasm. But instead of such an approach the RSS-BJP-VHP combine launched the campaign to demolish the Babri Masjid and to build the Ram Mandir and turned it into a communal fratricidal turmoil. During this campaign after having the government of Janata Dal at Delhi, dependent upon the BJP, it took full advantage to raise the communal tension to a high pitch. Widespread communal carnage that followed Advani's Rath Yatra took the toll of innumerable innocent human lives, destroyed homes and hearths, the peaceful and cordial relations among Hindus and Muslims were badly shaken everywhere and replaced by suspicion and fear against each other. Although both the communities suffered the same ordeal the Muslim minorities suffered the most. Advani's Rath Yatra, like Hanuman's tail with lighted fire blazed the Lankapuri of Ramayana went on spreading the communal fire all the way it passed through—from the historic Somnath temple in Gujarat to Ayodhya where Vishwa Hindu Parishad wants to build a Ram Mandir at the place where an old mosque known as Babri Masjid existed since the time of Babar, the founder of the Mughal dynasty in the early 16th century A.D.

No doubt that the popular response of the Hindus everywhere to Advani's Rath Yatra went surpassing the expectations of the organisers themselves as it was made up of the VHP, RSS and BJP. So wild was the enthusiasm to march to Ayodhya with more vigour and determination to destroy the mosque and build the temple that BJP also decided to withdraw its support to V.P. Singh-led minority National Front Government and precipitate general elections again.

In this background of national-communal-political tension the Hailakandi riot in Assam took place. The apparent cause that ignited the communal carnage was a plot of government land in Hailakandi town for long commonly used by all for all public functions including puja functions. Hindus recently demanded the said plot and started the permanent construction of a goddess Kali temple there. It is said that some RSS and BJP elements were behind the move. On 23rd October, 1990 Advani was arrested and tension mounted to a climax and call for Bharat Bandh was given. The same day the permanent construction of the Kali temple was also removed by police. It worked as a fuse to ignite the communal fire. Hindus became aggressive and Muslims who were opposed to the move of permanent settlement of the land to the Kali temple also did not lag far behind. The tension spread to the villages with heightening speed. Section 144 was promulgated but to no avail and subsequently curfew was clamped. But the large-scale disturbances could not be stopped. Arson and looting went on unabated. Police and administration practically collapsed. There were many more number of victims of riot than the number of rioters arrested. This speaks of the weaknesses of police administration.

Unfortunately or accidently the District Magistrate of Hailakandi at that time was a Muslim, and the Assam state government minister of AGP from Hailakandi was also a Muslim. This coincidence was fully exploited by the BJP. Venom was continuously spilled against the DM Abdul Malik and Minister Saidul Alam Chowdhury to incite the Hindus against the Muslims. Unfortunately they overlooked the fact of police and administrative failure and concentrated upon the individual Muslim officer and minister. This is the tactic of all communalists. But the fact remains that as everywhere in India riots are caused by the bureaucratic and police failures, because they are not less communal than the communalists. Immediately in a communal flare-up the local bureaucracy and police get communally divided and paralysed. The constant and consistent communal campaign carried on by the religious communalists and fundamentalists influences all belonging to both Hindu and Muslim followings. Communalism has become respectable amongst the bureaucracy, police and other intelligentia more and more because of the opportunists, power greedy political parties and groups who declare themselves as secular but ally themselves with communal political parties and also compromise on communal issues. Such collaborations and compromises with communal politics by the secular-democratic forces will surely and certainly help the growth of communalism, lead to religious nationalism and fascist chauvinism thus angering the Indian unity and integrity more seriously than at present. After all Hindus are 80 per cent in India and our people are deeply religious. Even a vague secularism that is preached by the secular democratic bourgeois parties are dubbed by BJP as appeasement of the Muslim minorities and the left parties views on communalism is interpreted by them as anti-religious. It is unfortunate that when communal polarisation is taking place with greater speed in this country embracing more people than ever before, the left, democratic, patriotic and secular forces are not putting up a strong resistance to communalism, because of narrow power politics and partisan opportunism. It must be stated here that it was the alliance or merger of former Jan Singh in Janata Party headed by Morarji Desai in 1977 and then all round seat adjustment between secular democratic socialist with left parties and national front led by Janata Dal during 1977 and 1989 which gave the best opportunity to BJP to emerge as a Hindu nationalist party. That is why the visit of BJP leaders like Kailash

Nath Misra, Burilal Sone and Purkayastha to the riot-torn Hailakandi in November, when prevented by the administration was resented by many otherwise well-meaning Hindus of Barak valley.

There are no two opinions that the communal riots that took place in October-November of 1990 were carefully rehearsed dramas enacted by the BJP in alliance with the VHP and RSS for a long time. There are two factors which came in handy to them. One is the fact that being on the border of Bangladesh, formerly known as East Pakistan, a Muslim country, millions of Hindu refugees and migrants were and are settled in Hailakandi, Karimganj and Silchar districts. These migrants are very susceptible to communal feelings because they are the victims of communal carnage in East Pakistan. Very few Muslims migrated to Pakistan or Bangladesh from Assam. Influx of migrants to Assam is a continuous phenomenon since 1947 till date. The original composition of population even in Barak valley including Hailakandi are badly affected. The linguistic, ethnic and religious identity crisis is felt by all groups of population. Interestingly the flow of both Hindus and Muslims from Bangladesh to Barak Valley of Assam is still continuing, the Assam agitation for 6 years against influx of foreign nationals and the Assam accord by Government of India and agitation leaders notwithstanding.

The growing apprehension of the Assamese that the unending influx of Bangladeshis to Assam will seriously undermine the demographic balance in the area; led to the prolonged Assam agitation. During that agitation the RSS and BJP while supporting the agitation, mixed up with the mass of the agitators, tried their utmost to turn it to an anti-Muslim movement, i.e. they introduced the communal colour into it. BJP clearly stated then that Hindus from Bangladesh cannot be foreigners and Muslims are the only foreigners and they alone should be prevented from coming and detected and deported from Assam. This communal divide succeeded to influence those who were the victims of Partition settled in Assam but not the indigenous people of Assam. The border areas adjoining Bangladesh, as stated above, were composed of mixed population. BJP's move since long has adversely affected the Hindu-Muslim relations here, more than elsewhere. BJP's propaganda based on the theory of transfer of population including transfer of some territory and redivision of the border also attracts some of the migrant Hindus near the border. Subsequent developments including the 91 election results conclusively proves that BJP's communal line has succeeded to divide the people and establish its base among the section of Bangladeshi Hindu migrants wherever they were settled in sizable number.

Assam is a land free from Hindu-Muslim conflicts throughout its history. Assam's Muslim minority population is very large; after Partition even when Bengal and Punjab were bleeding in communal riots and Jinnah was determined to add Assam into Pakistan yet Hindus and Muslims in Assam remained unitedly away from communal carnage. Only after Partition when lakhs of riot victims and refugees migrated to Assam some insignificant skirmishes and tensions between Hindus and Muslims were recorded. Assam however was never free from national and linguistic clashes between Assamese and Bengalees which is a different story.

As in the rest of India so also in Assam, the BJP in alliance with VHP, etc, is emerging as a recognised Hindu communal force. In Assam however, for the reasons stated above, they are mainly confined among the migrant sections of Bengali speaking Hindus especially in Barak Valley. They are trying to appear as a viable and responsible Hindu political force, as an alternative to the other left and democratic parties. The religious sentiments and feelings are fully roused by all fair and foul means. The Ram temple issue has been made the centre of rallying the Hindu masses.

The BJP being very insignificant force in Assam till the 1985 elections when they polled only 0.37 per cent votes has now consolidated its position came to occupy 3rd position with 9.63 per cent votes though mainly in Barak valley this being a danger signal for all secular-democratic forces of Assam and the outer north eastern region. It should be noted that Assam is a state where the percentage of the Muslim minority population is the highest in India after Kashmir, bordering a Muslim country, i.e. Bangladesh. There are three Christian majority states around Assam and there is a acute ethnic problem within the state. Aggressive Hindu communalism and chauvinism in Assam therefore is a grave threat to the traditional communal harmony and amity among the people and may create disastrous consequences to the region.

The alliance of BJP, VHP, Shiv Sena combine may bring unprecedented catastrophe to this land of Rama, Krishna, Buddha and Mahatma Gandhi by their policy of communal divide from top to the bottom level of Indian society. They are trying to divide every town, *mohalla* and every village on religious lines. Where there are no valid reasons why Indian society built by thousands of years of long tradition, a composite culture and pluralistic society, brought into being by great thinkers, reformers, and humanist rulers based on tolerance, co-existence, mutual respect and a cooperative common-wealth of India, should be disturbed and destroyed by religious communalism and linguistic or regional separatism.

By and large, longstanding communal harmony in Assam among the Hindus and Muslims is a historically established fact. It may be because the composition of the population, evolution of the Assamese society from the assimilation of various tribal communities without any strong influence of any religious fundamentalism and casteism. The Aryans, Mongols and Dravidians, etc, who migrated got assimilated in that society. Even the Middle-Age Hindu caste system had very little impact in the Assamese society. So also the Muslim migrants, the Pathans and Mughals by and large got assimilated in the Assamese way of life and they only maintained the religious identity. Secondly, Assamese Hindu society being moulded by the fifteenth century reformers like Shri Sankar Dev who preached Bhakti cult in the form of Vaishnavism, had a very strong positive influence over them to respect and tolerate other ways of worshipping God. Sufism among the Muslims was preached at the same time. It might have had a positive impact on maintaining communal harmony in this part of the country, until the advent of extreme Hindu chauvinism into this territory.

In the recent past, after the partition of India and with the present persistent and organized effort of the parties like BJP with their philosophy of 'Hindutva' has been able to rouse the feelings and passions of a large section of Hindus in the context of Ram Janmabhoomi issue and has no doubt vitiated the atmosphere of tolerance and amity.

Another factor which may have contributed to the Hindu-Muslim clashes in Hailakandi the other day is, as a result of continuous migration from Bangladesh. With BJP's the encouragement to Hindu migration as against the Muslims, the tensions between the indigenous and new migrants had already increased. At Hailakandi and its neighbourhood, the indigenous people are mostly Muslims settled there from long and new migrants, majority of whom are Hindus and that explains the cause of increasing tension although the Hindus and Muslims are of the same ethnic origin. Moreover, Muslim peasants are not generally averse to Assamese language and culture so most of them enthusiastically organised the Assamese literary conference at Hailakandi town some years ago and sections of Hindu Bengalese did not take it very kindly and it also became a source of psychological conflict.

BJP is talking of establishing Hindu Raj based on *Hindutva* the meaning of which they alone know. In a democracy, the majority rules, which is nothing new. But it is not a religious majority but a political majority. This sort of society nowhere in the world will go back to religious rule especially not so the Indian society. True, the 80 per cent of Hindus constitute the overwhelming majority of Indian population but there are Vaishnavites, Shaivites, Jains, Buddhists and Aminis worshippers besides the Muslims and Christians, i.e. non-Hindus who constitute 20 per cent. Moreover there are so many castes and ethnic differences in Indian society. Further whatever is the total percentage of non-Hindus, they are above 170 millions whom no political or social movement can afford to ignore.

The spectacular growth of BJP in communal politics is because of the opportunist political practices pursued by the different secular democratic forces in their greed for power. So when all these years of recent past the BJP, RSS, Shiv Sena and VHP went to taking on an offensive to rouse communalism and use it as their main political weapon to capture power, it went unchallenged. Similarly the Muslim fundamentalist also went ahead during the same period to help each other. The mass of the people were disappointed, the intelligentia were confused in the absence of a strong united principale political ideological struggle against communal offensive. As a result the BJP could take advantage to broaden their base.

The growth of communalism, particularly the majority communalism in India is a grave threat to itself. After all, if fascism comes to India, it.can only be through Hindu chauvinism. Such a danger has to be nipped in the bud by the combined forces of secular democratic and patriotic forces belonging to all religions, castes and ethnic origins. Secular damocracy does not and should not mean any discrimination against any religion. It must protect all rights of all faiths irrespective of majority or minority religious communities in India. Only on the basis of equality of all faiths, mutual tolerance and mutual respect to each other can all faiths live in peace and march forward together to prosperity.

17

Her Master's Communal Voice, on Audio

Kuldeep Kumar

Courtesy, The Times of India, 24 Nov., 1990

Two audio cassettes containing material propaganda are being openly sold in the Capital's music shops with the police blissfully unaware of their existence.

One of them, which blares out Hindu chauvinistic speeches inciting violence against Muslims, was brought out clandestinely some time before the October 30, 1990 incidents in Ayodhya. The jacket on this cassette shows Lord Ram with his bow and arrow and bears the following inscription: "Ramjanambhoomi, 'Jai Shri Ram', Bharat Mata Ki Jai." There is no clue as to who has manufactured this cassette and whose speeches it contains. This should *prima facie* make this an illegal entity.

However, the police does not seem to be even aware of the existence of any such cassette. When contacted, the deputy commissioner of police (crime), R. Tiwari, pleaded ignorance and so did the additional

Ccmmissioner of police, K.K. Paul.

The second cassette has been legally brought out but this fact alone does not mitigate the impact of its explosive, communal content. Narendra Chanchal, the star of all-night Bhagwati Jagarans who was catapulted into national fame with his song in Raj Kapoor's film *Bobby*, has packed it with his incendiary musical tribute to the "martyrs of Ayodhya."

The jacket of this cassette too depicts Lord Ram, armed with his bow and arrow, standing over the proposed temple. *Mandir Wahin Banayenge*. (We shall build the temple on the very spot) is the title and refrain of this cassette.

Vitriolic Tirade: The first cassette which has been produced illegally, begins with cries of *Bharat Mata Ki Jai* and *Har Har Mahadev*. Apparently, this cassette is a recording of a meeting held somewhere in Jagadhari town in Haryana because an anonymous male voice, while addressing, the gathering, specifically mentions *Jagadhari ke Rambhakton* (Ram worshippers of Jagadhari). Immediately after this, a female voice takes over with a vitriolic tirade against Muslims and all secular Hindus.

As this meeting in Jagadhari took place before the October 30 deadline, the woman speaker exhorts those present to sacrifice their lives for the cause of building the Ram temple on the very site where the Babri Masjid stands.

The woman speaker digresses into poetry in her message to Rambhakts, asking them to follow the example set by Hanuman, the supreme devotee of Ram. She explains: *Hanuman ne banayee jab raakh sarva Lanka, to Ramjanambhoomi ko kya soch aur shanka. Ho Ram ka mukhalif, aur Bharatiya bhi ho, sambhav nahin kabhi bhi, kah do bajake danka.* (When Hanuman could reduce Lanka to ashes, then what can come in the way of constructing the Ramjanambhoomi temple? Announce to the whole world without fear that whosoever opposes

Ram cannot be considered an Indian).

Ominous Call: Having repeatedly told the audience that for the past four years, Hindus have been discriminated against in their own country and have suffered untold miseries and injustices, the woman recites a longish poem which ends with an ominous call: *Jo hamari roti matribhoomi ko sukoon de, aur deshdrohiyon ko goliyon se bhoon de, aise sarfarosh ka hamen prakash chahiye, desh ke liye hamen Patel ya Subhash chahiya.* (We need people like Patel or Subhash who are willing to sacrifice their lives for the motherland, who can wipe away her tears and who can gun down the traitors).

The female speaker extolls people like Rahim and Raskhan who "looked for the dust from Ram's feet in the dust of this land" and castigates those Muslims who instead of identifying themselves with Rahim and Raskhan, have a sense of belonging with Babar.

Then suddenly, the voice assumes menacingly threatening overtones declaring that *Babri auladon ko ab hum Bardasht nahin karenge* (we shall no longer tolerate the progeny of Babar). This brings to mind the slogan written on the walls of Ayodhya by the Bajrang Dal in 1986: *Babar ki santanon se, khoon ki holi khelenge.*

The plan of the Vishwa Hindu Parishad (VHP) for October 30 becomes amply clear when the speaker praises the PAC (Armed peoples Constabulary) for being avowedly pro-Hindu. Not only that, she gives out an ominous warning : *Jab ek-ek Ali ki chhati par das-das Bajrangbali chade honge, tab pata chal jayega ki yeh sthan Ramjanambhoomi hai ya Babri Masjid. Tab pata chal jayega ki yeh desh Prabhu Ram ka hai.* (when 10 Bajrangbali, i.e. members of the Bajrang Dal will sit on the chest of an Ali, i.e., a Muslim, then it will be decided whether the place is Ramjanambhoomi or Babri Masjid).

Call for Bloodbath: The female speaker lambasts those Hindus who are afraid of a bloodbath in Ayodhya, asking them for how long they could avoid it. And then, she gives a call for precisely this: *Aao sab mil chalen Ram ka mandir banane ko, khoon kharaba hota hai to ek bar ho jane do. . . Samjh na paye baaton se ab laaton se samjhne do, khoon kharaba hota hai to ek bar jane do.* (Let us all go to build a magnificent Ram temple and if there is bloodbath, let it take place once and for all. Since others are refusing to understand, let us kick them and then they will understand. Don't worry if a bloodbath takes place).

She also incites those devotees who are ever willing to sacrifice their lives for the cause of the Ram temple, saying that before laying down their lives, they should first kill thousands of others who oppose it. The fiery orator warns the Hindus that October 30 will decide whether they or the Muslims will live in this country. Not only that, she informs them that on this magic date, the starting of the *kar seva* would in reality mean laying the foundation of a Hindu Rashtra.

Who is this female speaker, full of venom and hatred? Those who have met the BJP MP, Uma Bharati, or have heard her address meetings believe it is her. When this correspondent contacted Bharati, she said the cassette contained more or less her speech but somehow, another voice similar to that of hers had been mixed at a few places, mainly where explicit abuses have been used. "You," she said, "know this is how I speak and the speech is more or less mine."

The CPM has demanded the arrest of Uma Bharati for whipping up communal hatred and seizure of these cassettes. However, so far, the administration has failed to act on it. This is quite surprising considering the occurrence of communal violence in the walled city. These cassettes are easily available in bulk at the Lala Lajpat Rai market and from reputed music shops all over the city. Also, there is no reason to believe that their sale or distribution is only confined to the Capital.

18

Communal Riots in Varanasi

Yogesh Vajpayee

Courtesy The Times of India, 16 Dec, 1990

The looms that wove the famous Banarasi saris for centuries have fallen silent. Communal riots have devastated Sarai Nandan, Sarai Surjan and the nearby localities and villages south-west of the city.

Silver-haired men, whose nimble fingers produced the zari work, stare vacantly at the devastation around and ponder: "Is this the same city where Hindus and Muslims vied with one other to claim the secular heritage of Saint Kabir ?"

Women were burnt alive. Those trying to flee were clubbed and hacked to death. And those who managed to reach the police were beaten up and put behind bars.

"It was a nightmare," mumbles Mohammed Yaseen, a 52-year-old weaver of Sarai Nandan, shaking his head in disbelief. This reporter met him in jail, where he is lodged with his two sons.

It was 10.30 am on May 21 when Yaseen saw an armed mob approaching his lane. He hurriedly locked the door from inside and went to the roof. The mob had by this time started bludgeoning the door with axes and iron rods. Yaseen was relieved to spot a contingent of the police and PAC in the rear area and jumped down with his two sons. He was hoping to summon courage to save the womenfolk trapped inside.

The sub-inspector and his men, however, appeared deaf to his pleas. "They caught hold of us and started dragging us to a police van, showering lathi blows on us all along," he recalled. Mercifully he was spared of witnessing the plight of the women.

But others did. According to Akeela, Yaseen's 10-year-old daughter, the miscreants started smashing everything in sight as soon as they entered.

Set Ablaze: A group, meanwhile rushed to the roof where her mother Sitara, sister Shakeela and sister-in-law Sayeda were huddled in a corner. They were attacked with choppers and lathis. As Shakeela and Sayeda fell down unconscious, they were set ablaze.

A profusely bleeding Sitara Devi, with a hand chopped off, tried to flee but collapsed. She was rushed to the hospital where she died of her injuries two days later.

"What pains me is that this barbarism was inflicted by people we know... Young men who called my wife chachi and my daughter didi...," he sighs.

Similar tales were heard in Bajardeeh, Deopokhari anu Jokha village on the outskirts of the city. Whatever the rioters spared was ravaged by the police and the PAC men.

In Bajardeeh and neighbouring areas, inhabited primarily by weavers, violence erupted when a PAC officer started beating a social worker, Khaleel, who was trying to sooth frayed tempers. Scores of houses were damaged and set ablaze.

A 70-year-old weaver, Abdul Waheed, was sitting before his house in Jokkha village when a group of PAC jawans pounced on him and started battering him. Waheed died on May 21 and was hurriedly buried. Even his famiy members were not allowed to see the body. Not a single loom in this weavers' village was intact when this reporter visited the place.

Traders Worried: Although Varanasi has witnessed communal riots earlier, Bajreeh and adjoining areas had remained unaffected, says Ram Chandar, a silk merchant in Dashaswamegh Ghat, "However, last week's incidents may prove traumatic for traders," he fears.

Apart from the active role of the police, an almost total disruption of Hindu-Muslim relations seems to be the novel feature this time. However, more sinister is the fact that the riots were deliberately provoked, if not engineered, by people for short-term electoral gains.

Benia Bagh, site of a stormy BJP meeting, has lower middle-class Muslim households on three sides which makes it a communally sensitive place. A section of district officials feel that Mr S.C. Dixit, himself a seasoned police officer, should have known better than to insist on holding a meeting there. The trouble, according to them, erupted when provocative slogans at the meeting were answered by brickbatting from rooftops.

Mr Dixit does not agree. "If Mr Chandra Shekhar and Mr Rajiv Gandhi can hold a meeting at Benia Bagh, why can't I?" he asks.

The speed with which trouble escalated within an hour or so in areas under four police stations, with reports of bombings, arson and stabbings, showed how deep the roots of suspicion have spread.

Curfew Relaxed: Parts of the city were under curfew when it went to the polls on May 20. Although the authorities had formally relaxed curfew, trouble broke out in Jaitpura, Madanpura, Jangambari, Pittarkunda,

Lallpaura, Gauriganj and Shivala. One person was killed and over 50 injured. The next day proved worse with violence enveloping new areas.

Varanasi would have continued to burn but for the assassination of Mr Rajiv Gandhi which benumbed the city.

19

Religious Frenzy in Gujarat

Gautam Mehta

Courtesy, The Times of India, 16 Dec. 1990

The communal violence that rocked Ahmedabad and Baroda had no overt linkage between the second round of the VHP-sponsored *kar seva* at Ayodhya. The spell of violencc had already taken a toll of 27 lives.

Officials maintain that the current riots are no different from previous riots. But the violence spread to new areas this time and has also taken on a new form. Also, the myth that bootleggers and antisocial elements are responsible for the violence no longer holds good. The religious factor has emerged as a new, important cause that sustains the riots. For the first time, places of worship are becoming targets of violence.

The mass participation by members of both the communities in street violence is also a new aspect and is apparently fomented by the Ram Janambhoomi-Babri Masjid issue and was allegedly given an impetus by the BJP which has a score to settle with the chief minister, Mr Chimanbhai Patel.

The new phenomenon of pitched battles between members of the two communities, coupled with the political uncertainty in the state, has rendered the police force helpless. Unable to even gauge the gravity of a developing situation at the outset, the police repeatedly reached too late or with inadequate personnel.

Ineffective Police: Also the communal and disruptive forces themselves have realised that the police force, crippled by internal bickerings, is unable to prevent the spread of violence and therefore the government has to frequently call upon "the big brother", the Army, to restore law and order. This has on the one hand, demoralized the police force and on the other, strengthened the people's poor opinion of the police; thereby emboldening mischief-makers. As a result the frequent flag marches and deployment of the Army do not have the desired effect.

In the past, communal violence was confined to the urban and semi-urban centres. However, after October 24, as many as 18 towns in various parts of the state had to be placed under indefinite curfew.

Violence in the tribal belts of Banaskantha, Panchmahal and South Gujarat is also a new development that has baffled the government and the police. Though the administration realizes that these riots have not been caused by the traditional scapegoat—bootleggers, it has not yet taken cognizance of the slow but systematic penetration by Hindu organizations into the tribal and rural areas. Tribals attacking Muslim houses and forcing their families to flee may also have roots in the socio-political exploitation of the adivasis. But the immediate expression of their antagonism to the minority community has essentially been aroused through a subtle creation of Hindu consciousness among the tribals.

Women's Role: Equally surprising is the fact that women are no longer spared. Since October 24, the casualty list shows a significant rise in the number of school-going girls and women stabbed to death in Ahmedabad and other parts of the state. Cases of women committing violence is also a new development. The police have also come across many cases of women carrying sharp-edged weapons for their protection.

A definite element of organization is also discernible this time even if violence sparks off spontaneously. The large amount of acid bulbs, rag bundles, kerosene and explosive material used in street fights suggests that members of both communities were prepared for any eventuality even as intelligence officials remained in the dark.

The use of private firearms as well as the frightening phenomenon of masked scooterists opening indiscriminate fire in crowded places would suggest that it is a new game in Gujarat.

Finally, the two rounds of violence here brought about some new equations within the Hindu community. While the 1985 riots saw the backward classes combining with the minority group in view of the anti-reservation agitation, this time the Harjans and the other backward clases have joined forces with the mainstream Hindu community. Contrary to the belief that the Mandal controversy would deepen the chasm between high-caste Hindus and the lower classes, they seemed to have come together. But the backward classes became victims of communal frenzy in the predominantly labour areas of Bapunagar, Gomtipur, Behrampura and Saraspur in Ahmedabad.

20

Yawning Communal Chasm in Kanpur

Yogesh Vajpeyee

Courtesy Times of India, 28 May, 1990

"What the hell are you officers doing? We are being overrun, will you....come only after we are lynched?" The wireless set in the police control room here crackled. The men in the room looked at each other, fidgeting uncomfortably in their chairs, as more abuses were hurled through the set.

The shrill cries for help came from the beleagured policemen of Purva outpost in the riot-hit city. The new "acting" superintendent of police, Javed Akhtar, had been asked to take charge only two days ago and didn't know whom he was working with or even the names of Kanpur's roads. (The Kanpur SP, Arun Kumar, was earlier sent on forced leave on poll eve because he was "unsuitable" to the powers that be). The PAC had been taken off the curfew-bound areas on the orders of a senior police officer, known for his proximity to the UP chief minister, who constantly kept breathing down the neck of the Kanpur SSP, Subhash Joshi.

Chaos and a shattered morale characterized the efforts of the security forces to contain communal violence here, which took a toll of 23 lives in the first three days since the sparks became a fullfledged fire on May 19. Only the numbing news of Mr Rajiv Gandhi's assassination could stop the rioting.

It was the third outbreak of communal frenzy in this industrial city in the last one year. The first outbreak in April last year was essentially a clash between two mafia dons trying to establish their foothold in politics by communalizing the incident. All the six dead fell to bullets from policemen trying to contain them.

The riot that broke out earlier did have its origins in communal hatred. But in essence, it was an outburst of the minority community's anger with the police, specialy the PAC. Few cases of Hindus killing Muslims or vice versa were reported and the majority of the 24 victims fell to police bullets.

Well Planned: The uncontrollable violence that engulfed the city on May 19, however seemed to have been carefully planned and politically motivated. It started with aggressive BJP stormtroopers taking out an election procession in Muslim-dominated Lakkarmandi area and hurling abuses at the community. Some Muslim youths retaliated with a vengeance. Four persons were killed on the first night itself.

Next morning the city appeared quiet though tense. But rioting started again in the evening coinciding with the BJP protest starting in Navin Market, which faces the Parade area heavily populated by Muslims. Rioting soon spread to almost every part of the city's central business district and continued unabated till the Army was asked to move in on the evening of May 21.

Communal passions ran high among sections of both the communities. A Hindu shopkeeper was dragged out of a police jeep and lynched. A young Muslim bride was kidnapped and brutally murdered.

With the exception of three persons killed in police firing, all the deaths were due to stabbing, close-range shooting or burning. The police could not attribute any of the killings to personal motives. In most cases the police either did not reach the trouble spot or was too late.

Nobody disputed that the riots were triggered by the BJP stormtroopers' brashness. Senior BJP leaders sadly conceded that they had no control over the "young blood", meaning the new recruits to the "Ram Kaaj" (Ram's cause) drawn from the lumpen lot, seeking social legitimacy in the name of religion.

But the BJP's opponents also played their part in whipping up troubles. The SJP candidate for the Kanpur Lok Sabha seat, Ms Tasleem Ashraf, was mobbed and assaulted by members of her own community on the first day. Not to be left out, the CPM outgoing MP, Ms Subhashini Ali, lost no time in claiming that she was the real victim of the BJP hooligans and pointed to a partially burnt CPM office, allegedly damaged by BJP men to prove her point.

Divided City: Today, the city of Maulana Hasrat Mohani and Ganesh Shankar Vidyarthi, which kept aloof even during the post-Partition communal savagery, appears almost totally polarized along communal lines. "Not even in 1931, when the late Ganesh Shankar Vidyarthi was killed, did passions run so high and suspicion was so deep-rooted", says Nawabzada Kaari, a 70-year-old Muslim scholar. "Today's politicians appear to have succeeded where the British had failed. They have divided the people of Kanpur," concurs Dr S.S. Awasthi, an eminent historian at Kanpur University.

A century ago, when the first riots broke out here on April 11, 1890, to protest against the imposition of quarantine regulations by the British, Kokila Kumhar, a Hindu, and Akram Ilahi, a Muslim, were hanged from the same tree. The second major riots in Kanpur in August 1913 were also directed against the British government. The Khilafat-Congress alliance of the twenties cemented communal ties.

The two communities started drifting apart when Hindu revivalist organizations like the Arya Samaj with the stress on *shuddhi* (Conversion) and *Sangathan* (organization), the Hindu Mahasabha, Katha Mandal, and Mahabir Dal, became active. The Muslims reacted by forming organizations like Tabligh-ul-Islam, Anjuman-Hifazat-ul-Islam and Tanzeem committees. The 1931 riots, in which 400 people, including Vidyarthi, were killed represented the bitter harvest of this crop.

The events of the last years—the emergence of the VHP and the Bajrang Dal on the one hand, and the Babri-Masjid Action Committee and other Muslim militant organizations on the other—reveal a replay of the thirties. With the BJP ready to respond to L.K. Advani's call "to go all out for the kill", the stakes this time are higher.

A comparative analysis of Kanpur's last three communal riots gives a hint of the dangers ahead. The April 1990 riots were confined to a four-sq km area involving no direct assault by one community against members of the other. Political activity was restrained.

The December, 1990 riots were widespread. The epicentre of the trouble, however, was in Beconganj-Chamanganj localities.

With the lifting of the day curfew a day before, Kanpur appeared quiet on the surface. But underneath, lava was smouldering, threatening to erupt any time.

21

A Veil of Fear

Kumkum Chadha

Courtesy Hindustan Times, 1 September, 1991

New Delhi: it is well past midnight. Heavy rains have virtually marred visibility. A group of young boys - presumably rough-necks are all set to make a fast buck on the road between Garh and Meerut in Uttar Pradesh. Till wherever one can possibly see, the area is heavily waterlogged. A car can only swim through with water literally drowning more than half of it. They demand a price to get you out after which they suggest an alternative route which means a detour to a lonely stretch. Here another group awaits you. Fortunately help comes in the form of villagers who offer shelters "You are not one of us," they tell this correspondent, "therefore it would be better for you to stay with people of your own community. *Kya Karen ab yahi waqt aa gaya hai . . .*" (what to do? The times are such). Anwar Mia's words have a tinge of sadness. While we were being escorted to the place they considered "better" for us, the trauma of the incident was replaced by an uncomfortable question: Is history threatening to repeat the bloody saga of an irrepairable human divide? Are we on the threshold of the times Anwar Mia spoke of ?

Lamakhera is virtually deserted. A sizeable section of its population comprising a particular community has been driven out by dominant section. They were terrorized, beaten and forced to leave their homes and fields. Their houses were burnt and their belongings looted. Today with absolutely nothing they seek shelter in areas where their community outnumbers the rest.

It all began in June 1990 when lathi-weilding men allegedly prevented them from casting their votes. Later, the same evening they reportedly broke into their houses, beat them up, manhandled their women and looted whatever they could. *Ab tum kuch aur din ke mehmaan ho. Ab raaj hamara hai* . . . (Now you have only a few days. Now it is our reign) they had chorussed. They were given an ultimatum: Stay and die or leave and live. A deadline was set: Before the crack of dawn.

Fear drove them out. As also experience. For in the past they had borne the ire of dominant groups. Nabi Ahmed had suffered it by way of broken leg while Nanha had deep scars which silently told the tale of the numbers games "*Ham log Kya Kar sakte hain? Ham thore woh ziyada* . . . (what can we do? we are a handful, they are in a majority). It is this more than anything else which not only intensifies the feeling of insecurity but also makes them surrender completely. The suggestion of consolidating themselves to meet the challenge is expectedly scoffed at. But not without reason. For they have learnt and learnt it the hard way that confrontation means communal violence and communal violence means a bloodbath; A bloodbath where the odds heavily weighed against them; a bloodbath where the PAC plays a controversial role.

Tensions, they told us, had always existed. As also the assertions of dominant groups who appeared from time to time to extract their pound of flesh as it were. "But earlier," says Aftab, "it was different." Takes over Ahmed: "*Pahle baat murgi aur anaj par khatam ho jaati thi. Ab to ghar par charai ker di to hame bhagna hi paraa . . .kahte hai woh kaho . . .*" (Earlier they used to settle with livestock and grains. Now, they invaded our houses so we had to escape. They want us to say that). Chides Akhtar Ali : "*Woh Kya . . . saaf kaho kya kahte hain . . .Jee kahte hain Jai Siya Ram bolo . . .*" (What that? Tell them frankly. . . they ask us to say Jai siya Ram). Adds Mehdi: "(*Babar ko gaali dete hain . . .*" (They abuse Babar). Akhtar Ali's cue was all that was needed to give expression to suppressed emotion. With strong words. After which they stopped at nothing. The "accused" vary from village goons to the powers that be. From the local constable to the district administration. And from the state chief to the politics at the Centre. The crux being : Religious fervour has unleashed a reign of tyranny; it has encouraged criminals to get the better of minority groups; it has sent a message, through its political workers to either speak their language or quit.

The state government is attributed the same sentiment which is interpreted as a dangerous signal encouraging both communal and criminal elements. The district administration, as also the local police, is oblivious of the large-scale evacuation; they privately admit that they are helpless. Concludes Mehdi: "It is true that after the BJP came to power at the state the local administration as also the goons feel it a free for all. If the state government is not party to all this, why doesn't it do something to stop this reign of terror? why do they allow police atrocities?" Why aren't our cases registered? What are they doing about the evacuation?" Not the one to mince words Mehdi frankly says: *Jai siya Ram legaya hamara gaon ko dooba kar . . .*" (the Jai siya Ram slogan has taken its toll).

Lamakhera, about 30 kms from Bareilly, is only one

of the several villages in the area where the communal divide has taken its toll. And resulted in evacuation of a particular community. With the local administration seemingly oblivious. Perhaps partisan.

In Sainthal a particular community is consolidating itself. This is one of the few areas where an otherwise minority community is in majority.

The disputed site is a graveyard which has witnessed communal tension from time to time, including the one in 1988 when there was a move to fence the area and separate it from the Harijan colony alongside. There was a furore and allegations of a land grab with the idea being finally shelved.

The site has once again come into focus with a Harijan, Banke Lal, reportedly finding a statue at the graveyard and handling it over to a local resident, Krishna Swaroop Gupta, who is known to be one who has historical records and documents in his possession. It is to the same person that a research scholar Prem Bhatia, who is doing his doctorate, had come for the District Gazetteer 1911.

According to Gupta he made the records available which included a documentary evidence of an idol found and a suggestion therein that if the area was dug up maybe more idols could be traced. With Banke Lal's "discovery"a new dimension has been added to the whole episode with stories circulating that the statues have been found in the graveyard and there are possibilities of there being some more. There are also reported statements of Professor Udey Prakash Arora, Department of Ancient History Rohilkhand University, wherein he has said that the 200 acre expanse of land (of which interestingly the graveyard is a part) could possibly have idols of gods and goddesses, if proper excavtions are carried out. According to Professor Arora, who this correspondent was unable to meet, Sainthal is one of the historic towns of ancient India and the possibility of idols and statues in this area is not ruled out. Krishna Swaroop Gupta has also been quoted as having suggested a search for the statues, something which he vehemently denies: "I only made the documents available for research and simply handed over the idol which Banke Lal gave me to Professor Gupta", he said in a desperate attempt to simplify his role in what has now become a communal controversy.

For those whom the graveyard has an emotional significance see a well-chalked out design in this. As Kazi Zuber Ahmed explained: "This is where our forefathers rest. Can we allow anyone to come near this spot leave alone digging it up on the pretext of finding imaginary idols and statues? But this is what the other side is aiming at. They want to whip up euphoria so that our blood boils and then give it a colour of a communal conflict. *Pahle suar aur gaiy par phasad hota tha ab Masjid Yah Kabristaano par . . .*" (Earlier communal conflicts were a consequence of conflicts over pigs and cows now they are over mosques and graveyards). Elaborated Bilal Zaidi : "The whole purpose is to drive us out: Terrorise our community where they are outnumbered and create problems where they are consolidated. In Sainthal we are a force therefore they cannot confront us. Hence they want to create a situation which would prompt the district administration to deploy the PAC which would do what they would have liked to, were they in sufficient numbers . . . . They want to keep the controversy alive with one issue or the other till the by-elections." Election in Nawabganj assembly segment, of which Sainthal is a part, were countermanded following the death of an independent candidate.

Yet a common *baithak* remains : where the people of both communities sit together. Transcending narrow communal considerations. Here the need for co-existence is the prime concern - a concern which has more often than not fallen prey to political manoeuvres. "Respective vote banks", they call them, "which swell at the cost of our lives. And blood". Nayaab Hussain blames the political parties, fervently supported by Surendra. "It is essentially a political battle - one party pitched against the other to garner votes of respective communities and then give it the necessary communal colour." Akhmal Hussain Zaidi takes over : "What makes things worse is that our community is feeling insecure. An insecurity which has intensified and which brings with it the fear of being overpowered. And uprooted." Adds Virendra Kumar : "These may be illusions, but they exist". Everyone there agrees, as also admits, of the collective failure in not being able to create confidence between the two communities. They also realize - a little disheartened- that the political vested interests - and parties - will get the better of them : "They will not let us remove suspicion or sink our differences lest it upsets the vote bank."

The three scenes - though different - have a common thread : they narrate a tale of mutual suspicion; as also the fact that politics has played a dirty role to which the normally placid have fallen prey: often victim of communal and religious frenzy: a frenzy which no longer is on the surface. And a frenzy which is threatening our national fabric. The scenes, though for the moment, confined to a few areas, seem slated for encores despite the common *baithaks*.

22

Communal Riots after Destruction of Babri Masjid

N.L.Gupta

H.V. Seshadri on November 11, 1990 said that the Muslim community should take on a new line of thinking *vis-a-vis* national issues. It is high time they guard themselves against power brokers, who have been using them as power. They should now come forward to gracefully accept the reality that their real interests lie in relying upon the traditional goodwill of Hindus towards all religious groups and win their love and confidence. He said that October 30, 1990 had repeated an invincible spirit of confidence in Hindus. He goes that the Hindus will have to gird up their loins, keep their flame of determination and dedication ever bright and press forward till their final victory is achieved. It is this path advocated by Seshadri that resulted in the destruction and demolition of Babri Masjid.

He further said on November 18, 1990 that it is

Hindu society alone which can guarantee their (Muslim) safety. Governments could come and go, they could not assure them of their safety.

L.K. Advani said on November 19, 1990 in Faizabad that neither the military force nor the Government could guarantee the security of Muslims. They would be secure only in a Hindu society and a "Hindu Raj" On January 19, 1991 he further said "I hold Nehruvian perspective responsible for the fact that even after partition the Muslims of the country have not been integrated into the national mainstream." Atal Bihari Vajpayee on 10th February, 1991 said that majority of Muslims do not feel to be Indian culturally, they keep harping on their Islamic culture and refuse to join the mainstream.

Seshadri on February 3, 1991 said that the minority rights which were originally conceived for protecting the religious rights of non-Hindu groups have thus turned political and destructive of national integrity and ethos all under the protective comings of present day 'secularists' His hoisting the flag on Babri Masjid proved to be a Supreme symbol of success of the October 30 Plan. Government arrangements crumbled down before the "do and die", onslaught of the Kar sevaks; that the despotic *'Raj Shakti'* has eaten dust before the "patriotic" Jan Shakti. He further described the October 30 achievement as a struggle between those who consider themselves as Babar's progeny and those who feel proud of calling themselves the descendants of Sri Ram.

Daleep Padgaonkar of *Times of India* said Rath Yatra left in its trail much bitterness and bloodshed. The culmination of this itinerant carnival of hate and prejudice was the storming of the Babri Masjid and the planting of VHP saffron flags atop one of its domes. An epitaph on V.P. Singh's disastrous prime ministership could well be seen as follows : "He diminished India in the eyes of the world and infinitely worse, he diminished us in our own eyes." The October 30, 1990 plan to hoist flag atop Babri Masjid and damage a dome and remove Kalas was taken to its conclusion and culminated in the destruction and demolition of Babri Masjid.

Before that on December 19 an attempt was made to blow up the shrine and the whole disputed area at Ayodhya an attempt to blow up with dynamite the Ram Janambhoomi Babri Masjid complex was foiled. Four bombs of dynamite enough to destroy the whole complex were seized. Suresh Chandra was arrested and his associate Samanta from Maharashtra reached the Kuber tila near this complex around 6 pm and after 8 pm crossed into bushes behind Sumitra Bhawan. Thirty other explosive experts were in the town. They did not recognize each other. They knew only their job and were not even aware of the plan. Many of them were religious fanatics. Suresh had courted arrest when L.K. Advani was arrested on October 29, 1990. He was also arrested once in Delhi.

In January 1991 Bajrang Dal was directed by the VHP to prepare a list of temples which had been converted into Mosques during the Mughal rule. This work was to be completed by the end of March. So it is not merely Babri Masjid or Mosques at Varanasi and Mathura. On January 3, 1993 SS Bhandari, the BJP Vice President said that he does not foreclose the party's (BJP) option to take up the issues other than Ayodhya, including the liberation of famous mosque in Delhi, even though he said that as he knew there is no such intention. On May 14, 1992, the question of Babri Masjid and Ram temple was again revived. Kalyan Singh, Chief Minister of UP said on May 1992 that Ram temple is a national issue and his government would do all it can to make it into a reality, even though on May 28, 1992 he gave the assurance to the Home Minister, Government of India, that the disputed structure in Ram Janam Bhoomi complex was well protected. He said that the state government had done nothing against the statement made by him in the National Integration Council. S.B. Chavan, the Home Minister, Government of India, at the meeting ot the Standing Committee of the National Integration Council said that the deteriorating security arrangements of Babri Masjid is inadequate and urged the Chief Minister of UP, Kalyan Singh, to accept the advice of the Central experts. He further said that the UP and the Centre have different perceptions of security of Babri Mosque structure. He said that the UP government has paid scant attention to implementing a comprehensive security plan drawn by the Cental experts to protect the structure.

While these parleys and assurances were going on, riots broke out on June 17, 1992 in Rajasthan. Fourteen persons were killed and 70 were injured with 20 missing. In the first week of July, riots broke out in Gujarat at Ahmedabad and violence erupted at Surat, Rajkot, Dholka, Sindhpur and Marui. In the ensuing violence, 25 persons were injured and 1700 arrested in 67 towns of the state. Riots occurred in Jhatua in Madhya Pradesh. In Gujarat the VHP-BJP decided to take out 11000 Rath Yatras throughout the State against the alleged 'attack' on Lord Jagannath procession on July 2, 1992 and also wanted to highlight the socalled failure of the government providing security to religious processions. The situation in Ahmedabad, where municipal elections were due soon, threatened to go out of hand where the police was forced to fire 12 rounds and burst tear gas shells.The police fought pitched battle at many places. The BJP volunteers headed by Keshubhai Patel, leader oi opposition in the Legislative Assembly and others defied the curfew restrictions to March towards the temple at Jamalpur. Many leaders of VHP also courted arrest. Many pitched battles were fought near the Jamalpur Cole, Paleli and Yalka between the volunteers and the police. However, the situation was saved, by the Maharaj and trustees of the Jagannath temple in Ahmedabad who openly disassociated themselves from the politically motivated Rath Yatras and urged the people not to fall into trap being set up. Harish Khare, resident editor of the *Times of India*, said L.K. Advani failed to condemn the murder of an IOC. official (Muslim) in the presence of his family during these Ahmedabad riots. He said that in the attempt of VHP-BJP to take the Rath Yatra in sensitive areas, the people saw a calculated gratuitous attempt to provoke communal animosity.

In October 1992, communal riots again surfaced. In Meghalaya, 21 persons were killed in such riots. Mr Shinde, the General Secretary of the AKC told newspersons that "I suspect the handiwork of VHP-BJP elements and I have received reports to this effect during my on-the-spot study of the riot affected areas."

A communal clash took place between the two communities under the Kathar police station in Kota district on the issue of road construction near a religious place. Twelve persons were admitted to Kota hospital. The Rajasthan government ordered a probe in communal riots in Ajmer town on October 26, 1992. Thirty-two persons were taken into custody. The VHP had planned *Ram Paduka Poojan Yatras* in 12000 villages of Gujarat on the eve of Panchayat elections but had to be abandoned after 310 Yatras because of poor response of the people. Coming back to Ayodhya, on 11 July, 1992 the UP Chief Minister assured the Centre that all necessary steps have been taken to ensure protection of the disputed shrine.

On July 15, 1992, the High Court restrained the Government of UP from carrying on any construction activity on the acquired land. Next day, the Supreme Court observed that construction of concrete platform near the disputed shrine amounted to contempt of Court.

The BJP objected to holding the National Integration Council Meeting. V.H. Dalmia (VHP) said that the National Integration Council represented anti-Hindu forces. The BJP on 21 Nov., 1992, decided not to attend the National Integration Council Meeting. The BJP Chief Ministers of States also boycotted the meeting. The VHP as well did not attend. The UP Government on 29 November, 1992 gave an undertaking to the Supreme Court that the *kar seva* will be symbolic and that it would not allow any construction at the disputed 2.77 acre site. Even on 5 December. 1992 Kalyan Singh assured that no damage will be done to the disputed structure. However, other belligerent voices were raised. Acharya Vamdev said that he did not know what symbolic *seva* means. He said that *kar seva* means construction of the temple. Prof.Rajindra Singh of RSS said that the *kar seva* at Ayodhya would start on 6 December. 1992 without violating the Supreme Court directives. He said that the Sangh Parivar is averse to any confrontation with the Centre. He made clear that *kar seva* will include *Bhajan, Kirtan, pooja path* and construction work, and that the first phase would continue for 22 days. On 2 December. 1992 L.K. Advani said categorically that *seva* in Ayodhya from December 6 will not be stopped in any circumstances and that the construction of the Ram Temple will start simultaneously with *Bhajan, Kirtan,* etc. "We are prepared to face any eventuality arising from the *kar seva* and are ready to give any sacrifice for it." He went on to say that *kar seva* does not mean *bhajan* and *kirtan,* and that they will perform *kar seva* with shovels and bricks on the 2.77 acre land acquired by the UP government. He said "we respect the judiciary, but it did not mean that we would allow it to play with the sentiments of the people." He pointed out if an adverse verdict is given "we would still perform *kar seva* on the acquired land as the land belonged to VHP." The rule of law and sanctity of judiciary was to be ignored.

The *News Track* video shows the tension building in Ayodhya from December 3, 1992 onwards with the *kar sevaks* determined to demolish the mosque. It show

BJP leaders making forceful speeches and Mr Ramesh Pratap, an RSS leader leading a dress rehearsal of the demolition of the Babri Mosque on 4 December 1992 It shows the *kar sevaks* dancing and singing : "We will not sift sand, we will demolish the structure". And above all it shows the first few moments of attack. The saffron clad *kar sevaks* were helped by a senior BJP leader. The policemen surrounding the mosque at the same time walked away. Next moment *kar sevaks* attacked the mosque from the back. This could have been stopped easily by the police on duty. But there was not even a *laathi* charge. Except for a dozen policemen all had left. The persisting dozen ran away too as soon as the few stones were tossed at them.

About 300 *kar sevaks* broke into the inner circle. They seemed to know what to do and were carrying rods, pick-axes. A few seconds later the *kar sevaks* react and follow. The RSS workers supposed to maintain order were nowhere to be seen. There were too many men carrying rods, pick-axes and ropes. If it was not a pre-planned action what else was it?

On December 6, 1992, what happened was: at 11.30 am Advani and Dr M.M. Joshi addressed *kar sevaks;* at 11.50 am. *Kar sevaks* stormed the Babri Mosque and tampered with its walls; 12 noon security personnels withdrew; 12.15 pm. There was alert in Faizabad. The district administration sought more forces from State Government, 12.15 pm the UP Cabinet reviewed the situation, 1.20 pm red alert is sounded all over UP; 2.45 pm one of the three domes of the structure was brought down; 4.30 pm the second dome was brought down, 4.45 pm the third dome was brought down; 4.50 pm L.K. Advani, M.M. Joshi, Ashok Singhal, H.V. Seshadri appealed to the people to maintain peace, 5.25 pm Shanker Dayal Sharma, President of India asked the Prime Minister to initiate steps to uphold the rule of law and maintain public order; 5.30 pm Kalyan Singh government resigned. 6.30 pm the Cabinet met. By night all *kar sevaks* were fully in control and the idols of Ram Lalla which had been removed earlier were reinstalled amid chanting of prayers.

During the demolition on December 6, 1992 the *kar sevaks* assaulted brutally the press representatives. Three hundred pressmen had come to corner the *Kar Seva*. Many were stabbed, harrassed, beaten with rods, etc. A woman correspondent was stripped. It was a blatant attack on freedom of press. The All India Newspapers Editors Conference strongly condemned the attack on pressmen and photographers. The veteran journalist Raghuraj said, "We do not want such a Hindu State." Another journalist said, "The few of us who were here can tell you exactly how a fascist state functions after experiencing Ayodhya."

More than an hour after the shrine was stormed, the district magistrate R.N. Srivastava sent for reinforcements. Four companies of the CRPF and RAF were despatched from Faizabad but the road was blocked with bricks, stones and logs making their progress difficult. Uma Bharati, Sadhvi Rithambra and L.K. Advani had exhorted the *kar sevaks* to block the roads to Ayodhya so that Central forces could not reach there.

What followed the demolition of Babri Masjid ? A holocaust of communal riots, blood bath, brutality and basteality. Nationwide violence occurred for the next five days. On December 6, 1992, the *kar sevaks* torched the houses of Muslims. Stabbings and killings were rampant. On 7 December, 1992, at least 225 people were killed and 1000 wounded. In Maharashtra 60 people were killed, 40 were killed in Bombay in police firing; 41 people died and 150 were injured in Gujarat, 35 people died in UP, 23 people were killed in Rajasthan, 22 were killed in Karnataka, 22 were killed in Madhya Pradesh, 9 in Andhra Pradesh, 5 in West Bengal, 2 in Bihar, 1 in Kerala. In Ahmedabad 27 riots took place in Palanpur: 9 died in riots. In Ayodhya in another mosque *kar sevaks* installed an idol of Lord Hanuman, 5 *kar sevaks* were killed in Ayodhya, curfew was imposed and flag marches carried our.

On 8 December, 265 more persons were killed taking the toll to 500. Maharashtra toll rose to 130, in Bombay alone 94, in Gujarat it was 117 with 56 more deaths, in Assam 30 persons killed : 18 of them burnt alive in Dabalen area in Nagaon district, when there houses were set ablaze. In Solapur Baldana, Yawatmal in Maharashtra, police opened fire to quell marauding mobs. In UP 24 more deaths, were reported taking the toll to 59. Deaths, were reported from Saharanpur, Faizabad, Lucknow. Allahabad, Varanasi, Fatehgarh, Jhansi, Aligarh and Bareilly. Fresh violence started in Kanpur. Toll in MP rose to 48, and 34 in Bhopal. The UP Lucknow Bombay train was attacked after it left Bhopal, in which 35 passengers were injured, one seriously. Three persons were burnt alive in Bhopal in the old city; in Ujjain the toll rose to eight with a police constable and a homeguard killed by rioting mobs; in Gujarat the toll rose to 109 with 48 more deaths with 32 persons killed in Surat alone. Riots occurred in Dholka, Ankleshwar and Malupur. Indefinite curfew was clamped in Ahmedabad, Broach, Ankleshwar, Borsad, Palej, Prantiz, Junagarh, Madasa. Calcutta toll rose to 8; 24 more killed in UP riots, Mhow, Hamirpur, Jaunpur, Rampur, Ghaziabad, Saharanpur Fatehpur, Samlehal, Muzaffarnagar and Roorkee. Nine people were killed Kanpur, 2 in Lucknow and 1 each in Varanasi, Fatehpur and Allahabad. 900 arrests were made in UP, the maximum being 400, in Aligarh. On December 9, 1992, 260 persons more were killed raising the toll to 760. In Maharashtra 85 deaths took place raising the toll to 215, in Bombay alone to 149, in Assam the toll rose to 67, 25 deaths being reported from Nagaon district alone, in all 37 deaths reported; in UP the toll rose to 104; in Surat 24 persons were burnt alive taking the toll to 91, army being moved in the city; army also moved in Mehsana,

Sidhpur, Palanpur, Godhra, and Himmatnagar as the toll in the State rose to 168; in Rajasthan army moved in Diggi, Malpura area in Tonk district, following the death of 16 persons including 4 women and a child, toll in the State rising to 43; in Madhya Pradesh the toll reached 60, fresh incidents taking place in Bhopal which counted for 43.21 towns were put under curfew, army deployed in Ujjain, Bhopal and Indore. In Andhra Pradesh, the toll reached 21, in Bihar army was called in Ranchi, in West Bengal army was called in Nub where several places of worship were damaged; in Lucknow 17 died, 12 injured, places of worship damaged; in Kanpur 11 bodies were recovered from various localities raising the toll to 25; in Meerut, police firing took place resulting in 2 deaths; in Barabanki district in Rasauli town clashes took place on return of *kar sevaks*; in Moradabad, army was moved in; in UP 35 districts were under curfew imposed in 20 places; in Ahmedabad more army columns were deployed, toll rising to 43, in Assam 37 deaths occurred, 30 bodies recovered from Hogai where 40 persons had been burnt alive; in Kerala army moved in Kasargod district following large-scale arson, loot and attack on places of worship, country made bombs hurled at AIR in Kozhikode; in Karnataka incidents of arson and stone pelting took place in various areas, police opened fire at four places in Cuttack, shoot at site being ordered in Jaipur, 16 persons including 4 women and a child were killed in Malpura in Tonk district, violence spreading in many more towns in Rajasthan; in Gujarat, Dolka, Prantif, Mehsana, Palan, Idar, Himatnagar, Jambusar were put under curfew, toll reaching 153, 60 huts being burnt in Dolka, stabbing incidents taking place in Sinore town of Baroda district and Jamnagar city; in Bihar 6 were killed, curfew imposed in Jharia, toll rising to 16 with 3 deaths in Arorla, two deaths in Dhanbad and 1 death in Jamshedpur; in Orissa 150 houses including big business establishments were set on fire.

On 10 December, 1992, situation in UP worsened. The total toll reached 1000 all over the country. More than 50 deaths took place in UP raising the toll to 163, group clashes took place in Varanasi, Ghaziabad, Rampur and Kanpur, 35 being killed in Kanpur including 7 members of a family, the toll in Kanpur amounting to 62, in Ghaziabad army led a flag march; in West Bengal, toll reached 19, 9 killed in Calcutta and one in Kharagpur; in Assam the toll reached 76, in Rajasthan 3 more killed, in Bengal toll rose to 216, in Surat alone there were 185 deaths, in Bhopal 2 persons were burnt alive, in Ujjan 9 deaths, in Kharagaon 3 deaths, in Jawra one death, in Indore one death, in Kharagaon 3 deaths, in Jawra one death, in Indore one death, in Jabalpur one death, and in Numukh one death took place. On 11 December, 1992, the death toll reached 1100 with 150 deaths taking place today and number of injured rising to 4000. In Bombay 202 lives were lost, in Maharashtra 259, in Gujarat 237, in Ahmedabad 146, in Surat 165, in Madhya Pradesh 110, in Bhopal 89, in Ujjain 9, in Burhanpur 5, in Khargaon 6, in Indore one, in Jabalpur one, in Numukh one; in West Bengal one death took placc in Calcutta raising the toll to 32; in Assam two more were killed; in Kanpur 38 killed in stabbing and group clashes; in Aligarh 15 Kashmiri students of Aligarh Muslim University were thrown out of the train bound for Delhi by *kar sevaks* returning from Ayodhya on Tuesday afternoon between Tundla and Khurja stations two being hammered as well, three were missing, Farhat Razzaq died. On December 13, 1992, the toll in Delhi rose to 15.

The RSS chief Bala Saheb Deoras, while describing the demolition as unfortunate and improper, said, "I can understand the anger and anguish of our Muslim brothers due to the demolition. But they must also consider the fact that if they could be so incensed over the demolition of a mosque, which had no significance for them and where Namaaz was not being offered, the sentiment of Hindus must also be equally strong over the disputed structure at Ayodhya, Mathura and Varanasi. Here some of the holiest temples have been converted into Mosques. Neither the Center nor other political parties have bothered about the intensity of Hindus sentiments over these three places" Ashok Singhal said 6 December, 1992, should be celebrated in the same way as August 15, the Independence Day, was celebrated in the country. He further said, "None can stop us from restoring the prestige of the three disputed shrines in Ayodhya, Mathura and Varanasi. The Hindu of 1993 is not the Hindu of 1947. An invincible Hindu has arisen today. There is no question of condemning the Ayodhya demolition. It had to be done in the manner it was, God had will it that way." H.V. Sheshadri said, "It is undoubtedly a tremendous morale booster for the Hindu psyche. On October 30, 1990, hoisting the *Bhagva* flag was a symbol of self-assertion of the nations Hindu identity. But now, that standing monument to a foreign invader's insult to the nations honour and independence has itself been erased."

Kalyan Singh said that December 6 marked the emergence of "New India" in which Hindus will not remain number two. He described the controversial Ram temple partly built on the structure of Babri Masjid during the turbulent December days in Ayodhya as a "symbol of national pride, unity, self-reliance, self-respect and strength. L.K. Advani described Ayodhya as a symbol of secularism. He further said, "I am not at all ashamed of the Ayodhya demolition, there is no question of feeling so." Dr M.M. Joshi said he was not repentant of December 6 incidents. He said, "It has brought Hindutva to the Centre stage. The BJP has become the voice of the resurgent nationalism. It is redefining the political ideology of every aspect of national life, be it secularism, socialism, foreign policy or economic issues." Vamdev and Muktanand Sarswati of Sant Samaj said that the disputed structure should have been brought down after independence and this symbol of Mughal aggression could be done away with and that those who demolished the mosque on December 6 did a very commendable job.

S.B. Chavan, the Home Minister, Government of India said that the mosque was demolished because of the total absence of protection by the local police and the state authorities not allowing the central forces to reach the spot. He further said that the UP government betrayed the trust reported in it. The UP Governor said that the destruction of disputed structure was the result of a predetermined plan and not the spontaneous upsurge by a section of *kar sevaks*. The Prime Minister P.V. Narasimha Rao said that the nation was betrayed by the BJP and VHP which had agreed to hold only a symbolic *kar seva*. The President of India, Dr Shankar Dayal Sharma said that such acts causing damage to a religious structure were "absolutely against the doctrine and practice of Hinduism and all other great religions." He further said: "Those who have harmed the structure of the Masjid have caused injury to the centuries old ethos of India nurtured and strengthened by the martyrs of great leaders of India's struggle for freedom and national reconstruction."

The Lok Sabha passed the following resolution: "The House stongly and unequivocally condemns the desecration and demolition of the Babri Masjid at Ayodhya by and at the instigation of forces represented by VHP, RSS, Bajrang Dal, which has caused communal violation in the country. Such act of vandalism was carried out not only in violation of the orders of the Supreme Court but amounted to an attack on the secular foundation of our country.

"This House expresses its anguish at the happening and wishes to reiterate its resolve that it will ceaselessly endeavour to uphold the secular and democratic traditions of our country and for the maintenance of the rule of law. These tragic incidents which have been caused consequent to the sacrilege at Ayodhya demands from the Government all necessary steps to rehabilitate the affected people. It appeals to the people of the country to maintain peace and communal harmony."

A designated court on 8 September, 1997 decided to frame charges against 48 persons including Shiv Sena supreme, Bal Thakeray, BJP President L.K. Advani, M.M. Joshi, Kalyan Singh, in cases relating to the demolition of the Babri Masjid on December 6, 1992. The Special Additional Judge, H. Srivastava decided to frame charges against all accused under Sections 147, 153A, 153B, 295B, 505 and 120B of the Indian Penal Code for rioting, inciting violence and creating hatred between two communities. BJP leaders M.M. Joshi and Vijay Raje Scindia, VHP leaders Giriraj Kishore and Ashok Singhal and Bajrang Dal leader Vinay Katiyar were also among the accused against whom the court decided to frame the charges.

The judge also charged the District Magistrate and District Police Chief of Faizabad, R.N. Srivastava and D.B. Rai (now in BJP) respectively under Section 120B, 153A, 295A, 505, 201, and 214 relating to charges of conspiracy, dereliction of duty and failure to discharge official obligations during the demolition of the disputed structure.

The CBI which was instructed with the investigation into the demolition of the disputed structure, filed the chargesheet after examining 1000 odd people. In its chargesheet the investigating agency said the "conspiracy" to demolish the structure was hatched with the support of the then Kalyan Singh government.

Of the persons to be chargesheeted in the Ayodhya demolition, more than 10 were Members of Parliament.

Bal Thackeray, L.K. Advani, Kalyan Singh, Ashok Singhal, Vinay Katiyar, Moreshwar Dave, Pawan Kumar Pandey, Brij Bhushan, Saran Singh, Jai Bhagwan Goel,

Uma Bharati, Sadhvi Rithambara, Maharaj Swami Saleshi (MP), Satish Pradhan (MP), Murli Manohar Joshi, Giriraj Kishore, V.H. Dalmia, Champat Rai, Om Prakash, Mahant Avaidhanath, Ram Vilas Vedarthi, Dharam Das, Mahant Nritya Gopal Das, Mahamandleshwar Jagdish Muni Maharaj, Baikunth Lal Sharma, Paramhans Ramchandra Das, Vijay Raje Scindia, and Satish Kumar have been charged by the court under section 120B, IPC read with 147, 153A, 153B, 295, 295A, and 505 IPC and substantive offences.

Pawan Kumar Pandey, Brij Bhushan, Sharan Singh Jai Bhagwan Goel, Vinod Kumar Vats, Ram Chandra Khatri, Sudhir Kakkar, Amarnath Goel, Santosh Dubey, Prabash Sharma, Jai Bhagwan Pandey, Dharmendra Singh Gurjar, Ram Narain Das, Vinay Kumar Rai, Laloo Singh, Mr Ramji Gupta, Om Prakesh Pandey, Kamlesh Tripathi, Gandhi Yadav, Har Govind Singh, Vinay Bahadur Singh, Navin Bhai Shukla, Ramesh Pratap Singh and Acharya Dharmendra Deo face charges under Section 332, 338 and 201 IPC read with Sections 149 and 395 and 102B.

Srivastva observed that the criminal conspiracy for the demolition of the Babri Masjid structure began in 1990 and came to culmination on December 6, 1992.

Index